Dialogues with M

Talking with Twentieth-Century Men

Dedication

To those men
who were my ancestors
who were my best friends
who inspired and helped me
who were soul mates in disguise

Peter Watson Jenkins

Dialogues with Masters of the Spirit World, III

Talking with Twentieth-Century Men

Compiled by
Peter Watson Jenkins

Channeled by
Toni Ann Winninger

Celestial Voices, Inc.

Published by Celestial Voices, Inc.
1146 Waukegan Rd., Suite 118, Waukegan, IL 60085

Cover design by Robert Buzek Designs Inc.,
Lake Zurich, Illinois

Library of Congress Control Number: 2008906641

ISBN: 978-0-9798917-4-8

FIRST EDITION

Printed in the United States of America

Contact email: TheMastersInfo@yahoo.com

Our Publications Policy
Celestial Voices, Inc. is a specialist publisher of works produced with the sanction of the group of Ascended Masters who have commissioned them. We do not accept any submissions from authors, and we will not enter into correspondence concerning their ideas, or return unsolicited manuscripts.

Contents

Acknowledgments

The authors wish to thank
Sonia Ness for typing and copy editing,
Robert Buzek for cover design.

About this Book

People like to discover more about the famous people they admire. Some put pictures up at home of their idols, go to movies telling their story, collect old newspaper articles, autographs, and programs in scrapbooks, and even buy items of clothing the famous people once wore. Many visit websites put up by fan clubs, or by those whose creators want to honor their memory. But once these idols die, their book of life closes.

Or does it?

What if it were possible to talk with famous people *after* their death? What if they could tell us more about themselves and their life? What if General Patton could tell us about where he got the inspiration for his strategy in the WWII "Battle of the Bulge"? What if John Lennon and Dr. Martin Luther King could tell us what it's like to be assassinated—and explain how they feel now about their murderer? What if Joe Louis could tell us how it was to be admired as a champion boxer. What if Elvis could confirm whether he's ever been down again to visit planet Earth? How does Dr. Robert Oppenheimer now assess work he did developing the nuclear bomb? With 21 famous men to interview we had tons of questions to ask!

But it's true! We really can talk with them, and we really can find out their answers. It's what this book and its companion book on *Twentieth-Century Women* are about.

In *Talking with Leaders of the Past*, the first book in our series of *Dialogues with Masters of the Spirit World*, we interviewed 15 leaders, all born in the nineteenth century, including: Andrew Carnegie, Winston S. Churchill, Charles Darwin, Albert Einstein, Mahatma Gandhi, Adolf Hitler, Pope John XXIII, and Oscar Wilde. They answered the questions we shot at them, talked about themselves, and discussed what their life is like at "Home"—the place in the universe where everybody's soul migrates after they have died—which people sometimes call "the Other Side."

A lot of what we learned from these souls blew our minds. It was all so different when they talked about God, Heaven and Hell, the purpose of our life on planet Earth, why human beings suffer so much, and lots more.

Our first book was organized in cooperation with a group of Ascended Masters, spirits who live permanently in the eternal Home. Then the Masters encouraged us to produce two follow-up books of famous men and women of the twentieth century. The human interviewer was Peter Watson Jenkins. He's an author and former parish minister, now working as a clinical hypnotherapist. Peter drew up a very long list of famous people and presented them to the Masters for review. For many different reasons a lot of these people were not available for interview, so they were dropped from the list. Souls are not idle at Home; they are involved in their own past-life reviews and have further spiritual training to undertake. Many act as guides, advising the souls of people on planet Earth, or helping newly arrived spirits settle in after their time here. After being at Home for a while souls are usually given the option to return to planet Earth. We know those chosen by the Masters for our list of 21 famous men are outstanding subjects.

So how did we talk with these people?

Contact with the spirit world was successfully made by a leading American channeler, Toni Ann Winninger, JD. The Masters first asked her to start channeling just a few years ago, when she was getting ready to retire as a prosecutor in the Cook County State's Attorney's Office in Chicago. Toni's training as a lawyer has given her a real gift of mental accuracy, and her regular practice of very deep meditation has resulted in her amazing ability to allow the thoughts of those souls whom she channels to flow *through* her mind with little or no interference from her. Toni spends much of her time as a psychic advising private clients. She enjoys working with the same large group of Ascended Masters, which includes both spirits who have finished their task of coming down to planet Earth, and celestial beings (whom some call *angels* and *archangels*) who have never been down here in physical form.

Yes, we <u>do</u> know people are skeptical of channeling!

Psychics are really a mixed lot. Some of them, such as Echo Bodine, Sylvia Browne, Sonia Choquette, John Edward, Esther Hicks, Judith Orloff, and James Van Praagh, all have fine reputations, and deservedly have achieved great popularity. Many "street corner" psychics are also trustworthy, but, sadly, there are many wannabes and frauds who cheat and manipulate innocent people. But that's true in every profession—even religious leaders in churches, temples, and mosques, can be fakes.

As authors, we are more skeptical than you might expect, believing that we need to "test the spirits" as the Bible says, and also to test the claims of human psychics. We understand that some readers may prefer to treat this book as a work of fiction, but we sincerely believe that it is absolutely true and that, with Toni's channeling, Peter really did converse with the souls whom we have named. We stake our reputations on the claim that what is printed in our books is an accurate record of our conversations.

What if I don't know anything about these people?

It's easy! The questions that Peter asks fill in a lot of historic information, so we have not detailed every one's life story in this book as we did in the *Leaders* book. If interested, you can easily find out about each man for yourself by typing his name in an Internet search engine and harvesting the results.

Our aim is to help readers discover how and why these famous people came to be who they were, what influences affected them, and if they were influenced at all by their past lives. As we talked together we asked them to tell us a little about themselves as they are now, to explain in what way they like to remember their most recent physical life, and also to comment on our life on planet Earth today from their spiritual perspective back Home.

~ * ~

Note

We have used *italic type* to indicate Peter's questions and comments during each discussion. Replies are printed in roman type.

Glossary

Advisors. Souls who are given the task of advising incarnated souls.

Angel. A human term for a celestial being who, after being separated from Source, acts as a guide to those upon earth, but may or may not at some later time chose to experience an earthly body.

Archangel. A human term for a celestial being that is very advanced and experienced as a guide, whose soul has never incarnated.

Council. A group of guides who help us decide what lessons we wish to experience, and who help us make best use of the lessons we have learned.

Creator. See "Source."

Dimension. A waveband or stratum of vibrational energy. Planet Earth is at the third dimension. Home is at the fifth and higher dimensions.

God. See "Source."

God-Force. See "Source." Sometimes used as meaning "all souls."

Guides. Souls given the task of advising incarnated souls.

Heaven. See "Home."

Hell. A state of mind on Earth.

Home. Not a physical place but an energetic dimension of unconditional love and of conscious connection with Source. It is where each soul works with its guides, and council. Every soul who is not incarnated is consciously within the dimension of Home.

Incarnate. A soul who has gone down to planet Earth and is now in a physical body.

Shell. The living physical structure inhabited by a soul. No human or animal body can live without some connection to a soul.

Supreme Being. See "Source."

Souls. Individualized pieces of energy split off by and from Source, in order to have unique experiences outside the perfect. They are all particles of Source, so each and every soul is also Source. All souls are equal regardless of the human shell they have chosen to inhabit.

Source. The point of origin of all that is known by human beings, and all that exists. It is the energy of unconditional love, the highest vibrational energy anywhere, and is found in everything. The Source makes no judgments and does not reward or punish souls.

Transition. The soul's move from life in the body to life at Home. Physical death.

"I was in a hurry to be able to use the energy that I felt boiling up inside of me, trying to get out and come into expression."

Frank Lloyd Wright

1867-1959

Frank Lloyd Wright you were born in Richland Center, WI, the son of a Welsh Baptist minister. You later called both your homes in Wisconsin and Arizona by the Welsh name "Taliesin," and you changed your middle name of Lincoln to Lloyd. What did your Welsh connections mean to you?

A wistfulness, a connection with the Earth, and a connection with the flow of energy. As you are aware, the island of Great Britain is a magical place that allows one to be connected to the flow of the Earth, to feel the energy as it transfers from one place to another. To me, my Welsh roots—the DNA, the energy that was there—gave me the feeling I had for the flow that could be converted from the outside to the inside. From this built-in ability I derived the principles that created the flow of my buildings, that designed my windows connecting the various energies in a particular place, and that turned the buildings into homey, comfortable surroundings.

Where did your desire to be an architect come from: your past lives, or the Froebel building blocks you played with as a child, or something else?

It was a combination of things. I had been a builder, a constructor, in a number of my past lives. Sometimes it was building a physical building, and sometimes it was building a person—in other words, teaching, letting them know what abilities they had. So there was always within me the urge to connect things, to make things that were out of people's ordinary experience, so that they could expand and connect with their feelings. The building blocks that I had as a child kept drawing me to put into application everything that I had done before, but in a new way, because I had never before been a physical builder of individual homes.

In fact, you used geometrical designs and pre-cast concrete blocks and things that had designs on them, didn't you?

Yes, I did, because I could feel the energy of the symbols. It has now been recognized that Feng Shui has a terrific impact on the physical body. The various designs that I used were used in architecture in the world going back to the pyramids. I just modified them to be appealing and appeasing to the eye and the senses.

Where did your actual decision to be an architect come from?

It was sort of a gradual transition where all of the pieces just fell into place, and I realized everything that I had been thinking about and trying to work with would be best suited were I to build homes.

During your life you abandoned the Trinitarian faith of your parents and became a Unitarian. How do you view those religious traditions now that you are back Home?

It wasn't that I walked away from the religious beliefs of my parents; it was that I found they didn't serve me and have the same appeal to me as they did to them. My family needed specific direction. They needed to be told exactly what to think and how to think it and what the possible responses were for their earthly actions. I found that within the beliefs of the Unitarians, it was more left to individual persons to come to grips with their feelings. From back Home here, I see that they were all just lessons I had to learn. This provided a direction enabling me to think outside the box, which showed up in my architecture. It was an awareness that gave me the opportunity to connect with some of the feelings I had had when I was in a non-physical body, and to go with those feelings.

You were a young man in a hurry. You quit the university engineering college without a degree and then quickly left your first job with Joseph Lyman Silsbee to work with Louis Sullivan, and, remarkably soon, you took on all his residential design work. Tell me about that period and your two mentors.

It could truly be said that I was in a hurry. I was in a hurry to be able to use the energy that I felt boiling up inside of me, trying to get out and come into expression. With my first job, I was taught the basics of dealing with people within the profession, how you had to have—at least outwardly—a compromising demeanor, even if inside you were maneuvering to get things done your way. I was not given the opportunity, however, to really take the reins and create. When I started working with Sullivan, it was as if an entire world opened up to me. I showed him the designs I had, and we began almost to vibrate on the same level. I would now call it an enlightenment, that we were freeing energies from inside of us. He was not as concerned with residential properties as I was; I felt the additional component of the human person who would be affected by my energy, whereas that was not a factor in the larger, commercial buildings. He saw that my direction was residential, and after I had completed a couple of projects, they were so successful that he just turned over everything to me.

Then he sacked you for moonlighting—you were doing work on the side.

He felt that all my ideas should be used exclusively to bring money into the company. It's very common in this day and age for your employer to expect exclusivity; however, there were some projects that I just had to undertake that he did not want the company involved in, so in order to go in the direction that I felt I had to, I did a little moonlighting, yes.

Silsbee and Sullivan both taught you quite a bit.

They taught me the basics of what became my own individual style. They gave me the knowledge of how things had to be done and how to implement my designs. They did not teach me enough about business, because I wasn't as successful on my own as I was with them, but they showed me how to deal with people and which ones I had to deal with in order to accomplish what I sought.

Your pace was breathtaking. In 1889 you built a home in Oak Park, outside Chicago, for yourself and your bride, Kitty Tobin. Within the next 12 years you had designed some 50 homes, many of them in Oak Park and neighboring suburbs. This was before your Prairie Style period. Looking back at this start, what do you feel you achieved in domestic architecture?

I got away from what some would call the "cookie cutter" approach, that everything had to be built on the box, and every little piece had to be able to be easily put into a form. The important thing to me was the flow of the living space, and within that flow, how the geometries that people interacted with impacted each individual's energy.

Every single house was a new experiment. Every single house was a design specifically for an individual and his or her family. Even those houses which, nowadays, you would say were built on speculation were built with the owner's energies involved. I proved that you could take what people considered just brick and mortar and plaster and make it a living, breathing extension of the human beings who lived inside of it.

In 1904 came the Larkin Soap Company project in Buffalo, New York. Your innovative design for their Administration Building included air conditioning, radiant heat, plate-glass windows, and built-in steel furniture. Your designs for Midway Gardens, Chicago, in 1913 and the Johnson Wax Headquarters, Racine, Wisconsin, in 1936 were also big commercial ventures. Was technical innovation a common theme of all three?

You might call it a theme. I call it tools that were being overlooked by a lot of designers at that time, because these technical elements were not part and parcel of what they had learned to use, and change was very slow in coming to the average designer. I took into consideration who was going to be occupying the building and what type of energy they were going to need in order to fulfill the job that was going to be done in that building. When it came down to human comforts, current technology provided me with a basis to do it, so I took advantage of everything that was available.

Your radical designs sometimes caused headaches for owners. The Johnson Wax building, with its innovative Pyrex glass tubing and clerestories, leaked badly, and the three-legged chairs you originally designed were unstable. You were asked to try one out and fell off it, didn't you?

[laughs] Yes, I did! I would get these visions when I was designing something; they were very appealing to the eye and had an energy that was fantastic, but sometimes they were a little bit before their time. We didn't have the capability of putting the energies that I was downloading into physical shape—and I say "downloading" because some of my designs had assistance from non-physical architects whom I asked to help get the energy flows right.

Specific architects, or just generally asking the Universe?

Generally asking the Universe if they wished to participate, and of course, there was always somebody who wished to participate.

In your physical state were you aware of channeling?

No, I wasn't aware that I was channeling. I thought that I was just coming up with these brand-new ideas, although I was aware that there was an expansiveness about the origin of these ideas that meant they had to be beyond anything contained on Earth.

During the 17 years from 1900, you focused on designing open-plan "Prairie Houses." In addition to being distinctively horizontal to fit the landscape, they met human needs in new ways. They may even have inspired the Bauhaus movement later on, but they were not meant to be merely "boxes for living in," were they?

No. I guess you might call them incubation capsules, incubating the energy that was within people, bringing it out to let them know that they were more than just what everybody else was (if they allowed themselves to be) and that they didn't have to be categorized, that they could be expansive. The whole idea behind the Prairie approach was of unlimited abilities, unlimited energy, spreading out to interact with energies coming from all different sources. My desire was that a person within those areas would feel their connection to the Universe, that there were no "glass ceilings," as people say now, preventing them from moving above and beyond the pattern that somebody else had dictated for them.

It's interesting that you should be talking in terms of fluid movements of energy, because in fact you were sometimes very precise and particular. I remember the story of one house you visited that you had built some years before. You found that the furniture was not in the place in which you had put it, and you went around putting the furniture back in its "rightful" place.

[laughs] I was very aware of energy. I could stand in any room, in any location within that room, and know if there was anything impeding the flow of energy or air through that space.

Ninety-eight percent of the population was not as sensitive as I was to that. They went merely with their eye or what was convenient for them, whereas everything I did was placed with the idea of the flow of energy.

[Toni: He's showing me a wind tunnel, where they test cars and bike riders, and use smoke so you can see how the wind ruffles over them—indicating that he was his own barometer of how the energy or air was flowing.]

Your favorite Prairie house was, I think, "The Robie House" in Chicago, wasn't it?

I don't know that I had a favorite one. That was one where I felt that I had accomplished more innovations in a single place than I had been able to do before.

Did you make any mistakes that you would have preferred, in retrospect, not to have made in the design of the Prairie house?

Well, the only mistake that I might have made was not to be able to convey to people exactly what the Prairie houses meant to me, or what I was trying to accomplish with the design, with the flow of the energy. Some people saw them merely as living units. They didn't see them as living, breathing extensions of themselves that could help them to grow, and so, if there was a mistake, it was that I could not give my vision, my energy, to some of the people who inhabited my houses.

During the building of a Prairie house for Mr. Edwin Cheney, you fell in love with his wife, Mamah. Scandal followed, and with your reputations badly damaged, the two of you ran away to Europe. Was this a diversion, as some historians have suggested, because you had lost interest in the Prairie style and felt a failure in not getting much large-scale commercial work?

It's hard to tell you exactly everything that was going on with me at that time. There was a great degree of frustration within me that I was not able to convey what I felt about everything I did. I saw my work as being perfect reproductions that, instead of being honored in a museum, were given to a child to play with. So it was a diversion for me. It was getting out of my idealistic pattern of trying to help the world and change the way the world saw the interaction between buildings and humans, and just being able to be concerned about myself and go off and live.

After your return in 1911 you built "Taliesin" on land your mother bought for you at Spring Green, Wisconsin. What you were trying to achieve there architecturally?

As far as architects were concerned, I wasn't trying to please anybody. I wasn't trying to make a statement. I was just trying to create a womb for myself.

In 1914, personal tragedy struck that womb when your servant, Julian Carlton, set fire to "Taliesin" and butchered seven occupants, including Mamah and her two children. How do you feel about this tragedy looking back from where you are now?

I know now that contracts had been made between the various souls involved to experience things. I also was involved in those contracts, because, though my life had had ups and downs, it had been fairly smooth. I had never experienced a true sense of having my gut ripped out of me, as happened with that one act. I had been very aware of energy interaction with buildings and human beings, but I hadn't been that aware of the soul's essence interacting with the physical. It put me into a state where I had to examine priorities, stepping out of what is just bound by the physical, by the ego, and go into the emotional feelings generated by having such a thing happen to me. I had always felt protected and charmed, and thought it was my right as a human being to be able to say the world doesn't affect me if I shut it out. This was my wake-up call.

That call went on being sounded, because in 1922, after Kitty divorced you, you married Miriam Noel, then found out that she was a drug addict, and the two of you separated. Then you met Olga Hinzenburg, a dancer with the Petrograd Ballet, whom you eventually married, and she bore you a daughter, Iovanna. Her ex-husband, seeking custody of his daughter, Svetlana, had you arrested briefly under the White-Slave Traffic Act. Then "Taliesin" went up in flames because of a faulty electrical system. You were better known then to the public for scandal and disaster than for good architecture. Do you now see your behavior at that time as wrongful, and was karma involved?

From up here, I don't see it as wrongful; no one up here sees it as wrongful, because we don't judge. We evaluate if it was a lesson that enriched our knowledge of the human and soul experience, and yes, in that it was very successful. Although it contained what in human standards were a lot of disasters, to me it provided a lot of rich feelings, putting me onto paths that I needed to explore and understand. During that whole period of time, from the murders on, my physical world was in turmoil. I was depressed most of the time; I sought anything I thought could make me feel physically better. It brought me into a dream world where I wouldn't see negativity existing as long as I physically felt somebody wanted to take care of me. I was used and abused during that period, and I used and abused others. The only thing that was not true was the white-slavery case. Our coming together was by agreement, a true feeling that we could provide something for each other. Now I see that I learned more during that period of my life, as far as spiritual lessons go, than I learned in the entire rest of my life.

You had four sons and four daughters, including Svetlana, Olga's daughter, whom you adopted. Were you a good father?

It depends upon your definition of a good father. Was I there emotionally for all of the children? Not really. Was I able to provide physical needs for all of the children? Most of the time, yes. Was I able to give them some lessons in how to deal with the world and learn things about themselves? Yes, I was. Did they all agree [at Home] to be my children before they became my children? Yes, they did. So the agreements that we had made were exactly what I was able to produce.

Many of them have gone on to do very good things, haven't they?

Yes, they have, because one of the things I was able to provide for them was alternatives, that you don't have to go to the same beat of the same drum.

You sound like a Unitarian.

Fancy that!

Then came two of your most successful Organic Style houses: "Graycliff" on Lake Erie and "Fallingwater" at Bear Run, Pennsylvania. Tell us about them.

Since I had been up and down and all around, as you might say, the only place I felt a sense of comfort was in and with nature. There was a stability there that wasn't found in the airiness of my Prairie style houses. To be able to extend the energy of the outside and incorporate it into the whole sense of the energy of the house was my crowning glory. It showed that the planet is a living, breathing thing, and when you work with it, you create something that is unique, something that incorporates the living matter of a human into synchronization with the living matter of the planet. The houses had a totally different feel from anything I had done previously.

In 1936 you changed direction and built the "Jacob House" as your first of 50 Usonian homes (Usonian replacing the word American). They were less expensive, environmentally designed for solar warmth, with what you called a "carport" in place of a garage. Did you see this often-copied design as a way of influencing popular American architecture?

I saw it as a way for those who couldn't afford custom-designed houses to have some of the benefits that my experience had shown were good for the interaction between owner and home, and also a way to put a person into awareness of conservation.

One of your projects abroad was the Imperial Hotel, Tokyo. It was completed in 1923, the year of the 7.9 magnitude Great Kanto earthquake, which it survived. How do you view the current state of the world's preparedness for such disasters?

The world society, as a whole, is unaware of and cannot feel the energy of the Earth. They have a sense of superiority that they alone, as human beings, know that they are in control. It is an arrogance which time and time again is proving that they are not working with the Earth, that they are actually making an enemy of the Earth. She is showing them that their arrogance is their downfall, because while they claim to have scientific evidence that what they are constructing will withstand the shaking of the Earth, they are not taking into consideration the fact that the planet not only shakes but undulates. They think of it as a solid mass. They don't see it as a living, breathing thing, and in their arrogance they take account only of certain ways that a structure can be moved.

So this type of architecture is still faulty in your opinion?

Absolutely.

Is it going to be tested much in the near future?

It is going to be tested quite a bit in the near future—from shakings, quakes, weather-imposed tests such as wind and water. There are going to be a lot of things going on throughout the planet because of the arrogance of not caring, and of being unconcerned with what has been put in place.

You built several special buildings, such as the Guggenheim Museum in New York; the large Florida Southern College campus, including the Anne Pfeiffer Chapel; and on a smaller scale, Unity Temple in Oak Park; and your own sprawling homes: "Taliesin," Wisconsin, and "Taliesin West," Arizona. Which one satisfied you the most?

Of all of my buildings, the one that I felt the closest to was the Pennsylvania house, "Fallingwater;" I could feel the flow of the water within every board and tile in that house.

In your book The Disappearing City *(1932) you outlined "Broadacre City," the concept of a new type of suburban development. Were you to return to planet Earth today, how would you go about community planning in this environmentally conscious age?*

My biggest problem, were I to come back now, would be that I would have no memory of anything that had come about in my prior lives. Were I to come down as an architect, even with the sensitivities and sensibilities that I had in my life as Frank Lloyd Wright, I would be fighting the economic patterns on the planet right now. There are just too many variables for any really long-term planning to create a trend at this time.

What about the usage of fossil fuels for commuting, and that type of issue?

I don't know that I would have any effect on commuting unless I came back as a designer of motor conveyances. The use that the current inhabitants of the planet are making of the resources of the planet is sinful—if there were such a thing as sin. People will understand me when I say "sinful." It is against the basic principles of ecology, economy, and living in harmony with your neighbors. It is all based upon people thinking that they are entitled to whatever they want, even if it has a detrimental effect upon their neighbors, and until and unless the inhabitants of the planet shift and become aware of their interconnectedness with all of the other beings on the planet, I don't see any shift in the selfishness that is prevalent on the planet right now.

And is this leading to some kind of disaster?

The disaster has already started. The change in weather patterns, the melting of the poles, the increase in seismic activity based upon pressure put on the various plates of the Earth have all begun and will continue.

Are you going to come down to help us with that situation, do you think?

I don't have any plans at this time to do that. I am working as a guide with a few people who are involved in attempting to work on some of these situations, but I do not plan on being in physical form for quite some of your Earth years.

Thank you, Frank Lloyd Wright, for speaking with us.

I hope that I have explained a little bit about a soul's variances during its physical lifetime.

Commentary

Toni: The energy I perceived with Frank was matter-of-fact about everything. Whether we were discussing his extreme accomplishments or his scandals, it was all matter-of-fact. Yes, it did occur; I was a participant; it was just something I did to learn something. There were no emotional ups and downs with it. The only time he became somewhat energetic was in talking about the interaction between the soul having a physical experience and the physicality of the planet. When he talked about the ecology, the energy flow, and an interchange between the human being and the planet and the energy on it, he became much more animated and interactive. I found him a very interesting person. He gave me some visual pictures when we were talking about his different designs and how they affected energy—that was also quite interesting.

Peter: There were three aspects of special interest to me in this dialogue with Wright, and also a number of minor comments for his followers to discuss.

The ephemeral asceticism of his early period, with his use of terms like Energy and Feng Shui, came first. It felt a little odd that this businessman-in-a-hurry would express so different an aspect of his character as to remark, "...some of my designs had assistance from non-physical architects whom I asked to help get the energy flows right." But the individualism of this Unitarian free spirit clearly means more to him now than the aggressive "take it or leave it" architect who was adept at bending his ambitious clients to his iron will (and his ever-expanding budget). Perhaps it is rather easier, back Home, to recall aesthetic energy issues than business concerns.

Second, Wright helped us to understand more fully the issue of when and how the lessons that we prepare for ourselves before we come down to planet Earth may occur. These lessons—the incident of the servant who murdered Mamah and her children and set fire to "Taliesin" and, later, the electrical fire there—assailed him after a relatively calm early life. Once he had come to terms with them in his heart, his life appears to have returned to equilibrium. For those who are new to talk from the Other Side, "contracts" are made before incarnation with other incarnating souls, that they and we will mutually provide experiences which represent lessons that each wants to learn during the forthcoming human lifetime.

The third element, mention of coming planetary disturbances, is explored in greater depth in my dialogue with George Orwell, later in the book. This may be of special interest to architects who must design buildings that, like Wright's Imperial Hotel in Tokyo, are able to withstand earthquakes. This was the starting point of his dismal list of physical horrors to be visited on us by planet Earth in the coming days. He called the natural challenges a "disaster," and said that this situation had already begun to affect our life because of our human egotism and greed, which have made us enemies of Mother Earth "against the basic principles of ecology, economy, and living in harmony with your neighbors." Frank Lloyd Wright will not be on Earth to share the coming troubles with us who are left on the planet. He's sitting disaster out this time around—for a change.

"This is what the future is like, this is what the universe is like. It's not in the form that we see with our eyes, it is in the energy that is all around us."

Pablo Picasso

1881-1973

Your father, José Ruíz, was an art teacher and considered you a prodigy. Was it his influence and his genes which gave you early and lasting success, or were you endowed with genius like Mozart and Einstein?

I am a soul who had previous incarnations within my chosen physical profession. What you call a prodigy is not a person who is experiencing a first life within an art. There is a bringing together of previous lives which have laid the foundation for going forward and developing in different ways new aspects of the art. All prodigies come down with part of the tapes of their prior existences still playing in their heads. That is how at an early age they seem to be much more advanced than they really are because they are drawing on previous experiences. I chose to come into that particular biological family so that I would have the ability and the tools readily available for me to jump right in where I had left off in my previous lifetimes.

So genetics and environment do count quite a bit?

I don't know if you can say "quite a bit," but they facilitate the direction you have planned for that particular lifetime. Were I to have been born into a cobbler's family I would not have had ready access to the paints and the canvasses. I don't suppose people would have cared to have decorated shoes!

Tell us about your previous lives that were artistic.

I did a little bit of everything. Going back to prehistoric times I was one of the historians' pre-Neanderthals who recorded animals and migration paths on cave walls. I started art back in that time frame. I was also involved with a lot of oriental calligraphy which was very feeling—you're not only putting the characters down on the paper but you're putting your energy into them so that your message is conveyed on several levels at once. That is how I perceived my work—which to some seemed to be pure garbage but which had an energy in it. Some said my art had an idiosyncratic tendency, but people could not take their eyes off it because it was energy that pulled them in—the energy that I began to use a long time ago. I also did some renaissance art, painting chapel ceilings. I dabbled in folk carving and forming sculptures to get my energy into the clay or the marble. So I had a very complex history of mixing all the mediums that led me into what I accomplished in this last lifetime.

Were any of the people you have been currently famous?

Not by national standards. They were well known within their own small circles for being talented artisans. But they were no one whose works are now incorporated into any of the museums.

Among your early works, some, such as "Le Moulin de la Galette," were optimistic, but many were sorrowful, like your early 1899 "Self-portrait" in charcoal; or lonely, like "The Absinthe Drinker;" or like the 1903 portrait of your tailor friend Soler, full of melancholy. Were you unhappy at that time?

I was very aware of the depths of emotion that a person could sink to. I was going through a period of experiencing the depth of those emotions as a means of providing me with the energy to put that down on a canvas for another person to feel. Some people choose to be one level with their emotions, either a very low level, a very neutral level or a very high level, and they don't have the experience of feeling, of living and sensing the various beautiful experiences that can be had in the physical body. By that I mean, while it may seem strange to say that melancholy or depression is something we would choose *not* to have, it is a beautiful experience to know, so that you can rejoice in the opposite. I chose with those pictures to put people in an energy that would allow them to know if they were extremely happy or not. This let them know why they should rejoice in their happiness because they could be in that depression.

In your painting "La Vie," you were making a tribute to your friend Casagemas, who committed suicide. Can you explain the purpose of the picture?

Its purpose was my way of honoring him, of going through my physical grief over the loss of him, and attempting to get down on paper the energy of a transformation that can occur. As some people journal to get out their true feelings, I painted to express mine. It was a purging for me.

The setting was an artist's studio with a painting of nudes on a canvas in the background, then a male and female nude to the left and one dressed female figure to the right. Was there a particular meaning in this?

On a very esoteric level, we come in with nothing, we go out with nothing. That is the discourse of the nudes, meaning that all of our life is about the experiences we have in between birth and death. With this, the painter is able to paint his life, he is able to determine what he experiences, and starts with the unclad body form. Then he can experience whatever he chooses to experience; then he goes out with only energy, the knowledge that he has not taken away anything that he physically gained. It was all a metaphor of life.

Wasn't the dressed figure that of a woman?

That's because I was in a period [laughs] when women appealed to me. Also, in that setting, the artist's major model was the woman. Had I put a naked me in the painting it would have been condemned! The naked man and woman stood for the experiences which could be had in human form. The woman clothed was going through the experiences of life. The babies were the coming in. So for the coming in and the going out both couples were totally naked.

Another picture, "The Last Moments," has been discovered to have been covered up by "La Vie." What was that painting, and why did you destroy it?

It was too idealistic as I was painting it, and it did not make me feel that I was able to express the emotions that I had. I started it in total grief without honoring the entire process of life. To me it did a disservice.

This was your grief over the death of your friend?

Yes. It was totally inadequate to convey the feelings I had of the entire experiences of life and of the life that he had led.

It is said that, as a young man, you were inspired by the work of Courbet, Manet, and Toulouse-Lautrec. What did you take from their art and make your own?

Freedom! Freedom to do what the heart chooses to do. Also it was the energy they put into their paintings. Each one of those artists had a way to take and to capture not a flat surface but the energy of what was going on. Whether it was the energy of flowers growing in a lily pond or the energy of dancers and of human experiences, I took from them the energy of life.

Historians talk about various periods in your painting: The Blue Period was characterized by the use of a blue palette and subjects including prostitutes and beggars. Then after four years the Rose Period with light colors, pink, blue, beige, and rose, and a change of subject to harlequins and clowns —circus people. What was in your mind when making such a change of course?

This was the changing course of my thinking and experimenting. The Blue Period was a time of melancholy and depression for me. It was a time when I was considering what might be seen as the negative aspect of humanity—how badly one person could treat another, and the angst they would carry with them out of such an experience. In the backgrounds of my Blue Period, within the intermingling of the blues, there was that which created a boiling, twisting, roiling energy that took a person and said, "If you want to experience the deepest interactions that can be had in humanity, jump in and join me. You will experience sadness, you will experience depravation, you will experience the dark side of human life."

After I felt that I had had enough of the energy within that view of humanity, I chose to go on to the joyous, the growing, the lightness of the roses and pinks. It was as if sunshine were coming from the darkness of night into the brilliance of day—and also into the frivolity that surrounds people, so they could feel the happiness. Then, whatever they did brought them and others a way to contrast the blues, which were very deep and ponderous, with the roses, which were light and fluffy.

In 1905 you turned more to sculpture and large nudes, and finally, at the end of 1906, to cubism. How important to you were Paul Cézanne and your friend Georges Braque in this development, and how much came from within yourself?

The majority of it came from within. I was always aware of what was going on around me, but I caught on to what was being accepted by others a little bit—I still had to eat! It was observing what others did within the art and then taking those primary formulas and pulling out of myself what seemed to match. The sculptures were just what came out of my hands. I would go into a trance and just let my hands pull the energy from my core. When I went into the cubism phase, I was in an arena where I was attempting to communicate in the most primitive fashion with the essence of a person, saying that you don't need to have nice, beautiful, shapely forms (that I so dearly loved to work with). You could have straight lines! You could have primary colors! The combination you used with them could touch deep into a person and trigger emotions, trigger experiences. It wasn't for the inexperienced to get that out of the paintings but for one who picked up the energy of a painting. It was a new step. It was saying, "This is what the future is like, this is what the universe is like. It's not in the form that we see with our eyes, it is in the energy that is all around us."

Were you psychically aware of energy?

In the way you ask the question, yes. I didn't think of it that way, I just felt my way through life. I could feel a color. I could feel how the vibration of a color interacted with everything that was around it, with both animate and inanimate objects. I was aware of how a color impacted the mood of a person. It was that knowledge, experience, and the wisdom within me which allowed me to get feelings into my art.

What was the influence upon your cubism of African and early Iberian works of art?

Since I once had practiced them myself before they became known to collectors, it was like a revisiting of some of my background. I was an African artisan.

Artist or artisan?

Artisan, because at that time art was not only what was painted on the walls and put primarily onto wood to hang up, but it was also what was woven into reed baskets and into mats. So anyone who participated in artwork was multi-faceted, because putting colors onto a flat surface wasn't a way people could support themselves. They had to put art into the baskets, into something that had a useful purpose for other people.

So cubism became your hallmark. People have often asked about your works, "What does that mean?" Now, from your present position at Home, can you tell puzzled lay people what cubism is all about?

Cubism is about simplicity. It is about containment of various aspects of ourselves within boxes or cubes that lie upon, behind, and partially within other aspects of ourselves, and each aspect has a color vibration that affects the things that are near, within, or connected. It is part of the sacred geometry that is a form of communication within the universe. I never went into that as an explanation because it seemed to be [laughs] contrary to who I was at the time, and I didn't want the energy of what I was working on to be analyzed by the mathematicians.

You refused to accept payment for your very large, untitled, monumental sculpture in Chicago. You were enthusiastic but entirely enigmatic about it. Is it a woman, a bird, a horse, or an abstract?

It is a combination of what I felt was the energy of the City. It encompassed all of human life. It combined with that spiritual aspects of the angels. The morphing of the sculpture's outer appearance caused by the weather was representative of the experiences that we learn in life. The blending of the surfaces as the moisture rains down upon it shows everything in our existence is interconnected. It was for me a gift to a very active part of the planet, and those who go and feel the energy within it see what they need to see for the next step in their growth. That is why everybody sees something different within the sculpture.

Between the world wars your style mellowed somewhat and you did not embrace surrealism. Why was that?

Surrealism took the energy that I was putting within my pieces to a level that was on par with a mind that is on drugs. It wasn't part of the being and the feeling of what was real to the body.

You were truly prolific but did not care to sell a large quantity of your work. Was that deliberate?

In some regards, yes, because I chose to be surrounded by the energy that came out of me. Sometimes there would be so much of my energy in a painting or in a piece that, if I sold it, it was as if I had sold part of myself. It was easier for me to give it into the care of another and then I would be in many, many different places but never in exchange for a price.

Do you feel now, with some historians, that your post-World War II work has been rather neglected?

To be honest (as you would say), I don't care. I did what I did to have the experiences. What people need to feel, I hope they will allow themselves to feel through my work. There will be different times in the coming years on the planet when people will need different energies out of my various works. I hope that it is there for them, even if it is only for a small segment of the population. I did not paint, I did not sculpt pieces for other people; I did them for myself as an expression of who I was, where I was going, and what I felt. Those which were roundly applauded by people were of a vibration to feel and to accept. Those which were disregarded, like that period you mentioned, were so because people's focus was in a different direction from where my art was at the time.

In the non-material spirit world, how can souls visualize and appreciate art?

There's a difficulty in answering that question because we don't have visual sight as you do. We sense and live in the vibrations. Each of the various pigments within a picture gives off a vibration equivalent to the color within the spectrum. We can stand energetically in front of a picture and know what is there by the vibrations emanating from it.

So you visit Earth and stand in front of pictures?

Yes, sometimes we do that to have the experience, or we can bring up the imprint of that energy, either from experience or from a database.

You were a pacifist and a communist; you opposed Franco but kept out of harm's way in France. Did social causes actually mean much to you?

No. It was accepted that if people had an impact on the populous (artistically or not), they were supposed to have an opinion. So I expressed various opinions from time to time only to be left alone to do whatever I chose. Had I not been those things (pacifist, communist, etc.), I would have been pursued by people to become part of their cause. This gave me a label so that I was considered "harmless" and then they left me alone.

Okay, Pablo, one thing has defeated me. I lost count of all the relationships you had with women, some of whom you treated shabbily. Also I guess that no one knows exactly how many explicit paintings and lithographs you created of women in your last years. Were you obsessed with sex?

[laughs] In the physical form I went through a period of indulgence. That was to satisfy all of the animal yearnings that I had put on the back burner for some years. It would be considered by many to be excessive. I was simply in the position of being able to open my door and have it filled by those who wanted to come and experience the master! I courted a lot of that in sketches because the beauty of the energy of another human being, especially in an intimate relationship, is like a beacon that can be set ablaze. I recorded numerous, even hundreds of energy releases in what you call sketches. It's not for me now to judge what the human flesh did, but just to say that I experienced as much as I could.

With that in mind, are you planning to return to planet Earth soon?

I have contemplated it, but I have not seen a way in which I could really contribute to the art world, since the majority of art that really impacts people now is done graphically on computers. I get no energetic feel from that.

You could come down as an artist's model, perhaps!

I don't think so. I can't sit on the sidelines—I have to participate.

Thank you, Pablo Picasso, for talking with us.

It's my pleasure.

Commentary

Toni: When Picasso was talking about a piece of art, the emotional feeling he got from it and the vibration that was given off, I was right there, feeling the energy he was feeling. When he talked about the Blue Period it was like a pall of depression over all, but it was an energetic thing, not something you might consider sad. There was a depth of his sensing an emotion and being able to live within that emotion, able to see things through the eyes of those down on their luck or depressed. When he talked about the Rose Period it was as if there were bright spotlights on everything and the sun had come out (the Blue was like night) and everyone was in the open—I even smelled flowers.

The conversation about the Chicago sculpture was full of whimsy, almost as if he were saying, "Boy, did I pull the wool over a lot of people's eyes—but look what it started in so many lives." They had begun to look at art in a way that they had never done before, trying to connect with what it meant, with the energy it gave off. I saw kids playing on the sculpture in the city center with such happiness that people would think of art as something with which they could interact. He evoked a sense of completion and of satisfaction at having accomplished what he had set out to do. The popular response was more than enough payment; nothing else was needed in the physical sense.

In the Cubist Period it felt more like I was talking to a mathematician than an artist. There was a lot he was trying to accomplish by subliminal communication. I saw pieces of geometric figures—some completely contained in the art, but some only hinted at so people would have to go into the art to see the rest of the figure. It was almost as if there were words written within the figures, giving people a hidden message, very much like Light Language.

Peter: Although Picasso had some helpful comments about issues concerning individual paintings and his contact with past lives, this dialogue was dominated by the concept of energy of color and form. In talking with musicians in this series the concept of vibration has been very important; with speakers and writers the energy of words has been much discussed. When we talk with any soul at Home we make direct contact with an energetic being without a discernable form who communicates with others by means of energetic vibrational impulses. Back Home we do not stroll about the Elysian fields dressed in human bodies and clothes that look like Roman togas. Eyes and ears and speech organs are not needed. So the common basis of thought (even the soul's memories of lives lived on Earth) is always phrased energetically. In this brief encounter with Picasso, this bias toward explaining everything—color, shape, purpose—as energy is made crystal clear. This is why art, music, and fine speech are so important to us—they are the best means we have of experiencing life in our eternal Home.

"I knew from the very beginning of my life that I was to be a general, a great warrior and leader of men."

George S. Patton, Jr.

1885-1945

George Smith Patton, Jr., your father told you stories of military glory and your family came from a long line of soldiers from General Mercer in the American Revolution to some who fought and died on both sides during the American Civil War. What else prepared you as a child for your 36-year career in the US Army?

From the very beginning I connected with prior existences, going back to the time of the Roman legions, the great Napoleonic war battles, and the conquests of Alexander. Almost all of my prior incarnations were of a warlike nature, not necessarily in the heat of battle but in the preparation, the movement, the logistics of war. As a child I was bringing together all my memories of the things that had happened to me. To stimulate my memory cells, I devoured all the books and readings I could find on ancient battles, the majority of which I had participated in. Some of them I studied for the flavor of what other commanding generals had done. Although most souls come down with amnesia, I knew from the very beginning of my life that I was to be a general, a great warrior and leader of men.

You said on one occasion that you were the Carthaginian general Hannibal.

That's correct.

Who else can you name?

Marcus Aurelius—he was running the legions of Rome. I was the son of Genghis Kahn. I went back into pre-history (so far as written records go) in organizing the first humans in their joint conquest of animals and less-evolved humans. Within these incarnations my entire experience was about conquest.

You also absorbed myths like Homer's Iliad and Odyssey, and the works of Shakespeare.

The written word, in the way it is formed on a page, is very much the way you must form a regiment of soldiers in order to accomplish something. I studied every aspect of organization, every thought which came down, even through the chronicles of the oral traditions and the myths, to glean from them every piece of information I could find of how to sway people both with the written word and by commanding them. No possible interaction between humans escaped my attention. It was more than attention—it was scrutiny.

Yet I understand you were dyslexic. Didn't that reading disorder affect you severely as a child?

It only gave me more of an impetus to work hard "to get it." When I was finally able to accomplish what I did with a word, I knew I could accomplish anything. When I worked to glean from the written word the energy that was within, I had to convert the gibberish I saw into understandable lessons. These I used to teach myself to command people and in the conquering of that situation I conquered myself as well.

Was there a time of breakthrough for you?

Yes. Dyslexia was something that I held in check with the force of my mind. Whenever I did not totally concentrate it popped up in my teens and twenties. Even when I was at the military academy I had some difficulties.

You had to retake your first ("plebe") year at West Point Academy.

Yes, I did. It was as much the stress of the Academy as it was my excitement in knowing that I was moving forward with my dream and that I knew my destiny. So I was not able to exert the attention necessary to hold dyslexia at bay.

You maintained a belief in reincarnation all your life, didn't you?

Frequently in dream states, even in meditation or day-dreaming, I would go back and visit those scenes. As I began to travel, walking down roads and through fields I was transported back to battles in which I had taken part.

Did you use that information in your work?

I brought forward the wisdom I had gleaned from my past incarnations into the life of George Patton.

You had a softer side. While at West Point you renewed your childhood friendship with Beatrice Ayer. Shortly after graduation in May 1910 you married her, and subsequently she bore you two daughters. People say that neither of you ever had another sweetheart.

It was a moment of fulfillment for me when we married. In my mind, and in the lives I had visited, I had always been this harsh, thoughtless, sometimes almost callous human being. But I yearned for a physical connection to another being. Most females were frightened by my intensity. My darling saw through me, and she saw that in my heart all I wanted to do was to succeed in what I did. She was a nurturing nest for me, someplace where I could always go and be recharged, and she bore me two beautiful daughters who were the love of my life. It was a little tough for me, though, having daughters, because I could not pass on to them the military urges that were the core of me at that time. They in turn allowed me to feel the feminine side which is contained within all of us. It was only when at home or in their presence that I truly laughed.

Were you ever a woman in a past life?

Now that I'm back Home I know that I was, but during my last life the only memories I was able to access were of males in military settings.

I understand that as a soul you are without gender. How do you balance the male and female aspects of your being?

It's individually determined by whatever our desires and our needs are in physical form. For instance, my whole thrust as George Patton was to be a military leader in the perception of those who would follow me, and those who would cheer with me (or slightly above me). To be successful I had to be totally enmeshed in the military. Granted, I had to be fair, but ruthless in performance, knowing that my determinations might lead to the physical death of others. The feminine aspect of me was there but it was suppressed.

It is a choice. If, for instance, I wanted to be a military man but possessed a beautiful singing voice (possibly a feminine characteristic), I could choose to indulge myself with my singing, letting others feel the passion within me for something that wasn't military, but doing that might siphon off my effectiveness. So the choice made at the time is to concentrate on the energy of the experience your soul wishes to have in that body and not let anything interfere with it.

I had, as all souls have, a feminine and a masculine side, but I chose to conceal the feminine, except in some interchanges with my family. My presentation to the world was that of a very strong male figure—that was my choice. The choice that some other people make is to be within an ambiguity, to have their female energy primarily show while they are in a male body, or vice versa, have their male energy show while in a female body. My choice was just to have male energy as the outward persona I presented to the world.

Despite your initial failure at West Point, you ended up with the distinguished rank of Corporal Adjutant. Then you were commissioned as a cavalry officer. How did the Academy, your service in the US Cavalry, and becoming the Army's youngest-ever Master of the Sword turn you into an advocate of armored warfare?

I learned to move with the times. My first foray into the cavalry came from my love of horses and my remembrance of both being with Genghis Kahn and, during the Napoleonic wars, the importance of the cavalry—they ruled! It was during this period, after my initial failure, that the respect I won from being able to command people began to move me through the ranks. My entire being was devoted to the military, so it was very easy to become Master of the Sword, which was a preferred weapon at that time. My whole life was focused but I was also very practical, seeing how a man on a horse, charging across a field with a sword, could easily be picked off by a bullet. They were no longer gentlemen facing each other sword to sword. So in order to develop an edge and to come into compliance with others, the tank became the ultimate weapon of the period when I was in command. With the tank (and all that beautiful horsepower under you) it was still a matter of horses and of movement. You could ride upon that horsepower into battle with a "sword" (the cannon) that could project beyond the reach of the arm. It was the only thing that made any sense, and it gave us an advantage.

In 1912 you represented the United States in the first modern pentathlon in the Stockholm Summer Olympic Games. In fencing, you were the only competitor to defeat the French épée champion. You achieved fifth place in the event. What actually happened in the shooting competition where you had been leading prior to changing pistols?

Mechanical difficulties. I had changed pistols and because I had put so much emphasis on Bessie, the one I began with, I had not spent adequate preparation time in adjusting the sights on the back-up.

So the story that you re-drilled your first holes is false?

Yes.

A reporter misquoted your statement that "it takes blood and brains to win a war," and so your nickname "Old Blood and Guts" was coined. You are seen as ruthless and ferocious, a brilliant but insubordinate leader who was mentally unstable. Looking back on your life, how do you now see yourself?

Well, as I said earlier, in order to win battles there must be sacrifices. It is over the bodies of those who make a pathway, a bridgehead for us, that we are able to succeed. I did not relish the loss of life that was necessary for victory, but I was pragmatic about it. The idea that I was mentally deranged came from…I call it "my inventiveness;" *they* called it "my insubordination." I didn't feel that just because something had worked in the recent past of military planning, we should not be able to reach back further into the past, to the tactics of other master warriors, and implement those to the surprise of the enemy who was very well aware of our books and what we were teaching our men.

In fact this happened in the Battle of the Bulge, didn't it?

Correct.

You practiced what you preached when you said, "You can't run an army without profanity." One of your least racist remarks was, "I'd rather have a German division in front of me, than a French one behind." You were thought to be uncouth, bloodthirsty, and a racist who hated African Americans, Jews, and Russians. What other nationalities have you been in your past lives?

I have been just about all of the races on planet Earth at one time or another, and the thoughts I expressed were not of these races as a whole being inferior. My pronouncements dealt only with the effectiveness of the people on the battlefield under me. If they could not perform to the standards I knew them capable of, I would sometimes say some things I shouldn't have. I was talking at that time only of the characteristics of the people I was dealing with, not of the character of those very same nationalities I had lived amongst formerly.

You apologized for lashing out at soldiers with self-inflicted wounds. How do you now view the US military's recent treatment of soldiers and marines with PTSD and emotional injuries incurred in Vietnam and the Iraqi wars?

I cannot say that I have any pride in the way I handled some of those issues. My only desire at that time was victory, was success. I held myself to a very high standard of honor and service and saw anyone who shot or stabbed themselves, in order to shirk their duty, as weak and cowardly. I now know that was something they had to experience. They had to experience the depression and fear that was there, and the self-recrimination later on. Their souls had chosen that. I saw it only on the physical plane, that they were taking away from me another piece of equipment, themselves, which I needed in order to accomplish the job. So it was a sabotage of my plan.

The way that the military is now dealing with these issues is not nearly as far as they could go. They do not appreciate that the human psyche is a very fragile thing. Just as I could not see that stress could cause a person to become unraveled, they do not see the full extent to which the pressures (which now are even more hideous in some regards than those that were faced by my men) are now confronting others. Were I in human form at this time, were I to re-incarnate at this time as George Patton, my personality would call them all "shirkers and laggards" because of the personal standards I set for myself and expected others to have. But I now know that, once again, I would be inflicting my judgment upon them, when in fact this is the pathway they have chosen, and life's lessons go much beyond what occurs on the battlefield. It goes through the rest of their human existence, and they do need assistance in dealing with it.

You said, "There is only one tactical principle which is not subject to change. It is to use the means at hand to inflict the maximum amount of wound, death, and destruction on the enemy in the minimum amount of time." Did President George H. W. Bush drop the ball in 1991 at the end of the Gulf war?

[laughs] The Gulf War was not a conflict of the kind I was engaged in. It was not an all-encompassing war effort. It was what we would call a policing action, and as such there is not a vested interest in the death and destruction and annihilation of your enemy, but rather in

bringing them back into compliance so that they can be productive. So it is very difficult to say. I don't see them as a parallel. I think your history is going to have to determine that, and it will be debated, but it was not a war like those I fought.

Would you have gone to war in Iraq after 9/11?

A ground war as was undertaken, no. The type of war that I would have engaged in at that time would be to confront exactly what we were dealing with, which was a planned disruption, annihilation, terrorism. That is what you would fight terrorism with. When you are dealing with an invisible enemy you cannot go and become visible. When you are visible you are a target walking down the road. If you are invisible and infiltrate, then you are successful.

In the battle at Meuse Argonne, you led a team of six soldiers on a dangerous mission, fully expecting to be killed. Five died, you were wounded. In 1945, the day before you were to return home to the United States, you were injured in a road accident and died as a result. Did your soul have a choice each time of whether to live or die?

Our souls always have a choice whether to live or die. We determine when it is we are going to transition. We set up the circumstances for it. At Argonne I did not have a death wish. A lot of frustration was upon me at that time. There was a discussion that things couldn't be done or wouldn't be done correctly. It was my desire to show that they could be done, even if at a sacrifice. My final action came when I had learned everything that there was for me to learn as George Patton. I was going back into an arena where I would not be able to be out in the field at war, and I no longer had a desire as George Patton to go on.

You said, "There's only one proper way for a professional soldier to die: the last bullet of the last battle of the last war." Is the world ever going to have a last war?

The face of war that I talked about then is different from the face of war at this time. Then there were conflicts that were clearly defined. You knew when you were going to battle someone. You knew who your enemy was. You knew the loosely formed rules of engagement. What is happening on the planet at this time has totally gotten away from war as in my time and in previous centuries. It has gotten down to individual pissing matches between people, whether it be genocide of rival tribes in Africa, religious wars in the Middle East, or all-out political battles in the Americas. That is the face of war at this time.

So are the massive preparations for army against army conflict, and such weapons as nuclear bombs, no longer needed?

They no longer have their place in your current time. Warfare has gone back to improvisation, creating a constant question: what is next? The majority of the damage being inflicted at this time in places like Iraq is made with improvised explosive devices with screws, nails, broken glass doing much more damage without the potential danger of nuclear bombs. Not only does it do the killing, but it engenders fear in everybody as to where the next explosion will occur and what it will look like.

Now that you are at Home, do you talk with Eisenhower, MacArthur, Montgomery, Churchill, and your other wartime comrades?

Oh, yeah—we joke about personality conflicts, sensational things that we did, and things we did that we probably wouldn't have done if we'd thought about them beforehand. We talk about other lives that we lived together, so it's not restricted to our time within the twentieth century.

How about Adolf Hitler and Joseph Stalin? How do you get on with them?

They are souls just as I'm a soul. They had their duties and obligations, their contracts, and their desires of things they wished to learn, as did we. The fact that our ideologies and political convictions were different while in body form is totally immaterial in spirit form because we are all the same.

So they didn't go to hell?

There is no hell except what you create for yourself on Earth. The battlefield was hell. Moving into places we had to destroy, in order to be victorious in our pursuits, created a hell. Hell is a physical thing. It is not an energetic, spiritual thing. In spirit form there is nothing but unconditional love. We laugh at some of the roles we played, but there is no sense of regret or satisfaction, of one-upmanship, or anything else. It was just the choices we made for the experiences we had.

Have you made any plans for the kind of life you will have next on planet Earth?

No, because whenever I get into body form my major energetic thrust tends to be for war. I would not want to participate in any of the conflicts going on at this time.

Thank you, George Patton, for speaking with us.

I salute all of you who are doing good work.

Commentary

Toni: There was a dynamic energy about him, almost as if he were lecturing a group of people. I had the sense that he wanted to be understood but didn't really care if he wasn't. He was just going to be himself and be true to himself. He had a sense of confusion, however, when the issue of self-inflicted wounds came up. Could there really be someone who wasn't true to himself, who wasn't honorable or self-sacrificing for the cause, or who was less than totally passionate about what he did and had taken an easy way out? But then, with the energy of the Other Side, Patton said that he did understand—maybe that was the nature of a soul's mission. So first the energy was rampant George Patton: "These men are shirkers, cowards, running away from themselves and their country." Then there was a softening: "But this is the lesson they chose to learn."

Talking about current conflicts (this dialogue took place in December 2006), there was a head-shaking at the way the world has sunk into such a sad state. You can no longer go out and fight; you must do all this sneaking around, pulling the carpet out from under your enemy instead of facing him man to man, sword in hand.

Peter: We uncovered a good deal in this dialogue with the powerful Patton. The first was that it is not sissy to have feelings about your past lives. He was conscious of them, although, I suspect, rather unwilling to acknowledge his prior female incarnations. In that respect he indicated that there are no gender differences between souls in their natural state at Home. He did have a tender side to his nature. He suppressed his desire to sing in order not to compromise his male persona. It was only when he was with his true love, Beatrice, and their two girls that, he said, "I truly laughed."

We saw the working out of his male drive in the way he tackled a physical challenge—in his case, dyslexia.

This had haunted him through his youth into his twenties: "Dyslexia was something that I held in check with the force of my mind." This tough-minded concentration on the big picture comes through in many famous lives.

In life Patton was tough. He was profane. He blasted people for not coming up to his personal standard and was accused of being racist—a charge he stoutly denied—and uncaring of men who wanted out of the war. In this last situation his cosmic view of the fragile human psyche now leads him to complain that the military is not sensitive enough to the needs of troops in battle. This is a reversal for us to note, showing how far the human ego can get things badly wrong. In life he was always focused on the need to win at all costs. This was in no way phony—he lived as he spoke—but now he has a more balanced view.

Another aspect of our dialogue deserves attention. When Patton died he was about to return to the USA from the battlefield and enter civilian life, but he died in a traffic accident. About this event he said, "Our souls always have a choice whether to live or die. We determine when it is we are going to transition. We set up the circumstances for it." This is both technically correct and a little misleadingly brief. It is true that we set up the general circumstances for our transition Home before ever we come to planet Earth. The details of our death are worked on by the souls who guide our progress. Therefore, there are no accidents resulting in our death, in the sense that if it is not our time to leave our present life we will not do so. Nevertheless, the means of our departure will often appear "accidental" to human eyes—we were on the bridge when it collapsed.

The whole truth is complex in that our death is not simply arranged by our human mind, but rather, it represents a prearranged event. We may die because we have learned all the lessons we came for, or because we have agreed in advance with fellow souls to give them the experience of our death and living without us. Some human minds have intervened to drag out their passing, other minds may terminate their being here by taking their own life, but in general, the choice of when and how to transition Home is a soul matter, not a matter of human choice. Perhaps in Patton's case his wife and daughters needed to experience life without his immensely powerful presence, and that was his parting gift.

"I didn't care where the adulation was coming from, just as long as I had it, just as long as I was in the limelight."

Babe Ruth

1895-1948

George Herman Ruth, Jr., you were born in Baltimore, Maryland, one of eight children born to your mother, Kate, though only you and your sister Marnie survived infancy. Your father owned a tavern near the waterfront. Your parents worked very hard and found it difficult to find time for parenting. Tell me about your parents.

They were very hard-working, possessed people. When I say "possessed," I mean they were possessed of an elusive dream that they could accomplish prosperity. They did everything they could to create it. They got so entwined in the business that it, rather than my sister and I, became their life. We were like little decorations around the side. For the local community they were a center point of solidarity. Whatever happened that needed to be discussed, they enabled people to air their feelings about it, whether it was politics, issues in life, even the weather. Their place was where everyone came to feel that they had a voice in what was going on.

You were a little pub kid running wild, stealing, playing hooky, chewing tobacco, and drinking whiskey. When you were seven you were sent to live at the St. Mary's Industrial School for Boys and for the next 12 years were largely separated from your family. Was that all part of the life lesson you had planned before incarnating?

One of my life lessons was discipline, so I was put into a place where I would be able to examine what discipline was. Of course, as my life at that time showed, I had no discipline. I had no one to tell me what was right and wrong, so I made my own rules. I was left to my own devices and became totally incorrigible, and so rather than wreck all that my parents had built so carefully, I was shipped off. This was the idea within my life: to know what it was to have no limits, then to be in a situation where everything was limited.

But then when you went into the rest of your life, you maintained a pretty wild exterior, didn't you?

The exterior was wild, but the interior was controlled. While I knew my limits as to how far I could go with something before really impacting society or other people, inside I knew what it was I wanted to accomplish. I was very disciplined inside with being able to direct my energy when I needed to do something, as in making a living.

You were suspended once for alcohol abuse. How serious a problem was your drinking?

It controlled me. I was at that time rebelling against the discipline/non-discipline that my entire life had been, and I found that if I dove into the bottle, I could just lie around in that beautiful liquid—let it sustain me, let it nourish me, so to speak, and take me away from everything else that could possibly affect me. I was totally under the control of that liquid.

And it nearly destroyed you in the end?

It nearly destroyed me because I let it have such a grip on me that nothing else seemed to matter. I only felt good when I was in a state of total numbness, and when I didn't have to worry about what was going on. But then it started to affect the organs of my body—I think they call it "pickling."

Brother Matthias, the strong Prefect of Discipline at St. Mary's school, spent a great deal of time with you because you were so badly behaved. Tell us about him.

He was a true saint. He saw within me a spark of determined energy that, if it could be harnessed, if it could be directed, would allow me to accomplish great things. He was the total antithesis of my parents, who didn't see me unless I was in trouble, didn't care about me unless I was underfoot, and only just tolerated me. He wanted me to know who I was and how I was impacting all of those around me. He made me become aware of the results of what I was doing, and he would be the first one to appear out of nowhere when I broke any of the rules. It was almost as if he had a sixth sense of exactly how my behavior was turning and twisting.

Did he have a contract with you as a soul to give you that discipline?

Absolutely. He's actually a soul mate of mine—a soul mate being someone who has the most impact on you, and with whom you make a contract—and he was the one who was there to put my feet to the fire, to say, "This is what you wanted to deal with. You wanted to deal with discipline issues; here is how you can do it. Make the choice of whether you're going to learn this lesson or have to come back and do it again."

At St. Mary's you learned to play baseball as catcher and pitcher. Then, when you were 19 years old and six feet tall, Jack Dunn of the Baltimore Orioles saw you play and signed you up to play for his team. Was this the point at which you started to be called "Babe"?

It grew up around that period of time. The Babe idea was more a reference to the feeling that people got around me, rather than my physical appearance.

Jack Dunn was your guardian by law, wasn't he?

Yes, he became my guardian.

Weren't you called "Jack's newest babe?"

Others called me "Jack's newest babe," because he referred to me as "Babe." During that time I started spending more and more time with him. He realized that there was a wistfulness, a tenderness inside of me, like a babe that had not been exposed to any of the toughening of the outside world but had just floated and bounced from pillar to pillar without absorbing what was taking place.

Did you mind that the world called you Babe, not George?

At first I did because I thought it was a derogatory comment, but then it became such a term of endearment with people, and in a sense I felt I was finally being accepted as part of the family.

You stayed with the Baltimore Orioles for less than six months, then you found yourself playing in major league baseball for the Boston Red Sox. Was it a dream come true?

It was a dream but not of long standing, because I had never thought it possible. I had envisioned myself being a longshoreman or factory worker or something like that. I did not have any expectations. The ball that I played in the beginning was for fun and excitement, and it was during those first few games that I realized I was really good compared with the other people. Then it became a dream to see how good I could really be.

So you wanted to move to Boston?

I did want to move to Boston, yes.

In 1914, when you were 19, you married Helen Woodford. You bought two homes, one in New York City, the other in the Massachusetts countryside, and adopted a baby girl named Dorothy in 1921. But your marriage fell apart soon after. Why was that?

It was an impulsive decision on my part to get married. I so desperately wanted a family, and the opportunity arose because I was becoming a little bit of a cult hero in the prowess that I was showing on the diamond, and that drew people to me, but I didn't know how to be a part of a family. I was having trouble being part of a team, much less having the intimacy of a close-knit family.

Did drink get in the way?

Not that much. It was mainly trying to acclimate and assimilate, get used to what it was like to be close to a person, to be always with them, to have them depend upon you, to be responsible for the outcome of a certain situation on a personal level.

In fact, shortly after you adopted Dorothy, you met the actress Claire Hodgson. Did that affect the marriage?

It affected the marriage only because I saw stars twinkling before my eyes. I was finally coming to the realization that I was a somebody, and it went to my head. I also, of course, was in the prime of my life and thought that I had a lot of things to share with women.

Then in 1929 Helen died in a house fire, and your daughter came to live with you. Two months later you married Claire Hodgson, who was a widow. She was two years your junior and had a daughter, Julia, whom you adopted. Your girls gave you five grandchildren in all. What sort of father and grandfather did you become?

I would like to say that I was a good one, but it was a lot of trial and error. I was a much better grandfather than father, because as a father I sometimes became so frustrated that my emotions came out and I would blow off at the girls for no reason whatsoever. But, again, they were part of what I came to learn. In addition to discipline, I needed to have emotional connections to people and to be able to share things with them. When the grandchildren came along, without the stresses of having to be one of the sole reliable people in their lives, it was easy to spoil the kids.

You had an amazing career. In 1916, as a 21-year-old pitcher in your very first World Series game for Boston, you created a long-lasting record on the mound when, in game four against the National League Champion Brooklyn Robins, you pitched 13 scoreless innings in the 14-inning, longest complete game in World Series history. What did instant success feel like?

It was a validation for me that I really could make something of myself, but I wasn't ready for it. It went to my head. I became even more insufferable with some of the people around me who cared for me, and I also found it a very good reason to party.

You performed excellently for the Red Sox and batted 29 home runs in the next season, handily breaking Buck Freeman's single-season home-run record. But then Harry Frazee, the new owner of the Boston club, went and sold you to the New York Yankees. How did you feel about that sudden turn of events?

Well, it wasn't really a sudden turn of events. I was becoming pretty much of an insufferable bore when it came to being a team player, and I wouldn't do all of the little things that the club wanted me to do for promotion, etc., and my britches got so big, I guess, that they decided to let somebody else pay for the pants.

What did the Boston Red Sox and Yankee fans really mean to you, Babe?

I didn't care where the adulation was coming from, just as long as I had it, just as long as I was in the limelight. If people appreciated me when I stepped out onto the field, I felt a sense of worth within myself. I didn't have a loyalty to any particular group of people. I only had a loyalty to making myself feel good, so the fans were a vehicle providing me with the energy to feel good about myself. I didn't sense that any one group was better than any other, as long as they could put me up on that pedestal of being their hero.

With the Yankees, you quickly replaced your own batting record with 54 home runs in 1920. You bettered that record the next year with 59, and in 1927 batted 60 homers, your personal best. Your career total was a record 714 homers, with a record .690 lifetime slugging percentage. As a batter, how much did all these statistics mean to you then and now?

Then they were very crucial to who I saw myself as and who others saw me as. They were my credentials, my platform, my red carpet to whatever I wanted to do. Right now they mean nothing.

People breaking athletic records today raise suspicions of performance-enhancing drugs. How do you view that issue?

Well, unless alcohol is considered a performance-enhancing drug, they'd better take a better look at things. We didn't have the availability of all these things now occurring in athletics. We didn't control what we did. If we could go out and perform, the management didn't care what we had done the night before, or even what we had done the hour before the game. It was not unusual in some clubs to have a flask passed around in the dugout, so the only enhancing substances we used were those of the grain.

I suppose since you don't care about records now, you don't care whether somebody has taken a drug and beaten your record.

It doesn't make any difference to me as far as the spirit goes—that was just a life, something I experienced. If I were still in physical form, I would say, "Cheater, cheater, liar, liar, pants on fire!"

As an exciting batter (whom people still call The Great Bambino, The Sultan of Swat, and more), you so electrified the New York crowds that their numbers enabled the team to build Yankee Stadium, which opened in 1923. Your longest hit was at Navin Field, Detroit, when you hit a ball 575 feet from the home plate. Do you remember that moment?

I remember the impact of the ball on the bat. It felt different. It felt almost as if I had taken an energy outside of myself, added it to my normal energy, and brought it around with that swing to come in contact with the ball. There was an interesting feeling—I almost felt sorry for the ball as it was hit, because I knew it was going a long way!

Then there was the controversial drama at Wrigley Field, Chicago, in the fifth inning of Game 3 in the 1932 World

Series against the Cubs. Charlie Root was on the mound. The first two balls were strikes. Then you pointed toward the center-field bleachers and beat the next ball in a huge arc right out of Wrigley Field. Okay, you slugged a record-distance homer, but the discussion was about your gesture, and you gave various explanations to the press. Were you pointing at the pitcher or the bleachers, and was your gesture meant to be obscene?

The gesture was definitely not meant to be obscene. I enjoyed playing, and what I was doing was pointing first to the pitcher, acknowledging that he had gotten me with his first two pitches, that he had bettered me, and then I pointed over his head, where I was going to send the next one.

This was your last homer in the World Series, wasn't it?

Yes, it was, and a fitting climax to that day.

Surrounded by controversy, as usual...

Of course—that was my whole life.

You wanted to manage the Yankees and then, later, the Boston Braves. You turned down the Newark Bears, a minor league team. Then in 1938 you were passed over as manager by the Brooklyn Dodgers. How well did you cope with these disappointments, and with the end of your legendary career as a baseball player?

During that period I was going through a series of thought processes where I thought that I was the greatest thing the world had ever seen, as far as baseball was concerned, and that people who didn't take advantage of my prowess were depriving themselves of a superior intellect in baseball. As I see it now—what a pompous jerk! And I also realize that since I'd never been much of a team player, as a manager I had to be horrible. I didn't really appreciate the interconnection that had to be built between the players to make a cohesive unit. All I did was pit one person against another, as I had for my entire career pitted myself against the administration, against the owners, against baseball in general. That was what fueled my successes, but as a manager, it was death to a team in season.

Why did you get cancer in your neck and face?

The neck is where the vocal cords arise. The voice that comes out portrays the energy of the person. I was not being truthful to myself at that particular time in my life, as I had not been throughout most of my life. The cancer was for me a denial of the fact that I wasn't truthful. The face was because I showed a face to the world that wasn't the true George Herman Ruth.

In the end, did you learn all your lessons?

While in physical form, I did not completely learn everything I had chosen to experience. As I went through the review, as I left my body and went back Home into the energetic, spiritual body, I saw what I had done and felt the true depth and meaning behind all the situations I had placed myself in, and all of the anxieties that I had caused other people. I realized how I could have modified my behavior to live as a normal person would live (if there is such a thing as "normal"). In the end, I realized everything I had done, the lessons I had attempted to learn, how I had fulfilled the physical activity of learning those lessons, and then, once I was non-physical, I integrated the learning so I won't have to learn them again.

You said, "It's hard to beat somebody when they don't give up." Looking back on your life, what moment or achievement gives you most pleasure?

As I sit here it's very difficult to pick out one thing that gives me pleasure. All of them, in their totality, now give me pleasure because I did learn what I came down to learn. I don't take any particular pleasure in physical things, because they were all parts of the lessons that I came to Earth to learn.

Thank you, Babe Ruth, for talking with us.

I'm hoping that, from this discourse, people don't think any less of the legends of the human Babe Ruth because of the fact that they now see that what I did was learn spiritual lessons.

They'll have to learn, won't they?

They will, as I did.

Commentary

Toni: During the majority of the interview, Ruth's energy was like that of an immature child. Looking back now, he was very aware that his behavior wasn't what he would like it to have been. It was almost an embarrassment, but at the same time he was not apologizing for what he had been because, had he acted differently, he might not have learned the lessons that he needed to learn. In the latter part of the interview he became somewhat philosophical, analyzing how he now sees the reactions that people had to him—both the hero worship and the adverse "he's a pain in the butt; we don't want to put up with him." He now fully accepts both aspects of his life. It was interesting, because I could then feel a very spiritual person there, but he had really put himself back into the persona of the body in order to give us as much of a feeling of his human life as he possibly could.

Peter: It is amazing how so many of the individual souls whom we have encountered in this series have turned catastrophic childhood experiences into a springboard for subsequent major adult achievements. The little boy of seven running wild, getting drunk on whiskey, becomes a slugger who remembers his most recent life as having been permanently awash in alcohol. But somehow he just managed to keep away from ultimate disgrace. In the midst of roistering and womanizing, something inside him spoke of self-discipline. It was his youthful experience of tough outer discipline, rigorously applied by a hard-hitting cane wielded by Brother Matthias. I should have asked whether slugging the ball so hard and far was the way in which Ruth got his own back for the countless punishments he had received at St. Mary's school!

A lesson for us all is in the lack of concern Ruth feels about performance-enhancing drugs now, just like his apparent lack of pride in his amazing record as a baseball player. When, like him, we all finally return Home, we become quite disinterested in things we held so dear in our immediate past life. Passionate relationships (of both love and hatred) will normalize, and the record of personal achievements, which we may have prized, becomes an interesting by-product of one among many past physical lives. If ever there were a testimony to the old saying "You can't take it with you," this is it. Wealth, power, achievement all fade. What matters to the soul is whether it learned the lessons it set up for itself before incarnating, all presented in the experiences in its physical lifetime.

There was wistfulness in the great slugger's final comment, but no more than that. For him now, what counts is the soul lessons he learned during his time on planet Earth; not how many homers he hit. But I guess that won't stop people like you and me from spending fortunes on Babe Ruth memorabilia—or, for that matter, proudly writing our books containing conversations with him long after his leaving planet Earth for Home.

"I played each part of my life as though it were an elaborate stage show in which I wanted to engage the world."

Ernest Hemingway

1899-1961

Ernest Miller Hemingway, you are seen as one of the great English language writers of the 20th century. Aged 18, you worked six months as a cub reporter for the Kansas City Star *newspaper. Was the instruction you received there the key to your terse, vigorous, but understated style?*

I found it very restrictive, but it did have the effect of letting me know how important words were to reach people, and that being verbose generally loses your audience rather than titillating them. So I would say that it was a very good grounding for me to learn how sometimes a few words have much more impact than a paragraph.

Your time in high school was also important. You got involved in a newspaper there, didn't you?

We had an excellent proctor for the paper who would not let us go ranting off onto our little fantasy trails without putting facts down. That led to the newspaper job. It came to my writing after that. Those foundations allowed me to get into the energy of anything toward which I was trying to draw the reader. With that technique I built a whole universe into each one of my books, which would place the reader there with the writer.

If you were instructing young writers today, what would be the essential message you would give to them?

[laughs] It would depend on what they were writing for, because when you say "writer" it can be anything: a journaler, who conveys only his own thoughts, to whom I would say "Be truthful to yourself;" a textbook or catalogue writer, to whom I would say "Be true to your subject matter;" a dime novelist who is giving a quick thrill to people, to whom I would say (or am I not able to say this here!), "Be true to your eroticism, that which the people want." Then to the novelist I would say, "You have to create a universe. You have to create a world that will act as a vortex, sucking in the energies of what you are describing to the readers as well as sucking them into the very center. So with that you must be true to the energy you are trying to convey, and to the particularity, the flavor, of your scenario."

Your father was a physician, and your mother's passion was for singing and strict religious observance. Looking back now, do you see your supremely adventurous life as something of a reaction against the conformity of your narrow suburban Chicago upbringing?

I don't know if it was exactly a rebellion. I did feel very constrained in my home life. I had great respect for my father, his intelligence and his purposefulness, but his was a boring life. I loved my mother dearly, but there were some parts of her religious fanaticism that put a red flag in front of this bull. I could not have anything to do with it. I did get a richness of the arts from her, however, and I saw the beauty that is contained within all things if you let it loose and if you go with it. If it is a rebellion to take those things and know I did not want them (with the exception of the arts)—that I did not want that structure, that stricture—then it was a rebellion. But basically, I was being true to myself, true to the wanderlust that came upon me early, true to the need to experience whatever was placed in front of me, and to experience it to the fullest—not just to sip it, not just to take a little taste of it, but to immerse myself in it and become a part of it.

Many of your works allude to sexual ambiguities and destructive relationships between men and women. Grace, your mother, dressed you early on as a girl, calling you Ernestine. Later in your life F. Scott Fitzgerald's wife, Zelda, accused him of having a homosexual affair with you, but you often acted and wrote in a homophobic way. Can you shed light on your sexuality?

I would say it was everything for everybody. My mother dearly wanted a girl so my early times were patterned after those of a young girl. It was not until I began going to school that I got into a feeling for the sexes. The gentleness of the female that my mother shared with me early on never left me. To combat that I also sought out the most robust derring-do that the male would have. I tasted and experienced all of the possibilities that one may choose while in physical form. But I will not tell of my dalliances and alliances; that is for my partners to divulge if they choose. Needless to say I fully utilized the body I had, and enjoyed all the pleasures it made possible.

Your mother was neurotic, your father was self-destructive and blew his brains out. Two of your siblings also committed suicide. Was it hemochromatosis, a genetic tendency for excess iron to affect the brain, or the ECT shock treatment you received for depression, which resulted in memory loss, that caused you to end your life in the same way as your father?

If you were to chart the time frame of each member of my family, you would see drastic spikes and huge valleys. The drastic spikes were excesses of whatever we were into at the time. With my father it was being a workaholic, which he did in order to stay away from my mother, whom he found too difficult to live with. He was a very proud man and the thought of leaving her never entered into the picture. My siblings and I were cloistered in this environment for a number of years, where we saw the extreme of throwing yourself into something and then the extreme of losing everything you had, and suffering depression. The treatments of the time to deal with such depression were barbaric. The electricity of the shock treatment did interfere with various connections within my brain, which made it difficult to reconnect with some of the parts that were there.

From the time that the treatment occurred I never forgave those who performed it. As a lesson—now from Home—I see that this was to push me ever forward to learn new things to make up for those things that I had lost. But the pattern had been well established within me, and when I did not have something pulling me forward passionately, such as a book that I was working on, I would slip back into those depressions, and then be totally aware of what I was missing and what parts of me were like vast pits. That's what put me into the self-destructive mood.

When your father died you said that Catholics believe suicides go to hell. How do you now view such people?

In some cases it's very courageous (that is, in human terms). As a soul I know that before we come down we predetermine how we are going to live our life—not play-by-play, but the major lessons that we are going to undertake. When we do that, if we get into a pattern that's not working for us, one of the possible solutions (in golf you would call it a "mulligan;" in a soul's journey we call it a "do-over"), you put yourself into a situation where you are back in spirit form so you can return to Earth and do it over again.

So suicides have to re-face the tough experience they had chosen the first time?

If the reason they end their physical life is to start over, then yes, they have to do it all over again. Some suicides (a minority of them) are cases in which the person has made a contract to commit suicide so the family members may go through all the self-doubts and spiritual and emotional conflict that occur around a suicide.

Catholics say suicides go to hell.

Catholics say sinners go to hell, and a suicide—who has self-ended what they consider a life that will only end up in heaven or hell—goes to hell.

Are they correct?

They are not correct because there is no heaven or hell. Not up here anyway. The only place where we have a heaven and a hell is upon the Earth. I experienced both while on Earth. When on my adventures, and totally drawn by my passion, I experienced what for me was heaven on Earth because I was able to be fulfilled, to have a worth to my life, to have a passion, to have an energy. I was also in hell when I dropped into my depression. That was "pure hell," as they say. Nothing felt right. Nothing went right. I felt tormented, and in some cases, when medical science intervened, I was in hell. Now that I'm in unconditional love, I can see all that happens on the planet. I can remember the things that I went through in physical form, but as long as I choose to be myself, I am in unconditional love. If I choose to re-experience the things that I did while in body form, I can create an illusion for myself of that same torment, hell, or that same bliss, my adventures.

Then going Home to unconditional love is not really going to heaven?

It is much more than a human understands of heaven—where you go to the pearly gates and are greeted by Saint Peter who looks through the book and decides whether or not you have completed all of the requirements necessary to be in heaven, at which time the gates are thrown open and you are greeted down the white marble walkways by angels who float around. That's something from somebody else's novel! If you want to equate heaven with unconditional love, it is always being in perfect bliss, in a perfect understanding that all souls are connected, all souls are the same, with an interchange—you can make a choice whether to be present in a physical form or in our energetic form, which is much more comfortable. It's like being in your favorite bathrobe and slippers all the time. You don't have to worry about how you look; you just float around. That is unconditional love. There is no negative to anything.

So is going Home not a reward for being good?

No, it is an entitlement for the very simple fact that you are a piece of the Creator and that you are an individual soul.

All souls go Home?

All souls, regardless of what experiences they had in the physical world.

In the first World War you saw violent death starkly when a munitions factory blew up. Later, you were wounded by shrapnel, but you dragged a wounded Italian soldier to safety. How did these experiences affect you and your writing?

They were grist for my writing. The way they affected me was, in some cases, to show me that the depression I found so devastating was something only of my mind and spirit. That which can happen to a physical person hurts much more but at a different depth than the emotional pain I went through. It gave me a feeling that a solitary experience is something that you can learn from, but the experience of being with other people is a cornucopia for your benefit. You can pick and choose the notes that you want to convey as a thought to another person. It isn't something that is coming out of your un-experienced emotions. It provided me with a sliding scale of interactions between people which I tried to put into my writing so others could feel it without having to go through the mental anguish that I experienced.

In the Milan hospital you fell in love with a nurse, Agnes von Kurowsky, but she later married an Italian. Tell me about your novel A Farewell to Arms *and how you dealt with your disappointment.*

In human form I was a pip—a person who had a lot, wanted everything, was egotistical, and wanted everyone to cry with me when I was there. I played each part of my life as though it were an elaborate stage show in which I wanted to engage the world. I thought that as the writer I could totally influence everyone who came into my sphere. Instead, with certain matters like love, I found things had to be reciprocated on the person-to-person level rather than on the grand scale. Some people did not want to enter into my elaborate world. They wanted to have very quiet sharing moments, something that I had grown to...I won't say "disdain," but I did not go out of my way to share things one-on-one with anybody. To me, everything was to be done on a gigantic scale.

In Paris, Gertrude Stein and Ezra Pound were friends and mentors. You said, "Ezra was right half the time, and when he was wrong, he was so wrong you were never in any doubt about it. Gertrude was always right." Tell us about them.

They were such a lovely pair. Gertrude—I would have whisked her off into the sunset on an elaborate schooner, sailing around and keeping her all to myself. Her ideas came from her heart; the emotions she put out could be felt by even the table. She was exquisite and a beautiful person. I loved her dearly. Ezra would get onto a path and he would never get off it. If he were dead on, it was a beautiful result. If he got onto the wrong track, he would doggedly stick there and nothing could dislodge him. He sometimes said to me that once he began something he did not want to have to re-do it. So if things weren't as other people appreciated them or understood them, he just made up his own.

Why was Paris in the 1920s so important to the American literary figures of your "Lost Generation"? Why not Rome, or London, or even New York?

Paris was going through a time when they welcomed the Americans, when they embraced us. It was a time—for all of the arts, the fine arts as well as the written arts—when we were accepted. Rome was battling with its identity—of who it was—and did not want any of the young upstarts over there. During that time another thing that was happening in Paris was that they were having a little tiff with the British, as they always do. So supporting upstart Americans was another way to tweak the British. Therefore it was a very comfortable place for us, and they embraced all forms of the arts.

Tell us about your relationship with F. Scott Fitzgerald in those days and now at Home. Was he important in the writing of The Sun Also Rises, *your first successful novel?*

We became buds. We both loved our physical pleasures, the beverage kind as well as the pulse that went up into the heavens. He was very methodical in his approach to things, and at that time I had become a little undisciplined when I wished to sit down and compose the Great American Novel. He reviewed my outlines and my ideas and gave me some tips on how to put them together because he was so well organized.

He had just written The Great Gatsby *then, hadn't he?*

Yes, he had, and I was totally enthralled with the result—not that I wished to duplicate it, but I wished to engender the energy that he put into it. So I went through the various steps of my novel for him to give me tips and review it for me. Without him I would not have been so successful with my first approach. I did change my format slightly in subsequent books, in which I got more of a feeling of myself than I had with my first. He was extremely helpful. We laugh about it now. He says such things as that he might just as well have been the ghost writer on the book—which of course is not true! So we like to joke and have fun.

At least he is a ghost.

[laughs] He is a ghost, and so am I.

In 1927 you married Pauline Pfeiffer and moved to Key West, Florida. You converted to Roman Catholicism, visited Spain, and wrote Death in the Afternoon *about bullfights. Were you attracted by religious and social ritual?*

I was attracted by any type of ritual—it didn't have to be religious or social. Around that time there did not seem to be an order to my life. I seemed to be spinning a little out of control. I found order, as given in a religion, to provide a framework for stability. I found the ritual of the bull ring to be a definition of life, how a person presents himself to the world and how the world responds, and the care that must be given in order to maintain what you fight for so strongly.

On safari in Africa you wrote The Snows of Kilimanjaro. *In that short story the disabled writer awaits his death. Had you by then become aware of your own physical decline?*

I was more aware then of my mental decline than of any physical decline. I was having more and more periods of depression, of losing myself and not being totally in touch with things. I felt an urgency to get out of me what I wanted to present to the world, which was my energy through my books.

Was alcoholism holding you back?

My alcoholism was actually a self-medication to keep from feeling pain—both physical and mental unrest.

Then came your involvement in the Spanish Civil war on the losing Republican side. Your companion there, Martha Gellhorn, became your third wife, but that relationship was stormy. Now looking back on your marriages, would you agree that you were drunk and difficult to live with?

[almost shouting at first] I was horrible in physical form for anyone to have to put up with. That was part of my "charm." At that time people wanted to have the eccentric, to have the person everybody talked about. They just did not want to live with them day in and day out. I did not concern myself with anybody other than myself, but I needed companionship. I needed somebody there with me. I could not go through life alone. That would immediately put me into a depression.

In 1951, at your home in Cuba, you wrote The Old Man and the Sea, *which won you the Pulitzer Prize and the Nobel*

Prize for Literature. Back Home, looking at your literary work, which work now gives you the most satisfaction?

I don't know that I have a particular favorite. Each one spoke to a different period of my life and the different experiences I was having. For the overall human experience, *The Old Man and the Sea* had more depth. Within that book you can go through the entire life of a human person. You can see the ups and downs. You can see the compromises. You can see the unrelenting influences from outside on the person. It was also somewhat autobiographical about the decline you can go through at the end—as I was doing.

Were you ever a writer in a previous life?

Not to the same extent. I was a scribe in ancient Egypt, one of the first to use the method of conveying thoughts on paper (or papyrus and skin in that case). I was one of the monks who sat for years at a desk copying the Bible and the sacred papers. This life was my "freedom writing," where I wasn't structured and strictured and tied to the table, where I could get the experience that was conveyed on the paper and did not take the ideas of others and have to copy them down.

If you were to return to planet Earth today as a writer, what would you choose to write about, and in which medium: newspapers, books, plays, films, television, the Internet?

I haven't really spent any time considering that, but I think, were I to return, that with all the busy-ness of society, I would do something that hasn't been done before, and create an interactive medium that would encompass the very air around you, such as in holographic projection, where one could interact in his desired realm, whether it be as a lover (of course I've had a lot of experience in that!), as a businessman, as a family man (even if he had no family), and would be able to create his own illusion.

You've been talking to Aldous Huxley, I think.

Not really. This goes beyond anything that Aldous ever thought up.

Thank you for talking with us, Ernest Hemingway.

Commentary

Toni: When he talked about his depression I felt a sadness, almost like being in a dark tunnel and not being able to get out of it. But when he talked about his exploits, it was a lark, the enthusiasm of a young child in a toy store or sweet factory. He had such passion for everything he did, and he truly believed that the moment was to be experienced. Some of that came through the interview because he was performing, re-experiencing, conveying to people what they could get out of his books, even today. He did not seem to hold anything back and was very forthright in everything he said. It was as if we were walking down a street in Cuba or Key West, carrying on this conversation while he finished his cigar.

Peter: One of the little delights that these dialogues afford is observing the differences in the language used by each soul. In this respect Ernest Hemingway was true to form with crisp, tight sentences and plenty of visual imagery, using words like "cornucopia"—distinctively different from many of the others encountered in this book. Having said that, I admit that the channeling process has a softening effect. Toni receives the soul's words in vibrational form, which she automatically turns into English. Because it became clear that fast-speaking souls put a strain on accuracy, after making our assessment of the best word construction, we have taken the whole dialogue back to each soul in a separate session for it to confirm or correct our choice. Souls have had few problems; generally their contribution has been to add a sentence or phrase. Hemingway spoke slowly and used his words and phrases economically and lovingly. His soul made very few corrections.

One fascinating detail of the way souls look at the lives they have lived was touched on in our conversation. Hemingway explained that when it is merely looking at current happenings on Earth, or simply remembering its past lives, it enjoys the detachment and general feeling of unconditional love that surrounds all who live in the higher dimension of our spiritual Home. But when the soul actually revisits a life it has lived, and chooses to freshly experience the things it did while in body form, it can manifest an illusion of the very torment or bliss it once possessed. In his depression Hemingway suffered a personal hell, exacerbated by the clinical brutality of shock treatment therapy. This soul gently told us that entering into that memory again was no fun.

When he came to talk about Home, Hemingway waxed truly lyrical, the novelist's art dripping onto the page. He made it clear that heaven and hell are states of mind we experience on Earth alone. But his explanation of why this wonderful country of unconditional love, called "Home," is not heaven was implied rather than stated. Heaven is a concept linked in current Western religion to the favorable judgment of God—a place of reward for our having lived a good life. Home, on the other hand, has nothing to do with judgment, positive or otherwise. Home is the place of return for every returning soul—for all souls, we are told, constitute a part of the God-force, of which Source is the fountainhead of a love that is totally unconditional. "No," we were told, "it is an entitlement for the very simple fact that you are a piece of the Creator and that you are an individual soul."

The last exchange resulted in his whimsical idea of creating a new "interactive medium that would encompass the very air around you, such as in holographic projection." This reminded me of the tangible theatrical projection in Aldous Huxley's novel *Brave New World*. Here we were experiencing a glimpse of the soul's creative thinking. Life does not stop when we go Home. Souls continue to think, discuss, create, learn, and interact with one another. We may leave the shell of the body behind us when we transition from Earth to Home, but we keep our thinking faculties intact when we trade cigar smoke for bliss.

"My biggest lesson was that if you had faith in yourself, you could accomplish anything you sought to accomplish."

Walt Disney

1901-1966

Walter Elias Disney, your family came over to Britain with William the Conqueror, ending up in Ireland until your paternal grandfather immigrated to Canada. He failed to do well at farming and so your father went south to the USA. He also lacked business success and was violent toward you and your three brothers. Was your father a bitter man?

My father always had the impression that the world owed him something, and that he would not have been without means if his father had been more intelligent, more giving. He projected the feelings he had about his father onto us. It was like trying to pass on the angst of one generation to another generation. He was very bitter, never happy, never satisfied with anything he did, but he did not think out the moves he made—he just went on impulse and therefore was subject to failure.

How did that affect you in your life?

More often than not, it gave me a firm feeling of what *not* to do in handling myself in life. I started looking completely outside the realm of my family for guidance of how to develop myself, both from a prosperity angle and from a relationship angle.

When you were five years old your family escaped from the violence of Chicago and lived in rural Missouri at Marceline for four years. In this idyllic setting you seem to have been happy. Was it there that you discovered you could draw?

I had begun drawing a little before that, to escape things. When we lived in Chicago, we were always inside. Our parents did not want us outside, yet my father would complain if we were inside. It was a truly vicious circle. When we moved to Missouri, I was able for the first time to wander around the neighborhood. My eyes were opened to the beauty of nature, the way that animals interacted with humans and with other animals. I became totally enamored with life in general and recorded it as best I could with my sketches.

Horses and trains and...

Anything and everything that was different from what I had known earlier.

Then the family moved to Kansas City, Missouri, where you met Walter Pfeiffer at school. You spent a great deal of time with the Pfeiffer family. What was the attraction?

The attraction was a real family, a group of people who interacted—sometimes violently, but there was still an interaction, an acknowledgment of who the other members of the family were. Walter and I formed our own sort of family. It was a close-knit friendship outside the realm of blood relations, giving me for the first time a feeling of what other people could be and the possibility of depending on another person to accomplish something.

Returning as a family to the city of your birth, Chicago, you went to high school and studied in the evenings at the Art Institute. Was this the whole of your training in art?

Before I went to the Art Institute, I had gotten some art classes through the public school system, and it was the encouragement of my teachers that got me to the Art Institute—actually the contacts they made enabled me to become enrolled.

Had you been an artist in a previous life?

[laughs] Not art as you'd imagine it—not a grand master or anything like that. I had been a caricaturist who would do images of people to appear on such things as coins, and to put into the background of walls and the like, where the shaping of the concrete actually had the image of a person but not so plainly that you would recognize it. It was created to do homage either to the person who had designed the building or to the one in whose honor the building was erected.

When and where was that?

The latter was in Spain, and the time frame about the 1600s. The coinage work was done in Roman times.

You drew cartoons for the school newspaper. Did you know then how much cartoons and animation would mean to you later on?

I had no idea. I just knew what made my heart sing, and that I could give happiness to other people. Because there was so little happiness in my house, it had a profound effect on me to know that I could be the one who would take some burdens away from people as they laughed at my creations.

During the first World War you were too young for the army, but your mother helped you to join the Red Cross by lying about your date of birth. Did she want to help you escape from your father's violence?

She knew that I had a lot more in me and a lot more drive than my siblings. Yes, she wanted to protect me, but also to give me an opportunity to interact with as many people as possible. She could see that I had a craving for human contact, to know what people wanted and to be able to help them—whether it was with laughter or rolling bandages or making contact with their loved ones.

What sort of woman was she?

Mom was a long-suffering, quiet, loving, but extremely obedient woman.

You went to France and drove an ambulance upon which you drew cartoon characters. Had your drawing become a way of shutting out violence—Chicago, your father, trench warfare?

I wouldn't say that it was a way of shutting out violence. It was a way of shining a spotlight on something other than the violence. Nothing could shut out the physical things happening around you, but you could take your mind, your essence, and transport it into an area—right there in the midst of the bloodshed—that gave you peace and happiness.

Many of your films had villains in them that were quite frightening to little children. Was this your creation?

It was my creation, and it was a way to let others know that villains may be there. In most lifetimes there are villains—whether parents, diseases, landlords, slave owners, whoever—who can be overcome. They can become insignificant if you keep your hopes and dreams alive, if you have your faith solely in the right place. That important place is in yourself and in the power that you have as an individual.

After the war you returned to Kansas City with your brother Roy. He worked in a bank and you became a commercial artist. There you met Ubbe Iwwerks, who called you "Walt," not "Walter," and shortened his German name to Ub Iwerks (with one "b" and one "w," not two of each). Tell me about him.

Well, Ub was (and is) a soul mate of mine. We tend to reincarnate with each other and be important people in each other's lives. This was at a time in my life when I needed the stimulation to move out of the constraints of only doing work for other people. Instead I pursued my dream of transporting people out of their humdrum lives into imaginary places where they could be who and whatever they wanted to be. Ub was the one who was there. He was the cheering section, the one who gave me the possibility to move on. That was the contract that we had. Mine with him was to pull him up and take him with me.

When your business with Ub failed in Kansas City, you arrived in Los Angeles and tried unsuccessfully to get a job as a film director. But then came the New York distributor Margaret Winkler and your short animated film Alice's Wonderland. *Was Ub involved in that?*

Yes, Ub was involved in that, and the reason we failed in our first business was that it was too shortsighted for where we were supposed to go, so it was destined to fail before it even began, because that was not the plan of what our life was supposed to be like.

You began to create a team. You and Roy set up the Disney Brothers' Studio. Ub came from Kansas City to spearhead the animation. Virginia Davis also came from there to be the female lead in the Alice *series of shorts. Tell me about Virginia.*

She was sort of the "girl next door" who made you feel good. She was always the one who would be there cheerfully holding my hand when things seemed to be going wrong. She definitely was the twinkle in my eye. She was very wise for her age and saw past obstacles to a view of the whole picture. Virginia lived the part and loved it.

You ended up marrying an employee, Lillian Bounds, who bore your daughter, Diane. Then you adopted Sharon. Eventually you had six grandchildren. When souls return Home, what kind of affinity do you continue to have for those who have been your spouse and family—is your relationship changed in some way?

It is primarily an Earth relationship—unless they are part of your soul group, which keeps working together, keeps reincarnating together. It is the same as when you go to grade school and meet your best friend, and then you part because your families move to different areas. If you came together again in the future, you would recognize that you had had a past together, but you wouldn't be any closer to or entwined with that person than with anyone else who had such a minimal contact with you. It seems sacrilegious to a lot of people to say that a spouse is an immaterial contact, but in the greater picture of all the lives that each soul lives, if spouses or relatives are not part of the soul group with whom you continually reincarnate, they are but a little postscript.

Do you find yourself being involved in monitoring the activities of your loved ones, or when you get Home, does that fade away?

It depends if there are any contracts that you had agreed upon with that person before you came down to Earth and if you have completed everything related to that. For instance, you might have had a contract with someone to put them on the path to becoming an artist, or to develop something that would bring happiness and joy into the lives of others. After you pass on you would monitor how the progress is going, and see how many people they have been able to reach, how successful they are in developing new ways of inspiring people.

Into your life came cartoon characters, starting with Felix the Cat and Oswald the Lucky Rabbit. Then (in a Flip the Frog cartoon called Fiddlesticks*) there was Mortimer, a mouse with big round ears whom your wife called Mickey Mouse, and that name stuck. After you had added sound for his third short, called* Steamboat Willie, *Mickey took off and quickly became an icon. Walt, you were Mickey's voice for twenty years, but who dreamed up the original character, you or Ub Iwerks?*

The mouse was a character that kept creeping into my cartoons and little things that I did. What appealed to me was the big ears. With the ears I could create moods—not in the eventual Mickey Mouse because his ears were always pretty much the same, but in my early mice. If you look at them, you see that they would have a tendency to have one ear a little floppy if they weren't feeling too well, or have both ears down if they were sad or disappointed; it was a little signal that I used to try to bring an energy into the picture. It became kind of a joke between Ub and me. One of us would draw a little mouse with the ears indicating what our day was like and put it on the other's desk, so it was sort of a mutually agreed-upon signal between the two of us. Of course, once Steamboat Willie became such a fantastic person, his ears were always happy, and his smile was always there, and he became Mickey Mouse.

Then came your first big commercial battle. Charles Mintz had married Margaret Winkler and he now controlled the rights to Oswald, which your studio produced. Soon Mintz tightened the screws on the deal. You split, lost Oswald and many of your animators, and had to regroup. That's when Mickey came to the rescue. Animation technology also became very important in the race to succeed, didn't it?

That was what some people would consider a setback but it was really the driving force in the development of animation. It was what caused us to have to step up our game, to bring in the first string (we used to like different types of sports analogies), and putting that first string out there, we developed plays, animations, depth to our animation that nobody else had ever tried before. The amount of drawings needed to create some of our cartoons for a small short equaled what other studios used to create an entire feature. It became our hallmark to have such a depth and intensity to the characters, whether a Goofy or a Mickey or a Donald. We wanted to give the viewer a sense of their being with live persons with whom they could interact, even though the characters were only drawings on a piece of vellum.

Iwerks had been fully involved in the cartoons you released at that time, but you had a falling out and he left Disney Bros. and went out on his own for a decade. About the time of his return the animation crew went on strike. You have been described by historians as temperamental with him, and as a boss, and also very bitter about the strike. Is there truth in that charge?

There's a large degree of truth in that charge. When it came to my relationship with Ub, I considered him to be a brother, and I felt very betrayed by him when he initially left me. When he came back, it was very much the return of the prodigal son, but the energy that came with him, I feel, had a lot to do with the strike. There didn't seem to be any other reason for the strike to have occurred at that particular time. Some of the artists believed that I was showing him preference in bringing him back at an elevated position after his being gone for a decade, when they had been there and they had been the ones who had helped transform the art from what it had originally been to what existed at that time.

Your success was largely based on your grasp of technical change. First sound, then color, then multi-plane camera and tight organization made possible the gigantic task of the animated full-length movie of Snow White and the Seven Dwarfs. What do you now regard as your finest technical achievement?

I don't know if most people would consider this technical, but I think my greatest achievement was bringing my characters to life. Technically, people would say it was nothing more than being able to create a three-dimensional figure from a flat piece of paper, but to me it was much more than that. There was an energy; there was a life. More and more people came to believe that the characters were real, that they existed, because they brought a change into their lives. They brought happiness, a carefree feeling. The little character that they could hold in their hands became a symbol for them of where they could go in their life.

You hated organized labor. You spied for the FBI on union activity from 1941 to the end of your life, and in 1947 you testified in Congress before the House Un-American Activities Committee against several union organizers and the Screen Actors Guild. How do you view this activity now?

I believe the whole thing is very laughable now. I was completely in a judgment place at that time—it is a human characteristic to think that things are definitely right or definitely wrong. I thought that anybody who tried to regulate my hard-earned work ethic by saying that I must hire such-and-such a person, or keep such-and-such a person in my employ, or give them so much money, whether or not they were worth that amount of money, was un-American. That was my judgment. I did not think that these people needed to be protected. I could see in some of the industries, where dangerous things were being done around machinery, that the union served a purpose of providing safety factors, but you didn't need to protect my people from a pencil or pen and ink or piece of paper. I only asked that a person dedicate themselves to the job if they wished to receive money from me. Now I see that everybody was on their own pathway, and some of them needed that little push by the union to keep a job, to provide for their families, so it's now laughable to me that I got so passionate about what I thought was injustice to me.

Your films became the standard to beat. They were cute, upbeat, American as Apple pie. They celebrated small-town-paradise life with a cozy realism—great for the kids to watch. One historian has said, "His prettiness had no core or heart." Did your films help to create a worldwide image of America that isn't true?

I did not feel so at that time, nor do I now. The image that people took from my pictures created within them what they wished to see. While it depicted, as you said, small-town America, some people saw it as suburban America. Whatever matched their realism is what they saw. For those outside of America, what they could take from this were the possibilities of what could be done anywhere in the world. My idea was not to create a false impression. My idea was to stimulate the imagination and to beef up, embrace and encourage the feelings people had within themselves about themselves and those around them.

I must not fail to mention Donald Duck, Pluto, Goofy, Pinocchio, Bambi, and the gang, the full-length animated movies, The Wonderful World of Disney *on television, the theme parks you enjoyed so much, The California Institute of the Arts you sponsored, and on and on. You remarked that your greatest pride was "the fact that I was able to build an organization and hold it." Was the deeper truth that you had succeeded where your father and grandfather had failed?*

That was the postscript to everything that I had said about what I had accomplished. There was always that ghost hanging over my head that I would fail as my father had failed, as my grandfather had failed. It was a constant prodding for me to move forward, to accomplish whatever I could, and to carry with me those who were around me. As my father could not even take care of himself, much less his family, I took up the burden of taking care of myself, my family, my friends, and pretty much a large slice of the world.

During your life were you aware of your own soul?

I had inklings of it, and if you look at some of my movies, you see that in there I dabbled with the fact that we are much more than the physical. I also tried to let people feel as I felt, but only if they were open to it—never to drag them there and immerse them or brainwash them.

Then, having built a media empire, suddenly you were dead of lung cancer at 65. Smoking was the physical cause, but do you know spiritually why you were such a heavy smoker?

It pleasured me. I enjoyed the sensation of smoke in my lungs. I enjoyed the headiness it gave me, the dreaminess. It was a physical addiction so strong that at no time could I ever have quit while in that human body. It also was a planned part of my path, to give me an exit point when I had accomplished everything that I had come down to do.

Walt, what was the biggest lesson you had planned to learn in that lifetime, and did you learn it?

My biggest lesson was that if you had faith in yourself, you could accomplish anything you sought to accomplish, so that regardless of whatever obstacles were placed in your way, either by your family or by society in general, faith and trust in yourself would allow you to do what you wanted to do. I did accomplish that. I did take the noose that at some point I felt was around my neck because of my father's and grandfather's failures, remove it, shred it, and not have one thread of it interfere with where I went and what I accomplished.

I also sought to provide an environment to help others recognize who they were and what they could do, and how they could create an emotional environment for themselves different from the one they existed in. For instance, if a person truly sought to be happy and to be outside of the fact that their mortgage was about to be foreclosed or they had a terminal illness, they could come and they could—for a moment, for a day, for a week—be in total happiness, total faith in dreams, and yes, in total connection with who they were as an essence. I provided the means, and it was for each soul to use or not use, as they saw fit.

Your words create an image in my mind of a mature Bambi, with great horns, standing on a rock, and a cascade of music rising in triumph. Walt Disney, thank you for talking with us.

Did you ever consider drawing? That would be a great image!

Comment

Toni: There was such a dynamism in the dialogue. It felt like being in the midst of a hurricane sometimes, but it was always organized. He seemed to be able to be one step ahead of the blast of wind that was propelling him, so that he knew how to direct it to accomplish exactly whatever he wanted to accomplish. The sense I got was of an organizational mastermind. But everything was done with a sense of mirth. Everything was done with a sly smile of "did you get it—did you really feel what you could feel out of what was there?" It was almost as if we were being baited the whole time to go into a place of kid-foolery—just joy and happiness. I rather enjoyed it. The questions seemed a bit more serious than he would have chosen. I also sensed a driven, no-nonsense businessman who had his finger on the pulse of society and what it wanted or needed so he would be there to provide it.

Peter: Most people think of Walt Disney in terms of the movies they enjoyed as a child, or saw as grown-ups accompanying their own children. This dialogue with Walt, however, was about the man who made the pictures move. Certainly he had great artistic creativity, an ability to tell a good story, to make people laugh and cry, and to persuade little kids to hold on tightly to their protective parents when the baddie was about. But Walt did not lie when he disappointed a reporter by saying that the Disney empire (not Donald, Goofy, or Mickey) was his chief delight. He could have named his screen triumph, *Snow White and the Seven Dwarfs*, for which he was awarded one big Oscar with seven little ones. No, his pride and joy was his organization, which is now the largest media conglomerate in the whole, wide, star-struck world. This was his supreme creation, which he owed to his youthful decision to put away the financial disappointments of his grandfather and father.

Suddenly the theme all makes sense. Time after time in Disney movies the little runt, the forgotten child or animal, the despised Cinderella, finds that life can be turned around for the better. Walt's genius lay in realizing that his private goals were most people's dreams. So childhood delight in his bucolic freedom in Marceline became a dripping delightful depiction of an apple-pie-cute

Middle America that he never tired of representing in his movies.

We must try to distinguish between the warm, fuzzy atmosphere of his creations and the soul of the man himself. Walt admitted to dabbling with spiritual ideas in his films, all the while careful not to let them cause anybody actual distress. The truth, he admitted by default, was how badly he missed the spiritual steamboat. Now the "organizational mastermind" is itself, a soul, again. And does he care if the Disney empire is his no more? Of course not. He is eternally a soul, and that will never change. Walt left behind The Wonderful World of Disney for all of us to enjoy—at a price.

"The only thing that mattered
was getting on to that music, that vibration,
and feeling the connection with the whole world."

Louis Armstrong

1901-1971

Pops, you are held in very high regard as a jazz musician. You pretty much defined what jazz was.

I tried to think of music that spoke to the soul of the person—that conveyed souls, picking them up out of the humdrum problems they were facing and putting them into a place where they could float and be themselves, and be totally separate from the day-to-day problems they went through.

"Day-to-day problems" sounds like the story of your youth.

It certainly was. Just being who I was gave me an immense sense of the importance of providing for my emotional needs and my growth, a sense of solace, a sense of comfort and safety.

You were a tear-away kid. You were placed in the New Orleans Home for Colored Waifs. What would you call yourself?

More a "terror." [laughs] I was a high-spirited boy. The times and places led to that. Everybody was out there trying to make ends meet, and life wasn't that important to people. It was: go to work, do the grind, come back home, "party hearty" (as they used to say). I liked the excitement of that town.

Did you deliberately choose to have a father who would walk out on your mother?

Yes. I needed to be able to find myself at an early age. I needed to find out how I could affect other people, and it was what I was going toward with making that choice.

You were a hustler?

Definitely a hustler.

How do you now view your life as a youngster?

I view it as an education on the streets—education from the main group of society. It was fitting in, it was learning to cope, it was learning to go with the flow, and it was learning the music of life.

Did you ever ask why your people had to be so poor?

It wasn't a matter of thinking of them as poor, it was thinking: did we have what we needed to move on, to go to the next step of our life. There was always a way to provide for yourself, and that was the hustle you spoke of earlier. But if you put your mind to it you would find a way to get what you needed.

You put your mind to playing the cornet when you were in reform school, didn't you?

Right on. The first time I heard that it just made my soul sing. Then I took it up and I could put all of my wants, my desires, my sadnesses, my troubles—I could put all of them into the music and let them go away from me.

Was this the time when you discovered music in your soul?

I had heard it as I was walking the streets. I heard the music and it always appealed to me. The very first time I saw a funeral passing by, and heard the music of that procession, I knew of the connection to Home. That cornet was the instrument that called to me. That wail you can put in there—it spoke of the connection between the angels and the sinners.

Was the gift of music given to you by the spirit world?

It was part of me from before my life as Louis Armstrong. I had other lives where I was involved with music. The very first one was as a trumpeter in ancient Rome, in the Coliseum. The things we trumpeted there were not always good, of course. The good things were like the chariot races, but we also trumpeted the gladiator events, and what you would call murders, with the animals and everything. There was a wail that I put in, depending upon what was going on, which helped assuage the victim's soul as it was put into what would be considered its darkest hour.

Was that a direct connection with your life as Louis Armstrong, or were there other lives in between?

There were other lives in between, but there is still a direct connection between those two because of what the music accomplished in the Roman lifetime and in my latest lifetime. Once a soul learns something, or experiences something, or goes through a lesson while in human form, it becomes part of their identity, of who they are. They have the wisdom of that particular act and can access it in subsequent lives. With me, it was how music—how vibrations carried on what can be perceived by the ears as the very essence of a person—can change the pathway a soul was on in physical form. I learned that in Rome and I learned it in between lives as well. That was what I was seeking to do in my life as Louis Armstrong.

Did your big break come when Joe "King" Oliver took you under his wing?

Absolutely! We had been together before (had other past lives together) but I didn't know that until I got back here. We were together in this lifetime for him to stimulate me and to act as a catalyst to get me back into the groove, back into the memory, the flow of what I was inside.

You were playing at that time in the dive bars of New Orleans' Storyville section. Was that on the cornet, or had you graduated to the trumpet?

It was cornet at the beginning because that was cheaper and what was available. I was gradually turning over and converting as I got a little bit of money. I also had a benefactor at that time, a lady who was so into my music that she made sure I had a trumpet. She was Elizabeth Ashbury. She heard me play and she was moved by the music and thought that I could do so much more with a good instrument than I was able to do with the beat-up thing I was using. Elizabeth was an octoroon. (For people who don't know what that is, it's a person with just one eighth of black blood and the rest white.) She was elderly and died quite soon afterward.

As an octoroon she had passed as white for a lot of her life; then toward the end she was condemned for that little bit of black blood she had within her. She had accumulated a good deal of money during the period when she was passing for white, and that was what bought my instrument.

Nice lady. Another lady in your early life was Daisy Parker. She was a prostitute whom you married when you were 16, then you both adopted a little boy, Clarence. The marriage didn't last long. Tell me about Daisy.

Daisy I saw as a savior. Daisy I saw as a way to get some real credibility in the world, that I was no longer this street waif, this throw-away from the home. I figured that if we had this home—that I had envisioned as this nice little cottage with children running around and everything else—I would get a degree of respectability. Also I was trying to get the sense of having family, since my own family wasn't anything to write home about. I wanted to create a family for myself, but Daisy and I didn't see exactly straight on the same things.

What happened to little Clarence?

Clarence actually went to live with one of Daisy's relatives.

In 1919 you took off to play with Fate Marable's band in St. Louis. Were you on the trumpet then?

I went back and forth because they were totally different sounds, and because part of the time the music was geared toward cornet and part of the time toward trumpet.

You were still finding it tough living, I imagine. You did a little pimping in the '20s, didn't you?

I'm not proud of that! That was all part of that hustle I had from childhood—being a little kid, you did anything you could do to provide for yourself.

When you're back Home do you get censured for doing that?

Absolutely not—it's just the lessons that we learn; nothing is "judgment" at Home. Everything is "what did you learn from that lesson? What do you know you will never do again (in a subsequent life) from the lessons you've learned?" Everything you experience in physical form adds to your overall knowledge and your wisdom of the whole human experience. Whether, when we're in physical form, we consider it a "good" or "bad" experience, it's still an experience. So in spirit form it's simply more the wisdom of what you would choose to repeat or choose never to repeat in another life, were you to come back in physical form.

Looking back on your life, what are the main spiritual lessons you had to learn?

I had to try to overcome people trying to push me down as a black man, and I had to learn to bury the anger that was there—then at the end totally get rid of it. I felt a lot of injustice in my youth and in my early days about what was being done to me that was not humane. The lesson I had to learn was that I had to live with myself, and in living with myself, if I was comfortable with where I was, it did not make any difference what other people said. I wanted to reciprocate in love to people who treated me in all-which-ways.

My way of reciprocating with love was to go into my music and let them feel it, let them be picked up (it also picked *me* up!) so that whatever was going on outside of the bar, the restaurant, the concert hall, wherever I was, just didn't matter. The only thing that mattered was getting on to that music, that vibration, and feeling the connection with the whole world, and the connection with the spirit which is the totality of existence.

You were yourself, Satchmo (i.e., satchel-mouth), playing the part of a black musician. You wiped your face with a handkerchief, and in the fifties some fellow black musicians accused you of being an "Uncle Tom."

[laughs] There was no truth in that. I was myself.

When you grow up with certain mannerisms, you get older and other people don't like them, but the habits are what they are so you don't get rid of them. When I played, I perspired, and I had to wipe my face because if I didn't the mouthpiece would just slide right away from me. And if it did slip away from me I couldn't play.

So the Uncle Tom accusation wasn't based on fact?

No, not based on fact at all. There was quite a lot of misunderstanding about what I was doing with the music. My music, in order for it to go out into the world and get more people, at one point *had* to be geared toward the whites. That's when my fellow colored thought that I was trying to be Uncle Tom.

In fact you supported Dr. Martin Luther King, Jr., didn't you?

Right on. The man was phenomenal. He did more for the people than anyone else in existence at that time.

What about your spat with President Eisenhower over the school desegregation in Little Rock, Arkansas?

[laughs heartily] There was a lot more made of that than actually was there. I kinda liked old Ike, you know. He had his ideas and was true to them. He didn't have a real good sense of humor, either. I couldn't take things that much seriously. Little Rock really cut me up because I was getting to the point where I was being accepted for who I was, but then people just like me weren't accepted because they didn't talk to the soul. When I played, people didn't see me; all they did was hear me.

Was that your greatest achievement?

My greatest achievement was talking to the soul. I was able to dig in and shake that soul and let a person know they had one.

After you married Lillian Hardin, she pushed you out of Joe Oliver's band into Fletcher Henderson's Orchestra in New York. You rejoined her in Chicago's Dreamland Café, then you were off to Los Angeles. Wasn't it very exhausting being a successful musician?

Your life wasn't really your own. It was dictated by schedules other people set up. It was tiring, but when I got out there and I played I didn't feel anything but the euphoria of floatin' on that music. It was the times in between when the body got exhausted.

Were you equally able to "float" on the music when you were just doing recordings with Louis Armstrong's Hot Five and Hot Seven?

Oh, that was a great time because we didn't have to worry about what people were thinking. We just jammed ourselves. We'd have a piece of music we were working on and we *never* kept to the music. We just let our souls play, and we played off of each other. We joined a chorus—it was like listening to the Celestial Chorus in the heavens. We were all there—we were a part of it. We were floatin' on it. It was easy to do because there was nobody there to react to what we were doing, and we *sang*.

Satchmo! <u>Celestial</u> Chorus? Do they play jazz in heaven?

They play everything in heaven. It's church music that you hear, but it would be awful boring to have it there all the time. You know, with the upbeat of the angels—I mean, they like to jive, they like to get down, they like to boogie, and they sure can't do it to, excuse me, *Ave Maria*.

What about scat singing?

It's easy, but the thing is we don't have vocal chords. So it's easy to get the vibrations up here with all the music, but it isn't always easy to get that lip going.

Was Lillian Hardin a good musician?

She was.

She played the trumpet and the piano. Why did you break up with her so soon?

She wasn't as ambitious as I was. In some ways she wanted to push, and wanted things her way. I was just floating with what was going on. She would have liked to settle down a little bit and get into a pattern and do the domestic thing. At that period I did not see myself being put up on a cupboard shelf. Any time I wasn't able to be myself, be spontaneous, because I had an obligation to a spouse or a family, was to me putting me up on a shelf or gluing my feet to the floor. That wasn't for me. I wasn't ready at that time to be out of the flow. I liked that flow, where I was and where I was going—I liked the whole rhythm of my life and didn't want anybody else to change it. I felt the need to get up on that musical vibration and take off.

Did you and your third wife, Alpha Smith, have the same problem?

Yes. I was drawn to women who had the nesting instinct, because that was what I had searched for so much when I was a child. So I was drawn to these women but that wasn't the lifestyle I was accustomed to. There was no way that I could find to accommodate both. I couldn't find a way to be safe in the nest and be able to fly.

Your mother, Mary Armstrong, wasn't a nest builder?

No.

You were also raised by your grandmother, Josephine Armstrong.

Josephine was a little bit of a nester but I was much too much for her to handle. She was a dear soul who gave me some of my love of music. Boy, could that woman sing! She had the voice of an angel.

Your last wife was Lucille Wilson. At that time the Louis Armstrong All Stars were touring everywhere. Was she not fazed by your work?

They were going everywhere, and that woman just loved life. She loved excitement. She loved me—she loved caring for me. She would be the first one to have the suitcase packed if we had someplace to go. She liked the excitement of the whole thing and wasn't jaded by it. She was into her sweetheart!

You had a fruitful relationship with Joe "King" Oliver. What did he mean to you?

I had two sides: the side that I was the greatest musician in the world, and the side that was a little timid, not wanting to get swatted down by somebody 'cus I was in the wrong place. That had kinda been my experience as I was growing up. If I had gotten in the wrong place at the wrong time I got swatted. He was my balancing act. He was the one who knew my talent, who knew the depth of me, and at the same time did not want me to go out brashly and offend people, but didn't want me to stay hidden in the closet. So he created this fine line of making the connections that needed to be made, and prodded me to move when I had a tendency to sit in the back room making a little music with my friends. He gave me my push.

Joe Glaser, your manager, also helped you a lot.

Joe was the organization man. He was the one who got me in the right place at the right time with the right connections. I sometimes gave him a rough time because [laughs] I wanted to be more "off the cuff" and he wanted to be scheduled and go forward with things. He helped me organize who I was and where I was going, and he also helped me play around a little bit with music and decide what was going to go and what wasn't. He greased the wheels to keep me going.

Did comparisons with other good musicians, such as Charlie Parker, help you at all?

I loved Charlie's sound but I wanted something unique to me. The time I was on the Earth as Louis Armstrong saw the growth of the blues. Some people say it was the birth of the blues; it wasn't. It was the naming of the blues so far as the general population was concerned, but it had always been there among the people. This was bringing it out, naming it, and selling it. There were some great people there who just contributed. There was a mixture between blues and jazz, and the birth of country around that time. Music was a way for people to get out of their everyday life and to dream, to feel, to express themselves, to live through their trials and tribulations by singing how they felt about them.

Some of the musicians there who influenced me were little people who wrote their own music and sang in the honky-tonks. Everybody who sang from their soul influenced me. Everybody who played that wailing sound influenced me. There wasn't just one person. I absorbed the vibrations like a sponge, took it in, felt it, and blew it out.

There's a soul in church music, but there's a sadness there; there's not an exuberance. What blues and jazz did was to speak of everyday life. It spoke of how a person could move forward. It spoke of how if life was getting you down you could turn that baby right around. Everybody who was around there at that time—Charlie and the whole group—we let our insides speak for us, our souls, our beings; and we did it in a way that we began to vibrate with other people so they got sucked into that puppy and we just went!

At one point you had physical difficulty playing the trumpet, so you took up singing and created a whole new world in jazz vocals.

Yes, I did. It was a combination of things. I was having problems with my teeth and got into a little bit of an infection. It made it difficult for me to blow, but I sure could still wail!

What were your favorite songs?

I don't know I had any favorite—anything that made the soul sing, anything that made me fly, anything that I could see brought joy to other people and got them to the same place that I was at.

How do you view music that's being made these days?

Not very well. [laughs] I guess the hip hop and all the Goth-type stuff speaks to the kids who are there today, but it doesn't float the soul. It just makes it jump up and down. And when it jumps up and down it rattles the brains and you don't know what's going on. It doesn't take you and let you wail, let you sing, let you fly.

Are you going to come down again and show us, Satchmo?

I'm kinda having fun up here, jamming and making sure there are vibrations going out across the planet and different places, so I don't have any plans right now.

Keep up the jamming, Louis Armstrong. Thanks for coming to talk to us.

Thank you for having me.

Commentary

Toni: Armstrong's feeling was of mirth, joy, exuberance. It was like, "Let's get up and boogie around the room. Let's float on that music." There was almost lyricism in some of the things he said. You could feel the rhythm. It seemed to me as if some of it might have rhymed. It was often done tongue in cheek, but with a verve—it was alive.

Peter: Satchmo was as funny as he was laid back. I was almost duped by his lively description of music at Home where he now lives, and which he called by the vernacular "heaven." It all sounded so funny, with angels who like to jive, and a celestial chorus. Then, when I asked about scat singing he came down to reality with a sigh: "It's easy, but the thing is we don't have vocal chords." Still I loved his gentle, impish poke at *Ave Maria* and church music. The connection with his musical past lives was also fascinating, with the wail of the Roman trumpet resounding in his youthful cornet playing.

He told us quite frankly that he was a hustler and a pimp, of which he wasn't too proud. He was clearly a difficult man to be married to, and one senses that his managers really had their work cut out to have him stop playfully jamming and get on the road and into the next performance.

Armstrong was very clear about judgment. There is no judgment made on homecoming souls. Everything is "what did you learn from that lesson?" he said, insisting that the trip to planet Earth is all about learning lessons through physical experiences. "Whether, when we're in physical form, we consider it a 'good' or 'bad' experience, it's still an experience," he asserted. It is the foretaste of the spirit world's hardest lesson for us to grasp. Even our making choices that the world generally considers evil (like his "little pimping") can be a valid soul lesson in the spiritual realms.

It's a pity he didn't stay longer—I was beginning to wonder how well Toni's channeling would handle a little scat singing.

"If there were no radicals there would be no progress on the planet, good or bad."

George Orwell

1903-1950

Eric Arthur Blair, you are better known as "George Orwell," a pseudonym you picked for the publication of Down and Out in Paris and London. *Why did you choose that particular pen-name?*

There was a man whom I greatly admired, whose first name was George. He wasn't anyone famous but he impressed me as a person who really had his act together. At that time I was going through a period when I was floundering and did not seem to have any stability, and I thought I could use a change in name so that I could grow into the person I envisioned as myself. "Orwell" was a play on words. I would either become what George was, "or well" I would be like the rest of the world.

So it had nothing to do with the River Orwell?

No it had nothing to do with the river! I let people think that because I did not want them to think I had no firm foundation for where I was going or what was going to happen to me.

You wanted to destroy the manuscript of Down and Out, *but although you asked Mabel Firez to scrap it (and save the paper clips), she took it to Gollancz and they published it. Were you a bit ashamed of having been a highly educated Eton boy who had taken the most menial jobs Paris and London could offer?*

I was embarrassed by my entire life and by what I considered to be total failure. When I put pen to paper I saw it as a way to rid myself of the demons of my inner turmoil. When I saw that finished manuscript I thought that I didn't want to claim it, and I didn't want to allow people to feel the agony of my life at that time.

So you didn't deliberately take menial jobs—they were forced on you?

They were forced on me if I wanted money to be able to survive at that time, as I did not have any money forthcoming from any other source. So it was what I needed to do in order to survive. I was not doing it so as to get fodder for subsequent writing; it was a survival tactic.

Living in Paris at that time was the "lost generation" of American writers. You were not part of that group.

No, I wasn't part of that because I didn't have their dreams. They had very set dreams of what they thought they could do and how they could reshape things. I just needed to survive. I did not have the stimulus to go forward then and hadn't found whether I had any valuable, marketable abilities.

You suffered a lot at that time. Did you then contract the tuberculosis from which you died at forty-six?

Yes.

How much of your life was planned in advance: The choice of your parents? Life in Burma? Life as a writer? Tuberculosis?

Everything is planned before we come down. By "everything" I mean the major experiences we wish to have. We don't always choose exactly how we are going to have an experience. We do choose our parents as a means of setting the stage for what we think we want to work with, knowing exactly what are both their strong points and their failings, so these are the first mini-lessons we have to deal with.

Did I choose to return to Burma before I came down? No. I chose to be able to experience different cultures and different ways of life. The return to Burma at that time was partly a running away from my life to a place where I did not have to take responsibility for the aspirations other people had for me.

Like going to study at Oxford or Cambridge?

Yes. It was very easy for me simply to disappear in among people who did not have set agendas.

Was tuberculosis planned?

The exact form of the ailment—no. It was planned that I would have some chronic, subsequently debilitating disease so that I would have to fight for strength among all of my fights for survival.

Did you plan to be a writer?

I planned to be expressive and to be able to communicate to a lot of people. It was either going to be with writing or doing seminars. I found that I enjoyed more the solitariness that writing afforded me than I did constantly being out there on the front line in front of thousands of people.

In your essay "Politics and the English Language," which links authoritarianism with linguistic decay, you said, "The great enemy of clear language is insincerity." What do you now see as having been most influential in your development as a thinker and writer?

[laughs] When you take a look at the totality of my physical life, I had a lot of time to think, to explore, and to compare what was going on in the world around me. During that period I found initially that when somebody said something to you, if you simply received their words you did not necessarily have any idea what they were saying! You had to take their words, the context within which they said them, and the feeling that they put behind them. I was pretty much the same. I floated to and fro until I realized that you had to portray yourself to another person as who you were through your thoughts, your words, and your actions. If you didn't, if you hid behind the words and became flowery, and if you said what you thought someone else wanted to hear so they couldn't get the gist of who you were and what you wanted—then you were being insincere. I craved sincerity in life. I wanted to know that what was presented to me was what the person or the assembly or the nation really felt.

Who were your mentors in expressing that feeling?

Some of the great thinkers and philosophers. There was no single person, although Descartes comes to mind on account of the sincerity he put within his words and the depth with which he explored ideas. Some of the philosophers who took people to task for their insincerity impacted me highly, but there was no one person on whom I fastened.

Among writers, it is said that Somerset Maugham was very important to you.

I very much admired his style and his heart, which showed in his writing.

You savored British upper-class life at St. Cyprian's School, Wellington, and then Eton College. Then you went on to spend five years in the Indian Imperial Police in Burma. Were these various experiences of authority the roots of your future radicalism?

From two disparate angles—first, being able to have authority and being able to lord it over others in the police and also even with wealth, considering various classes of people; second, the realization of what I was doing. The realization came that there was an imaginary barrier existing between the authority figure, which I presented, and the people who sometimes could almost be terrorized by my presence. I thought that if I were there (as I later experienced in my menial jobs) it was only a matter of luck, as in the toss of a coin, which role you played.

Eton was the dice falling in your favor?

It was the crème de la crème, the top of the mountain.

Were you then a rebel at Eton?

I began to become a rebel at Eton because I saw that, as the amount of money people possessed increased, the less they cared about anybody but themselves, and the less they thought they were affected by rules and regulations. It rankled me that just because people had wealth they should be considered better than those who polished our boots. In that regard I rebelled against my peers who dragged me up and onto an exalted balcony overseeing the rest of the world.

You were brought up and died an Anglican Christian. How strong were your beliefs then, and how do you understand belief in God now?

At that time I did whatever was expected of me. I could not totally feel everything they were trying to tell me when I was at church, so you might say that I was a sideline member. I was there to be seen and to have an identity, but I was not much of an active participant. There was something about it that was not able to answer the questions inside me about the interplay of humanity that I was seeing all around me. From my position now, I know we all choose to experience exactly what we experience; there are those who choose to be in the higher echelons and those who choose to be in the gutter. So any formulation of injustice that I saw during my time in human form was illusory.

What is the place of God in all this?

God is within all souls, and there is no single entity who is the commander-in-chief of all.

When you were at the bottom of the ladder, didn't you blame God for allowing you to fall so far?

For a while I went through a period of blaming everybody but myself and, of course, since God was a convenient figurehead, I blamed Him.

After working among the "proles" in Paris and London you wrote your first books and essays about that experience and about your days in Burma. School teaching was brought to an end by your ill health. Then you became a part-time tramp. In your subsequent novel, A Clergyman's Daughter, *did the heroine, Dorothy, represent the essence of these experiences?*

I guess you could call it "the essence." It was a hope of allowing people to understand the energies that could be involved in a human life being played between the belief systems that come from the family and the church. It was one of my attempts to acquaint people with all the pieces of the puzzle, to let them see that we are not a soul who is having a solitary experience. We are a soul who is sharing an experience with other souls, being interactive with the path that they are on.

You were Dorothy in a sense?

In a sense, yes.

Then The Left Book Club commissioned you, and you wrote The Road to Wigan Pier *about working poverty in the industrial North of England. In it you criticized irresponsible thinking by middle-class leftist radicals. How do you now view radical thinking and the gap between rich and poor in the world today?*

[laughs] There hasn't been much of a change; we just use different terminologies. Souls wish to experience such things as poverty, and forms of slavery, which a lot of working-class situations are. Radicals are those who lay down what they consider to be iron-clad ways in which things ought to be handled and how they should be affected. Regardless of how radicalism is presented, whether it be through physical action, pamphlets, broadcasts, there is a monetary push and the sole purpose is always to impose your will upon another. Without money there is no power, there is no force behind radicalism. There has to be someone who is footing the bills. There are radicals spread throughout the planet at this time, and they interact with business, religion, and politics. It's rather fun to sit and have a more universal outlook. My view was of my world, which was also being played out in the world as a whole—I was examining a microcosm that really exists in a macrocosm.

But isn't radicalism a good thing, trying to put things right in the world?

Radicalism brings change and that change may be perceived as either good or bad, depending on where you're at. If there were no radicals there would be no progress on the planet, good or bad. So radicalism shakes the tree and causes the fruit to fall.

You married Eileen O'Shaughnessy in 1936, and the two of you ventured off to fight in Spain for the Republicans against Franco's Nationalists. There you experienced communist brutality and nearly died of a bullet wound in your throat. Tell us about that adventure.

It was everything that could possibly be experienced! It was poverty, starvation, living on a shoestring. It was man's inhumanity to man. It was exploring various idealisms which to the holder were the only truth. The experience of being wounded also brought me back to a sense of my mortality, versus immortality. During that time I did get glimpses of my immortal soul, but I was totally aware of the fact that the body I was inhabiting was of limited duration. Spain was a fantastic schoolroom for me—being able to examine all of the interactions of humanity, and being able to have a companion with me who allowed me to experience the human side of existence.

Did you meet Hemingway and his girlfriend?

Yes. I would say that I was more laid back than he. There was an edge to everything that Ernest did. There was always a playing of "How am I going to use this? What am I going to do with this?" There was an intensity to him that I did not have at the time.

You were treated badly by the communists, weren't you?

Yes. They were in suppression mode. They did not feel that anybody but the people they were dealing with in that particular part of the world should have any input into what was going on. They feared the fact that someone coming from the outside could examine everything that was taking place, and potentially could report it beyond their sphere of influence. The ideology that ran through almost all of them was one of total control by whatever means necessary. They seemed to take a perverse pleasure in inflicting pain and suffering upon people—just because they could.

You became strongly anti-Stalinist and later wrote, "Every line of serious work that I have written since 1936 has been written against totalitarianism and for democratic socialism." Was this the fulfillment of your soul's life purpose to do so?

One aspect of it, yes. The purpose of my life was to allow me to experience the various differences of human existence that I did experience. My soul's path was to be able to enlighten as many people as possible about things they might not have been able to see because of the predispositions given them within their own circle, such as their family and church and local politics; to be able to take and throw up a billboard saying, "You're not seeing this even though it's right in front of your nose;" and to give people an opportunity thereby to exercise their freedom of choice and so to enrich the life lessons they were then experiencing.

The so-called billboard you used in 1945 was your highly successful anti-Stalinist allegory Animal Farm. *The book asks if it is healthy for society to focus power in the hands of one person. How about the power of the American presidency today?*

The American presidency today is not on a par with Stalinism, because Stalin was supreme. There are some supposed checks and balances within the political realm of the United States, in that they do have a Congress, a Senate, and a Judiciary that have some influence upon the absolute power that the President might want to assume. With Stalin there was only Stalin—he had absolute power; so there is a difference.

Another thing impacting this is the influence in your current time of the media, which does not allow things to happen in secret. The media lays out the entire event, the entire direction that the President chooses to follow—almost at the instant he decides to do it. Stalin could wipe out entire villages and ideologies and it may never have been heard about by anyone alive at that time.

You've been talking to President Thomas Jefferson!

Yes. [laughs]

For a short time, you were a war correspondent for The Observer. *Tell us about your friendship with David Astor, the owner of that newspaper.*

David thought it was quite entertaining to have somebody on his staff who had the varied experience that I did. One who would appreciate wealth and what it could bring, who would know of what it was like to be in the tenements and to experience deprivation. One who had experienced the effect of different ideologies in different countries. While he was a very wealthy man who traveled somewhat, he never went below that echelon which he thought was his by right. So to get the influence and the feel of levels below him, he needed to get them from someone else. But he did not trust anyone who was a part of that lower estate. He trusted me because I had the credentials of coming from somewhere near his rank.

His body is buried in a grave next to yours. Was there a particularly close relationship?

Not that close. He admired me more (I must say) than I admired him. It was as if I were the embodiment of what he wished he could become.

In World War II you worked for the BBC in government propaganda. Did that experience provide the germ of your idea of the "Ministry of Truth" and "Newspeak" which you developed later in the book 1984*?*

What it did was to put me into a realm where I realized how persuasive the human voice was and what we could do with it. Several of my experiments showed how influential the spoken word could be. This did not occur to me until I was involved with that propaganda era. I saw that if we wanted to build up confidence, taking fear away from people, we could do it to a large degree with the spoken word. Then it hit me that truth was what I had been seeking in so many places that I had been to, and how powerful the spoken word could be for truth.

Limiting acceptable word choices, "Newspeak," a language in 1984*, is fabricated to render coherent thought impossible. Have we reached that stage in Western patriotic political spin?*

No, we have not reached that stage because there is not a governing body which imposes a Newspeak upon what is taking place. In the *1984* scenario you could not vary from the accepted wording, so you did not have words to express what you felt and wanted to get across to others. In the Western political genre at this time what you have is people speaking with empty words that have no feeling in them. It is not a case of being restricted to using only certain words. There is even the invention of some words that you give new meaning to, in order to convince people that you are right with your political spin. If you were to analyze the average political dispatch at this time, you could interpret it in half a dozen different ways, all of which would have a lot of truth in them.

There are many theories about the choice of the date 1984 as the title of your book, which had been entitled "The Last Man in Europe." Why choose that specific date?

A homage to my dear Eileen. [*His wife, Eileen O'Shaughnessy, wrote a poem:* End of the Century, 1984.]

In 1949, you gave your friend Celia Kirwan, who was engaged in government anti-communist propaganda, a list of 37 writers and artists you thought unsuitable as authors because of their pro-communist stance. Had you joined Big Brother's thought police?

[laughs] That was one period when I thought I had all the answers. Based upon the mental research I was doing for my novel I thought I knew everything. It was strictly based on my judgment of what was good and what was bad.

So you weren't a Senator McCarthy in disguise?

I masqueraded as one.

Do you regret or accept it now?

I would accept it as something I had to experience, because I wanted to feel what it was like to put myself above others.

So having fought for Winston Smith (the protagonist of 1984*), you became one of his tormentors?*

Yes.

Although Animal Farm *and* 1984 *have been the popular focus of your reputation, you are seen by many as a supreme craftsman of beautifully written English. Which book or essay do you regard now as your best piece—the one which gives you most satisfaction?*

I don't have a particular favorite. It was as if my writings formed a diary, chronicling changes I was going through. Each one is reflective of my position at the time of its release. It is rather difficult for me to decide which of the individual phases I would choose to replace—or cherish—because each one has its own significance.

Will America's so-called "global war on terror" develop in the future along the lines of the grim world society you envisioned in 1984*?*

No, it won't get that far because there are too many Earth changes that are going to take place before it would become a "Big Brother" society.

The Masters currently talk of great physical changes occurring to planet Earth on December 21, 2012. Some of those souls with you at Home seem to support that view. Do you?

Yes, at the winter solstice. What is going to happen is due to the influence of the planets on the insignificant little planet Earth, as all the planets line up across the solar system. Planet Earth is currently shifting on its axis due to the pull of these planets. There is going to be yet another polar shift (there has been a number of them on planet Earth in the past). At the time of the polar shift there will be an electrical change in everything, so that some machines will not work. Influences on the planet have been dependent upon the electrical force field around the planet, preventing people from communicating and going through the various levels of existence up into the ether. This electrical field, which has formed a protection for them, will be gone. That is why there will then be a commingling of the energies that are normally non-physical with the energies that are physical.

Please explain further, as I did not fully understand what you said.

Planet Earth and the atmosphere above the planet have a magnetic charge. This magnetic charge has been sufficiently strong to make it difficult for the soul that is within the physical body to connect easily with the energies that are outside of it in the universe. As the poles begin to shift, these electrical impulses are lessening, so that it will become much easier for a soul to communicate with energies outside of itself, because there is not a barrier.

I read recently that the resonances of the upper atmosphere have gone up from 7.83 Hz to 11 Hz. I don't know if that report is scientifically accurate.

That's the sort of thing that is happening. What it is allowing is that the vibrations will be closer for the human body's receptivity—like a dog whistle: you are getting nearer to the point where you will hear the dog whistle.

So what will be the result of this shift?

At that time, and leading up to it, the souls who are presently on Earth will have much more understanding and connection with their prior experiences, because the electrical energy will not prevent them from accessing their subconscious as much as it does now. So there will be a blending of all of the past lives and all the information that people have. Then the choices they are making now within this physical incarnation will be influenced by what they have done in the past. They will have more understanding of the fact that we all exist in unconditional love, and that we are here to experience things. They will have an understanding of some of the things they are now choosing to experience, and those that they really don't need to experience, such as blowing up their neighbors.

So there will be a big spiritual and emotional change. Will there also be big physical changes on earth?

To some degree there will be large physical changes because of the shift of the polar axis of the planet, but they won't be in the awareness of those who are spiritually connected. These changes will be in the awareness of those who refuse to connect with their spiritual aspects, and who just want to remain in the ego-based society where they can control others.

Do you mean that physical changes will not be catastrophic?

It depends on who you are. Are you rooted in the physical, or are you relaxing into your spiritual self? If you are rooted in the physical, it will seem like Armageddon as described in the Book of Revelation. If you are spiritual, it will be an ascension into the realm of higher awareness.

If people said that this is "only Armageddon chitchat," what would you say?

I would say that in physicality we create our own illusions. If the illusion we wish to create is nothing but solid and nothing but physical, yes, that is true. If we wish to expand and become part of the spiritual knowledge and connections that we have, we see that this is but an illusion, one little piece of a play in which we are actors.

What do you mean by "spiritual knowledge"?

Spiritual knowledge is accessing that part of the unconscious mind which contains the wisdom that has been experienced in other lifetimes. It is what some people call the Akashic records. Each person has a whole library of all of the lessons they have learned in previous incarnations. In physical form, until they reach a vibration where they will be able to reach up to that part of themselves which lies outside, they cannot have a knowledge of it. All the changes that are going on will allow them to access and re-integrate in a physical form the lessons they have learned before.

Some groups practice learning spiritual "ascension," but is there a natural way for individuals, not involved in such group activities, to achieve the same thing?

Yes, because it works in people connecting with their soul, and riding the energy of the soul into wherever they choose to go.

Many will ask how they can connect to their soul.

The simple answer is to identify with who you truly are—not your name as this body, this "shell" that you have been given; not the identity of who you claim to be: mother, father, lawyer, doctor; but the essence of your soul, this soul that has been experiencing things upon the planet. It has learned the lessons and no longer needs to have the duality of this environment we call humankind, and it gets out of duality to where there is no fear, no hatred, only unconditional love.

So our recognition of our soul is more than mental and emotional?

Well, you can't just open up your chest and say, "Hello in there, I want to be part of you!" You have to do some work. You have to find out what it is that is holding you into this physical body for the purpose of having additional experiences. If you have had your physical experiences and you are no longer concerned to go on having them, and wish only to reconnect with the universe, with your soul, with unconditional love, and you eschew all the connections that you have to the physical (the ego, the control, the need to know), just going with the flow of the energy, you then ascend in vibration because you have cut away all the heaviness that holds you into the physical body; you ascend into the vibration of the spiritual. For most of you the only contact with the spiritual has been talking with us, your guides.

Will children find this easier than adults?

Absolutely, and particularly the children who are now on the planet. A number of them, whom you call "Indigos," "Crystals," and "Star Children," have chosen to be on the planet at this time to be part of the migration, and to add additional energy to the planet to help other souls to awaken. In your social experimentation there is the "100th Monkey Theory" that, after 100 monkeys do something, all monkeys will know about it. The same thing is true of energy. If energy rises to a certain point, that level is felt by all, whether consciously or unconsciously.

What you say will be frightening to many people. Is it good to frighten people into a new spiritual awareness?

I don't accept the word "frightening." Fear is something that exists only if you insist on holding on to control. If you know that the universe is extremely benevolent and of unconditional love, you surrender yourself to that energy and then you have no fear. If you wish to know exactly what is going to happen next, that's wanting to control what is happening. While you maintain a stranglehold upon control you relegate yourself to an arena of fear.

Thank you, George Orwell, for talking with us.

My pleasure.

Commentary

Toni: At the beginning George tried to be open and forthright, but he had some embarrassment about many of the steps he had taken. I felt his genuine love for language and what you can do with it. Several times he flipped words around and clearly cherishes oral communication and what it can achieve. Language came across as being the root of everything. Experiences provide you with something to write about. It felt as if he were still engaged in writing. Then, when talking about 2012, he became very calm, almost as if he were an historian examining what had happened—examining 2012 in retrospect rather than talking about a future event. I have been told by the Masters that they have no sense of time, that for them everything exists at the same time, which was the feeling I got from him. It was an historical record rather than a prediction or predetermination of what was going to happen. There was a very unusual feel to it. Instead of the liveliness of the majority of our dialogue, it was a contemplative "this is the way things are."

Peter: Such was the importance of this dialogue that I decided to ask the Masters to add their comments, first about 2012 and second about radicalism.

The Masters' comment

The 2012 Phenomenon

Masters, I notice a tendency people have to run for cover when big events of this kind might take place, such as the panic among Christians at the end of the first millennium AD. Is society also going to treat the changes that will take place in 2012 with panic?

It depends upon the position people are in. If they are completely third-dimensional [Earth-centered] and have no connection whatsoever with their spiritual aspects, there will be some panic. There is no doubt about that because, as these polar shifts begin to occur, there will be an increase in seismological activity, earthquakes, and weather anomalies, which people will take as a sign of punishment by their fire-and-brimstone gods, instead of realizing that it is only a periodic shift in the planet. Those who are of a spiritual aspect, and know that the only reality is what we create for ourselves, will simply choose to create a different existence. They will separate their contact with physical experience and the manner in which they are having the physical experience at the time, and move it to somewhere else to continue or to go back more into their soul energy.

Spirituality is about moving from the Earth's third dimension to the fourth dimension [the spiritual]—getting out of feeling that only what you see with your eyes and feel with your hands is important, and going into energetically existing within your heart, where you feel and you sense what is going on. With that perspective, if you go out into a tornado you can marvel at the magnificence of the energy that is there, or you can fear for your life because that's the only thing that's precious to you. As your house is wiped out by a tornado, you can say that it's just a starting point because you have to move on, or you can fall into depression saying that God has taken vengeance upon you. So it is all a matter of perspective and of getting out of judging things, and going with the flow of what's happening—with the knowledge that everything that's happening is something you wish to experience.

It is not a question of where you are but of who you are. It is being responsible only for yourself, and not assuming that others have to be responsible for you, or you for them. It is the same as in all the world's conflicts going on now. Each person who participates, say, in Iraq, is there because it is what they need to experience, and people sitting back at home cannot judge the rightness or the wrongness of what they have done. Know that you don't need to have that experience right now, or in some fashion you would be open to experiencing it. The only thing we should be concerned about is what we are doing with our personal experiences.

How do we answer people who are truly concerned about the physical changes? If we believe this cataclysm is bound to happen, is it counter-productive for us to "take care" of our situation, in case we survive it?

[laughter] The first thing to explain to people is they should not assume that all this is going to happen exactly on December 21, 2012. That's a physical moment when the planets are going to form a line. The total effect of the energy will be determined by the planetary influences and how the bodies receive them. A body that has given up some of its physicality will be lighter and will not be as affected by the cosmic influences. If people choose not to release the energies that hold them in the third dimension (i.e., they have to have physical possessions, or emotional ones such as exerting control), that makes them heavier and their vibration remains earthbound, very "solid," so to speak. If they are going through a process of giving up their physical attributes, however, and they are going into and connecting with their soul in the spiritual realm, then their vibration will rise because they are not clinging to the physical. They are trying as much as they can to become and rely on the etheric (that which is outside of us, the non-physical). Those people who are completely physical will be affected by every ounce of energy that is affecting the physical aspects of the planet. Those who have given up some or all of their physicality will find themselves unaffected because the storm will pass right through them—it will not have anything to grab on to. It will be as if they have become gossamer and the wind goes right through.

So will those people survive the events of 2012?

Physically or spiritually? All souls will survive, whatever happens to the planet. Physically there will be an Armageddon. Souls who have embraced their spirituality, their true nature, will be leaving the physical realm (sometimes called ascension) and going to an etheric realm. That's not to say that the illusion they create for their life will not be within the physical body. They will be creating a place for themselves which is outside of the chaos created or caused in the purely physical.

When you say there will be an Armageddon, do you mean that everyone will die physically?

If souls have not completed learning all their lessons within the duality of Earth, they will move into a dimension where they may continue studying. They may choose to complete these lessons in an approximation of their current physical body, or they may choose another. If they have completed all their learning, they may just return Home. Exactly what will be apparent to human eyes will vary with the enlightenment of the soul. Some will continue in the drama of a deteriorating world, and others will create a utopia.

Any other comments?

Our intention in telling you these things is not to be Chicken Little: "The sky is falling!" Not our intention at all. This is just the cyclical termination of an age which affects the Earth periodically about every 26,000 years.

It is also important to note that the entire process is still shifting, depending upon the intentions of all the souls currently on the planet.

Radicalism

So the radical is really barking up the wrong tree?

Without a doubt.

Does that mean that nobody can do anything to improve things on Earth?

Unless the thing you are trying to improve is done in cooperation with the other souls involved.

Then unconditional love is a part of the earthly experience?

It is part of the soul experience, if people recognize that they are souls.

If unconditionally loving radicals wish to improve the lot of the working class, are they right to be radicals?

Only if the radicals appreciate that all they can ever do is to inform people, and then it is the people's choice of what to do with the information. If they think that by their action alone they are going to change things, that is erroneous. This is because something can only be changed with the cooperation of others. If someone chooses to provide for others, he can get the money so that goods and services can be given for those people. But then if they do not use them properly, all that effort will have been for naught. However, if those people do take the goods and use them to ameliorate their lives, to correct the way they feel about themselves, and to finish the lessons they had (such as poverty), and if they choose to go into a state of equilibrium or even of prosperity, it is incumbent completely on them to take those steps. The very fact that money and goods have been provided for them will not cause them to take those steps unless they choose to do so.

If, as has happened, a group seeks to visualize calm, peace, and good behavior in a local society, and then new positive attitudes increase in that locality, is this a form of radicalism?

If radicalism means having a hand in changing a force, then yes, it is. If radicalism implies enforcing your will upon another person, then the answer is no.

Mother Teresa was saying that the correct way to pray for peace is to visualize peace exists. If enough people visualized peace in a conflict zone, would peace break out there?

The people over there are all engaged in war. All they know is war. They don't have it in their consciousness that peace can exist. If, all at once, they are embraced with this idea that peace is possible, they can use that energy to supplant some of their thinking that conflict is the only possibility. People create their own reality, and all reality is an illusion. If they have no other reality but only war, only conflict, and they choose instead to have the opposite, which is peace, they can with their actions, and the energy they put out, change their illusion from one of war to one of peace, which then becomes their reality.

Is there an energetic force for good that can be set up by people?

One can be set up, but there are so many variables having to do with the intensity and the intention of the senders, as well as the truthfulness and the reception of the receivers.

I'm thinking that Gandhi was only one person.

And that one person did create miracles.

Thank you, Masters.

"Finally, I came to the realization that my life could not be one of total play. I had to go forward with a life purpose of accomplishing something for the betterment of society."

J. Robert Oppenheimer

1904 –1967

Robert Oppenheimer, after World War II, General Leslie Groves, the army officer in charge of the atomic bomb project called you "a genius—a real genius." Were you aware as a boy that you had unusual talents?

I didn't really consider my talents unusual. I just had this insatiable curiosity to always know why things worked and to get things to work beyond their capacity and in different ways, so I was always tinkering and taking things apart and making reapplications of some of the machinery.

Do you accept the idea of genius?

I don't really have a concept of what genius is, because from a soul level you realize that if you have done something in a prior life and then bring it into your current life, it would seem to those who haven't had that additional experience that you were much beyond them, possessing what would be called a genius. Did I have the physical human capability of doing things beyond what a lot of people could? Yes, because I pushed myself, and I tapped into the feeling, the energy, of things I had done before.

What had you been in previous lives?

I had been an alchemist, for one thing, and I had done the mystical qualities, as some people say, of transmuting various substances from one thing to another thing. Now I wanted to do it within the confines of physical science so that people would be able to use, understand, and not consider it witchcraft.

Had there been other lives besides that of the alchemist?

I was an alchemist in at least two lifetimes of import. I also had been involved with energy transference, mostly what you would call energy healing at this time.

Were you a shaman?

I wasn't considered a shaman because I was in the Tibetan area. I was considered a high, holy monk in that realm.

You and your brother, Frank, were sent to the Ethical Culture Society School where you had a broad education ranging from mathematics and science to classical and modern literature—the humanities but no religion. Did you enjoy your childhood?

My childhood was one of constant exploration, which was exactly why I had come down into this lifetime.

As a boy you were interested in minerals, weren't you?

I realized the qualities that minerals contain and that they were able to convey different types of powers in different ways. I saw that the magnetism of a mineral could affect other minerals, could convey some of its properties to other substances, and that various substances were fast conductors beyond anything in use at that time.

Was Felix Adler's educational system, which you experienced in the Ethical Culture Society School, a good one?

It was good if you had an inner drive. A lot of what occurred there was somewhat directed, but if you didn't have the inner urge to push and go as far as you could with things, there was a level of accepted progression for the students there. I was not satisfied with their progression. I wanted to go as far as I could within each realm—that is in the science and mathematics. I dabbled in the other things because I had to and needed some well-roundedness, but they did not grab my heart.

Later on in your life, you didn't turn to your parents' Judaism (they were secular Jews), but you showed a fascination with Hindu literature, and in your thirties you learned Sanskrit and read the Bhagavad Gita in the original text. What was there in this study that shaped your outlook on life?

I was drawn to it because it felt right, which of course you now know goes back to the fact that I had been very involved in that religious sect in another lifetime. What I found in it was an absence of people telling me, "This is the only way it can be." I found a fluidity that allowed you to take your inner feelings and use them to explain why you were having those feelings. I didn't see it as a law-controlled system of beliefs. I saw it more as, "This is an example of what you can do; now see how you can fly with it."

Many of your companions in the scientific field were atheists. How would you describe yourself, then and now?

Most of my colleagues were atheists because they did not believe that one God, one man in a white robe, was responsible for everything and controlled everything, and that there was judgment to be wrought if you did not follow the whims of that bearded wonder. I had a sense that there was a power that was responsible for all, but also that it was a pervasive power that instilled in all of us the desire to be able to match the power that came from Source. There wasn't exactly a term for my beliefs at that time. I just had a feeling that belief systems used for control didn't let us feel who we were. Now I am part of Source, as I was then, but now I know it, feel it, and totally understand it.

At Harvard you successfully studied not only your chemistry major but also a wide range of liberal arts subjects. Later, as a physicist you worked brilliantly on a variety of issues, but colleagues felt your contributions were so diverse that you did not received the recognition you deserved, especially for your work on gravitational collapse (concerning neutron stars and black holes). Would you agree that you had a lack of focus?

[laughs] My focus was always what appealed to me at the moment. I searched for explanations that would satisfy me as Robert Oppenheimer. I did not do my work to satisfy awards committees or endowment committees or anything else. I worked for myself, to enlighten myself, to train myself, to educate myself in whatever was my focus at that moment. Did I have a single point that I wished to go toward? No, it was too boring to focus just on a single point. So to others it appeared that I was a crazy ball bouncing off the walls, going in all directions, but I always got to the point I was searching for before I moved on.

Percy Bridgman taught you thermodynamics at Harvard, and you went on to the Cavendish Laboratory at Cambridge to study experimental physics. Tell us about that time.

That was a time of being a kid in a candy shop. I was being provided with tools and means to research what I wanted, to find out the answers I needed. It was a fantastic time in my life. [Toni: He's showing me the world opening, with rainbows and fireworks.]

After Cavendish, you moved from experimental physics to theoretical physics at the University of Göttingen under Max Born. Why did you make that change?

Finally, I came to the realization that my life could not be one of total play. I had to go forward with a life purpose of accomplishing something for the betterment of society. My love at the time was being able to take these tools that I had gotten and apply them to something that I could get all people to understand.

At Göttingen University, you made many contributions to quantum theory and published a famous paper with your teacher on the "Born-Oppenheimer approximation," which helped to simplify future calculations. This brought you recognition as a physicist. How much did praise for achievements of this kind motivate you at that time?

It had no motivation for me whatsoever. I was, as I had been throughout my life, a carefree person who just wanted to explain things. I put my efforts into digging down to the root source of things. Praise from others meant very little, except that I had accomplished a way of letting others understand a little of what I understood. It also opened doors for me.

Back in the USA from Germany, you started teaching physics at both the California Institute of Technology and the University of California, Berkeley. At Caltech you met Linus Pauling. Tell us about that friendship.

Linus was like a playmate. We had a lot of the same dreams. We had a sense of irreverence toward some of the administration principals, and we had a little bit of a rivalry in trying to best each other in accomplishing things. It was as though I had found a playmate.

Why did the relationship end?

Linus had a little bit of an egotism problem and wanted to take our work just to the point of gaining recognition, whereas I wanted to take it to the point of accomplishing something—which could be the same, but in this case was not. His idea was to stop at a point that would be blown out of proportion as being magnificent, instead of just a way station on the road to accomplishing something greater.

So the charge that you broke up because of your interest in his wife was false?

Absolutely false.

You did have a romantic attachment with Jean Tatlock, who had a strong interest in left-wing causes, and your wife, Kitty, was the widow of Joe Dallet, a communist commissar who had been killed in the Spanish Civil War, and she was also a radical. Please tell us about these two women and what they meant to you.

I think what you would say right now is they were my comic relief. They were so different from the theoretical work within the laboratory. They were both very earthy, very concerned with not only their causes but the way they could ensnare people into their causes. It was taking my passion for science and seeing it directed toward the human, and it was something that allowed me to retain a balance within my life.

Your friendship with Jean pre-dated your meeting Kitty, didn't it?

Yes, it did.

Did you and Jean remain lovers after you married?

We remained friends, but she went on to other alliances.

Why did she commit suicide?

She reached a point of frustration with not being able to have people feel the depth of her desperation toward change. She could not fathom a life of ordinariness, of the way people were just ignoring all of her causes, and the world she saw falling apart because of people's lackadaisical attitudes.

You were an active financial supporter of the Republican cause in the Spanish Civil War, and belonged to an active cell of communist sympathizers. Several of your students were Communist Party members. Historians say you might also have been a party member. This became a big public issue in national security hearings during the McCarthy era. Please give us your side of the story.

I was what people would call a communist because, at the time, I felt they were providing an opportunity for all people to experience what the democratic class system denied the lower classes. It was strictly from an idealistic point of view. Once they became very embroiled in politics, I did not choose to remain allied with them.

Did you actually join the party?

Yes, I did.

Is there anything about the subsequent debate over your party membership and all the things that were said one way or another that you'd like to comment on?

No. That was fodder for small minds. They didn't understand that it was an idealism issue with me, and it was not a political "let's wreck one thing to bolster another."

The President did eventually try to reinstate you a little bit with the award you received.

Yes, and that was more to assuage the conscience of the country for what I had been able to provide for them.

You were called "the Father of the Atomic Bomb." As you look back on your many other achievements in physics, do you feel they have been overshadowed by nuclear fission?

Absolutely, because that was one small paragraph in a very large book, but most saw it as the sledge hammer in the tool box.

The atomic bomb was a little paragraph?

Well, as far as all of the work I had done, all the things I had proven, it was just one insignificant part. It became important because of what nuclear fission foretold. It foretold power—as a war tool, but also energy, as has developed with the nuclear power plants. It has provided fuel for naval vessels and it will, at some time in the future, provide fuel for space vehicles.

You became the chief advisor for the United States Atomic Energy Commission. Do you still endorse nuclear power generation, or, in view of nuclear waste disposal issues, are there more Earth-friendly sources of power that you now prefer?

That is a very difficult Earth question to answer. Because of the amount of power that can be provided—if it is done in a cleaner, more proper manner, which has not been explored—it is still an excellent source of energy. As I mentioned, nuclear fission will be used in space vehicles. Now when you look at the size of the power source for naval vessels, you wonder what the size of a space vessel must be in order to use nuclear fission, and if you use the same construct it would be the size of the Pentagon. But that is because further research has not been done into how the breaking of the atom can be accomplished in a smaller space, providing the additional propulsion or power in a very small unit without the nuclear waste that is currently being produced.

You'll raise a few eyebrows by saying that! People will ask when this is likely to happen.

It will be around the corner when you get other people, who want the answers to the questions in their heads, to start looking and working.

Nuclear fission does not have to be destructive of the world?

No, it does not.

We have learned from souls on the Other Side that they do not harbor regrets for decisions they made in former human lives. Now that you are back Home, what sort of evaluation do you make of the development of the atomic bomb and its use in Japan at Hiroshima and Nagasaki?

As you say, we have no judgment over here of the rightness or wrongness of what occurred. The souls in human form have freedom of choice, based on what they perceive to be the choices they have at the moment. The U.S. government perceived that the only way to end a war that was overtaking so much of the planet was by providing such a superior force that it would hang as a guillotine over the aggressors' heads. Their solution at that time was to show the effect of that guillotine, which could only be done by the detonation of the bombs. There has been much said and debated about whether one was enough, but the thinking of the government was that, were they to have stopped at one, the question would always be there: Was it the only one? They sought to have finality, and that could only be accomplished by engendering that sense of fear and doom via a repeat performance.

So you see it justified in spirit terms or merely in human terms?

I see it justified in human terms because we don't judge. We evaluate, and our evaluation is that a lot of people's pathways hinged upon the detonation of those bombs, both what those people had sought to accomplish and the experiences they had sought to have.

On a lighter note, "Oppie"—if I may call you by the name that your students gave you, I believe that in your past life you were not an opera fan, but have you seen Doctor Atomic, *the opera that is about you?*

[laughs] I tuned in on part of it and found it hilarious. It is so strange when you read, see, or hear other people's opinions of you, and more power to them if that's their interpretation.

Do you visit Earth much?

Visit, as in interacting with? No. Do I monitor what is going on? Yes. Do I sometimes try to send messages to people who are working on things to help, when they ask? Yes. I work now as a guide to many of your scientific minds, but as with all guides we don't interfere or initiate contact; we just respond to requests, when appropriate.

From the Earth perspective, one has the impression of Home on the other side, where you are living, as being somehow at a physical distance. That's because we think in physical terms, and I'm quite sure that must be wrong. Help us to understand the physics of being at Home.

At Home, we are not solid; we are not molecules; we are not even nuclei with electrons running around us. We are the electricity; we are the vibration that can be perceived around the activity of an atom. This allows us to be present in your body, if we choose, to be present in the air you breathe, to be present in a book that you are reading. But our sense of consciousness does not have to be pinpointed to one particular place. Our consciousness may be open, like a person in an opera hall listening not only to the singer, but also to the instrumentalists and to the rustle of other audience members and the ushers' conversation behind. You can be aware of whatever you open yourself up to, and it is not restricted within a band of—as you might say—an orbit from the point of consciousness.

Could you please repeat that idea in a different way? That was a difficult one.

Think of an atom: The reach of the atom is the extent of the electrons circumnavigating it. Contrarily, the consciousness of a soul does not have a point of origin, so it is not restricted. It is pervasive.

You're not in a physical place.

We're not in a physical place. Our consciousness is everywhere, in everything. How it would apply to an individual is that in your human form, if you chose, you could tune in to a conversation in China, Alaska, or the center of the Earth—or the stars in space. Wherever you put your consciousness, you are present.

Thank you. Is there anything in the historical record of your life as J. Robert Oppenheimer on which you would like to comment further?

Well, you mentioned several points that were of note or were commented on by others during my lifetime—my associations with people and political ideologies, the direction I was going in life. None of that is of any importance to me at this time. I see it as the historical record of one human experience of a soul.

Is there anything in that life that is of importance to you at this time?

No.

Surely, it was not a throwaway life?

Oh, very definitely not a throwaway life, but my perception now of importance indicates judgment, something that is of more significance than anything else. The strained knee I had as a six-year-old, because of the experience it brought me, is as important to me as my work at Cal Tech.

You had a self-destructive tendency, with bouts of severe depression throughout your adult life, and chain smoking led to the throat cancer from which you died. Were these problems a by-product of the intensity of your mental power?

They were a by-product of my body's trying to deal with the immensity of the energy my soul could generate. They were like safety valves that would sometimes erupt, go off, so that my whole body did not destruct. Think of it as a release valve on a boiler.

Would you say that ill health is often a release valve?

For a lot of people it is, because it is a way to redirect the energy, which is reaching too explosive a point for the human body, the shell, to completely contain.

Thank you, Robert Oppenheimer, for talking with us.

It has been my pleasure.

Commentary

Toni: He felt to me like a little kid explaining why he had done what he had done—not caring what anybody thought, unconcerned about criticism as he had absolutely no regrets. He gave me the feeling of having lived the life he wished to live, focusing on whatever excited him as a human being. Even when he got serious and dedicated himself, it was like continuing to play, but with a destination. It was a fun, free-flowing interview. I had the sense that he is an older soul who has now truly grasped the concept of human experience from the soul's perspective.

Peter: It was made abundantly clear in this interview that when our soul goes Home it assesses its human performance, during its past life, in a startlingly new way. Such a change of perspective is commonly reported by those other souls with whom we have discussed the matter. Were that not so, it might seem eccentric of Robert Oppenheimer to dismiss in such a light manner that time in his life when his work on atomic fission made a huge impact on world history. However, I do not think he was being cavalier. The Manhattan project, which he led, did produce the most destructive weapon on Earth, but he seemed genuine in his opinion that it was by no means his most important contribution to the field of theoretical physics in which he excelled.

The idea that "you can't take it with you when you die" applies to our achievements as well as our wealth, power, influence, and reputation. This is because our souls do not come down to Earth to achieve fame but to learn lessons leading to our better understanding of the complex nature of divine being. Having said that, I felt there was a sense of playful intellectual elitism that carried over from the life itself into our dialogue. (Too bad it didn't go further—no doubt NASA would have been glad of a few tips from Robert on how to miniaturize a nuclear engine to fit into a spaceship.)

When it came to explaining the "physics of being at Home," as I termed it, the soul was very clear and helpful. We have to get away from "third dimensional" physical measurements of distance and time. From Home, the eternal soul can be anywhere it chooses—instantly. But despite its ability to observe our doings on this planet, the soul (residing energetically in the realm of unconditional love) brings no judgment to the human antics it observes, even when the humans concerned are making nasty big atomic bombs.

"The '36 games were, for me, the culmination of all my training and proved that the color of your skin didn't make a difference; it was the heart, it was the energy within you."

Jesse Owens

1913 –1980

James Cleveland Owens, you were the last of seven boys in a poor African American family of ten children, growing up on a farm in Alabama. Then your sharecropper father moved you all to Cleveland, Ohio, in search of a better job. Life was tough, wasn't it?

It was very tough. My brothers and I were always looking to see if there was some way we could help ease the burden, some little job we could do or some way to help out the family.

Delivering groceries, that sort of stuff?

Delivering groceries, shining shoes, whatever work was available.

You actually worked in a shoe repair shop, didn't you?

That was one of my jobs, yes.

It seems appropriate for someone who wore running shoes eventually. Did you ever make running shoes?

No, running shoes were a little different. This was mostly leather goods—rebuilding uppers and putting on new soles, things of that nature.

As a child you weren't particularly robust. Were you a rather sickly boy?

I was very affected by weather and by dampness—mostly lung problems. Now people would call it a type of asthma.

Did that clear up as you went along, or did you have that feeling all your life?

It was always in the shadows, but it didn't really affect me as I grew up. From my late teens and twenties, it started dissipating. As I began to strengthen my body more, it wasn't as impactful.

When you lived in Alabama, seven children made it pretty crowded, I imagine. What sort of home were you in?

Well, it was probably what most people would call a shack. The thing in Alabama is that the weather is favorable, so it doesn't make much difference if you're sleeping out on the porch or if you're sleeping in a bedroom—you were still able to get those restful hours in. We were kind of packed up in the house; in several of the rooms we just had mattresses laid on the floor, and we'd sprawl wherever there was room to sprawl.

Your elder brothers and sisters were able to pick up the burden of earning money before you were, I imagine.

My eldest sister became quite a washer woman, as they were called then—she took in laundry from people. She also helped out in various homes. My second-eldest brother worked in a lumber yard for a while; he was what they called a "strong boy"—he was the one who moved the large logs around for the cutting machines.

When your father took you to Cleveland, did you all go together, or did anyone stay behind?

The eldest ones stayed for a little while so that they could provide funds to send to us up north. Of course, my father was looking for a job that would pay some money because there was not a lot of good employment in Alabama, and Mother really didn't have a chance to work too much outside of the house because of taking care of all of us, although she did take in some mending work for people.

Now, your name was James Cleveland. How did you get the name "Jesse"?

[laughs] I had kind of a southern accent, you might say, and when they asked me in school what my name was, I said, "J. C." because that's what my brothers and sisters called me, and I guess it came out "Jesse."

And it stuck.

It stuck, and it seemed like a pretty decent name—it was different from all of the just plain Johns and Bobs and Daves and everything else. There weren't a whole lot of Jesses at that time.

It was biblical—were your family members Bible Christians?

Mom was a good Baptist, and she read that book to us every night.

When did you discover your love for running and jumping?

When I began to be able to run and jump. On the farm, I had started running a little bit with my siblings, but I could never keep up. Once we got to Cleveland we didn't have any money for cars or public transportation or anything like that, so mostly we walked from place to place, and it always seemed like I was late, so I ended up running.

You finally ran all the way to Fairview Junior High, where there was a gentleman called Charles Riley. Can you tell us about him?

He was just the sweetest person in the world. He treated me almost like a son, but he was also a disciplinarian, and he saw that what I needed was some direction.

He was a junior-high track coach, wasn't he?

Yes, and his way of discipline was for a kid to become part of the team. The thing was that in order to be able to be a part of the team and contribute to the effort of the team, you had to practice and practice and practice.

You couldn't practice with the team because of your work.

He found ways to set up schedules for me. From the school angle, track is a team sport, but to the athlete, it's basically an individual sport, so when he saw my interest and potential, he set up a schedule, and a lot of it had to do with running every place I went—running home from school, running from school to work, running from work to home—and when I had the time, it would be a couple of extra laps around the block, not just going straight home.

Later you wrote, "In order to make dreams come into reality, it takes an awful lot of determination, dedication, self-discipline and effort." Was this the point at which you learned those disciplines?

Absolutely, and I got them all from Coach. He was the one who showed me that if you put your time and effort into it, you could whittle down those times when it came to a race.

You had to work your way through college didn't you?

The family still didn't have any money by the time I got ready for college.

Were there no scholarships available?

There were scholarships available, but they went to people in certain categories, and I didn't fit comfortably into any of those categories.

Those were the white folks?

Primarily, yes.

Were you aware of that discrimination?

I was aware of that discrimination from the minute we hit Cleveland. There was a big difference, because we came from a town that was mostly black down in Alabama. The Cleveland neighborhood we lived in was mostly colored, but we had contact throughout the city with the whites, and that was my first brush with discrimination.

Your next school was East Technical High School in Cleveland. Was that also segregated?

It was primarily segregated.

You took part in the National High School Championship in Chicago in 1933, and in the 100-yard dash you matched the existing world record of 9.4 seconds. Tell us about that experience.

I had no idea how fast I really was up to that point in time. I just kept following what had been drilled into me, what you needed to do to succeed. I wasn't racing against other people; I was racing to do the best that I could do, and the time was just there at the end. When I went to Chicago, it was the big time when I realized what discrimination was like, and being called "boy," and being segregated from some of the other athletes, and it made me mad. It made me really mad. So I think part of my time in that race was due to the fact that I was proving something to them.

That was the beginning of the very big effort that you made later on in your life, wasn't it?

That was the start.

Finally, you got to Ohio State and you did well in the NCAA championships. You might have been the "Buckeye Bullet" to your team mates, but in the rest of the world you were discriminated against as a black man. In what ways did discrimination actually affect your life?

The thing I would say is that it was a tempering for me—as in tempering steel, where you become harder and harder because of what you go through, what you face. It was a time of discovering that I didn't have to be defined by what other people said of me. I could be defined by who I knew I was.

It must have hurt to have been made to live off campus with the other African-American athletes.

Well, it did and it didn't. It took us out of the constant conflict with the whites. It was a place we could go and relax and be ourselves, so from that aspect it wasn't bad. But it did take away from the richness of the experience, not being able to commingle with the other athletes. On the teams there were always those who were totally colorblind and those who saw nothing but black and white.

Didn't you have to eat in different restaurants and sleep in different hotels when you were on the road with the team?

Everything was segregated then, but it was just accepted because that's the way it was in the entire world at that time—from our perspective.

You were, in fact, sought after by several universities, weren't you, but you never actually got a scholarship, and you had to work part-time jobs to pay for school?

The schools that sought after me, wanted me, but they imposed even more restrictions.

Ohio State was the best that you could get?

Ohio State was more colored-friendly at that time than the other places I visited. I did visit a couple of places and could see right then and there that it was like they weren't recruiting an athlete—they were recruiting a shoe-shine boy who could do other things. That was the impression I got. And because those scholarships weren't available and I was as determined to get an education as I was to get the training I needed for my running, I had to have jobs, but it was nothing new to me, and I accepted it as a part of life.

With all your running success, did you actually finish your degree course?

Not on time, but I did go back and finally get it.

Do you have any views on the way men and women are awarded scholarships today?

There are some of the same prejudices now between the sexes as there were between the colored and the white. In a lot of universities there's discrimination between the colored and the white except in certain sports. The colored are very well received in sports such as basketball and football, but when it comes to track or tennis or golf—sports of that nature that are considered the province of the genteel white—there is still discrimination.

On a percentage basis, basketball does better than football because they're smaller teams. If you take the percentages of black athletes within basketball now, they are almost given the world.

In May of 1935 at the Big Ten meet at Ann Arbor, Michigan, despite injuring your back when you fell down stairs that week, you broke three world records in the 220-yard dash, low hurdles, and long jump, and equaled the world record for the 100-yard dash. Did you then realize you were a great athlete?

Still at that time I wasn't doing it to make world records. I was doing it to prove what I could do, both to myself and to those who were trying to hold me down. As great as my accomplishments seem on paper today, it was very fleeting recognition. At the moments the records were broken, there were huge accolades and much cheering. But as time went on, it still didn't get me better lodgings, better food, or other things that I needed to take care of.

Did your running skills have anything to do with past lives in which you had been an athlete?

Well, as they say, funny you should ask. I was one of the first marathon runners back in ancient Greece. At that time it was all about the races and just training for the races—different from this lifetime, when I was doing it because I wanted to do it, not because it was a job I had to do. So it was revisiting the creation of a fantastic, perfect body, but it was for a different reason.

Can you access that life now and tell us how athletes were treated in those days?

Athletes were just below the kings at that time. We ran for different groups—the senate was a group, the hierarchy was a group, the philosophers were a group—and every group had their stable of athletes. We were like race horses, and we were pampered and touted as long as we produced and brought honor to whatever group we were running for.

Then came the 1936 Berlin Olympics. You said, "For a time...I was the most famous person in the entire world." Adolf Hitler dreamed of proving that Aryans were the superior race; at only 23, you proved him wrong by winning four gold medals. Tell us about your experience at the games.

The '36 games were, for me, the culmination of all my training and proved that the color of your skin didn't make a difference; it was the heart, it was the energy within you. And again, there was that little bit of anger motivation, because although I did not speak German, it was very apparent in the stares and the whispered comments I heard as I went through Germany that I was the despised interloper. It made me mad that I could not walk the streets as other people did and enjoy the games and the goings on, so I just took that internally and created this machine inside of me that would go full blast to prove that what is important is the heart, not the skin color.

Does that response best describe your life purpose?

My life purpose was to be put into a situation where I had to deal with adversity—financial hardship, skin color, weakness of body and having to build it up—and in all of this to find that the important thing is the heart and soul inside. That is where the energy is. That is what can transform (what they call "manifesting" now) your life into what you want to experience.

Do you get to decide your life purpose beforehand, or is it given to you before you incarnate?

Each soul, before coming into a body, meets with advisors, sometimes called a council of twelve (at times it's not the whole group but just the main guides who are going to help you in that particular lifetime). You take a look and ask what it is you want to experience in that lifetime. For instance, to compare this life with my Roman life: In that lifetime I was lauded and given everything I needed and treated like a prince, and this life was to see if I could create the same results with the exactly opposite "building materials," so to speak.

That decision was jointly made by you and your council?

Well, the decisions were solely mine. The possible scenarios were contributed by some of my advisors.

Just for my records, you just said the Roman life, and previously you said you were a marathon runner in Greece. Was it Greece or Rome you were talking about?

I was in both. [laughs] The biggest one, of course, was Greece because that was the beginning, but it carried on into Rome, where the human body was absolutely adored and honored.

So you were mainly talking about the Roman situation?

Yes.

Hitler waved at you but didn't shake your hand, and neither did the American President congratulate you. Back in the USA they put on a parade in New York for the Olympic team, but you were forced, because you were black, to ride the freight elevator at the Waldorf. Then the officials withdrew your amateur athletic status and all your job offers fell through. That must have been doubly distressing after your triumph.

There were a lot of things involved in everything that you have just mentioned. I don't feel Hitler ever really waved at me. He waved at the crowd when the event was over. At no time did I ever expect to be able to get near to him because of his fear that I would contaminate him.

When it came to the President, he was riding the sympathies of the country at the time...

This was FDR.

...and I did get a private note from him, but it was not considered seemly for me to be touted in public by him. The reception in New York was just a continuation of the way my life had been—that no matter what I was able to accomplish, the only thing that could be seen by 98% of the population was the color of my skin, and that automatically made me lesser than they and relegated me to the freight elevator.

Did you have reason to feel that the situation was becoming less racially discriminatory as you went through the rest of your life?

I saw that changes were being made, but each one was hard-fought for. When I monitored the situation within the military services during the war, I saw that my brethren had just as much difficulty fighting to do their jobs as I did fighting to use my physical prowess.

Eventually, President Dwight D. Eisenhower named you "Ambassador of Sports," and President Ford awarded you the Medal of Freedom. Was that a symbol of success?

It was a symbol not only for me, but for the race as a whole. It was a symbol that intelligent people were no longer going to accept that the color of your skin made you more or less than anyone else. It was an acknowledgment of how hard-fought the battle had been and that as difficult as it was, we did not break under the yoke that we were forced to bear.

After you came home, you went into entertainment, ran against horses, led a jazz band, tried dry-cleaning, and then you went bankrupt. Finally you found your voice as a lecturer and motivational speaker. Did you eventually accept your need to break out of feeling poor?

There were a lot of things going on within me emotionally at that time. I did somewhat buy into what my siblings and others of my color were telling me—that I was this great savior—and I figured that if I could be a savior through physical prowess on the track, I could be a savior in anything I wanted to do. I jumped into a bunch of ventures I knew nothing about, and the reason they failed was because my heart wasn't in them. I was trying to substitute monetary acquisition for the drive my heart had for physical accomplishment. Then it finally dawned on me, after all of my crashes and burns, that the important thing was to be myself, and what I was, was a person who learned to use the forces within me, who learned to climb out of the pit by force of will and discipline. That was my expertise, and that was why, when I turned to motivational speaking to convey to others my experience and how they could utilize it, I became successful.

You championed ideas of hard work and loyalty. Were you a religious person?

Mama always had us in that Bible and believed in the Good Book and the words that for her meant the Bible—"Do unto others as you would have them do unto you;" "Turn the other cheek"—there were all kinds of things she was always instilling in us. To me, my sense of self was a connection with the Creator. The ability to transform a weak body into a perfect running machine showed the impact of the energy of the Creator in all of us.

And now that you're Home, you can verify that that is true.

Now I know that we're all the same.

The Jesse Owens Foundation awards college scholarships to young people. When you get Home do you maintain an interest in such programs, or do you lose interest in the things you have done and the causes you embraced?

Well, that's kind of a difficult question to answer. Do we maintain contact with what's going on? Of course. Do we make any judgments about the rightness or wrongness, the goodness or badness? No, we don't. We just see them as trends that are occurring in the human population at the particular time that we're observing. Do we campaign for causes? Absolutely not! But we don't lose our curiosity about what's going on.

You had three daughters. Did you continue to watch their progress, as well?

Absolutely. There's a difference there, because they are souls whom I helped become physical, and I watch over all souls with whom I had intimate contact.

Did smoking kill you?

It was a contributing factor. It weakened the lungs that I had strengthened. It was something that became a comfort and an addiction and something to escape to when times seemed hard. As I got older, I wasn't the completely idealistic young man I had been during my high school and college time. I was a realist about a lot of things, and particularly as each endeavor I went into failed, there was always that cigarette to keep me company.

How do you view the use of performance-enhancing drugs by athletes?

That's their pathway. I can only see that in so doing, they take a very pure machine, the human body, and interfere with its inner workings, so that for a time it exceeds the output it could have had without the interference. They don't care that the drugs can potentially cause harm, because their ego is saying that what they have naturally is not good enough. Those are the people who go down to study self-worth issues, and their way of working with self-worth is to say, "I can do it some other way. I don't have to go inside. I don't have to know who I am. I'll let the pharmaceutical companies shape the way I want to be."

Thank you, Jesse Owens, for talking with us.

It has been my pleasure.

Commentary

Toni: The sense I got of Jesse Owens was that we were talking more to the physical embodiment of him than to the soul, but the soul was always there. I felt that it was very important to him to let us know all of the physical responses to what went on—his experiences with poverty, dedication, discrimination, and dealing with the issues of everyday life. He could very easily have gone into the spiritual implications, but although he did touch on them, they weren't as important to him as making people understand the plight of the African Americans during that period. So it was more as if he were directing this interview than our just getting an open view of the soul that had been Jesse Owens.

Peter: There are many little clues to the authenticity of those whom I have interviewed. With Jesse Owens it was his use of the contemporary term "colored" where we might, more respectfully, say "African American" or the still-accepted "black." With his use of language and his very clear account of the impact of racial discrimination on his life and, especially, on his career as an athlete, Jesse evoked an emotional response in me that few other souls have equaled. His triumph not only exposed the lie of the eugenics-besotted Nazi concept of Aryan superiority; it also played a vital part in the great upward movement of African Americans to gain honest recognition, civil rights, and (hopefully soon) a true acceptance in the land of their birth.

Jesse did acknowledge that treatment afforded black athletes in colleges has improved over the years. But the fact that "genteel" sports are still largely reserved for white students challenges our sense of fairness, and our spirituality.

There was an enjoyable twist in the story of success. Jesse was not only striving to beat his past track performance. At the soul level he was striving to learn a lesson by achieving recognition and success as an underprivileged human being in contrast to his former lives as a super-privileged and pampered athlete, first in Greece and then in Rome. This layering of experiences past and present serves to make us more aware of the complexity and finesse with which ideas are worked through on the spiritual level of the universe. Those of us who in our present life are favored and pampered might do well to think about the prize runner from ancient Rome who came back as little Jesse Owens.

"People said, "Oh, you don't have to train so hard because you're going to knock them out in the first round." My response was the only way I could knock them out in the first round was to train."

Joe Louis

1914 - 1981

Joseph Louis Barrow, you were born in Alabama, the seventh of eight children in an African-American cotton picker's family. Did you choose your parents?

I chose the environment, which in essence chose my parents. There were a number of things that I wanted to deal with. I knew I was going to be a boxer, or a fighter, and I wanted to have an energy surrounding me that had power behind it and quick reflexes.

Your father died when you were only four. Was your stepfather a powerful man?

Physically he was extremely powerful. The power in the house, though, was Mother.

Were you a fighter as a kid?

We called it "scrapping" then. We had our share of scraps around the house.

You were one of the young ones, up against your bigger brothers and sisters.

That's how I got as tenacious as I was, being on the bottom of the heap—sort of like the runt of the litter having to fight its way to the top.

You weren't the runt—you were seventh out of eight. There was one after you.

Well, size-wise I was kind of the runt.

Had you been a fighter in a past life?

I had been military in a number of different lifetimes, so in that regard I was into fighting or into engagements. I had not been a pugilist, specifically, in any prior lifetime.

Did you concentrate on a particular theme in your lives, or were they varied?

Totally varied. Some souls, though, do concentrate on the arts, or on control issues, or on victimization until they can come out of it. I sort of popped around from one thing to another.

Were you ever a woman?

Oh, absolutely. Everybody has been.

Were you gay or lesbian?

No, that's one lesson I have not chosen yet.

When you were twelve your family moved north to Detroit in search of work. You worked in the automotive industry, and you learned to box at the Brewster Recreation Center. In 1934 you won the National Amateur Athletic Union light heavyweight title. You turned professional the same year. Did you have any idea at that time to what success boxing might bring you?

I wasn't looking toward a future or national ratings or anything like that. It was a matter of just seeing what I could do. In the beginning when I started boxing, I had a very low estimation of myself. I thought that I was just average. Although I knew I could do what I wanted to do, I didn't think I could be the best at anything, so when I started winning at boxing, the idea started creeping in that this was something at which I could possibly be the best.

It's a long ladder up to the top, isn't it?

It's an extremely long ladder, with a lot of falling back as you climb up.

Who was the major influence on you as a young boxer?

There was a gentleman at the gym who had been a bare-fisted barroom brawler, he used to say, but he was one of the first professionals—never really made a name for himself but was able to make a living at it.

Do you remember his name?

We just called him Jesse.

And what did he teach you?

He taught me that if you put your effort into it, if you were disciplined, if you looked just to each fight and not for some mythical prize on the horizon, that you would be able to hone your skills so that from each bout you learned something and you got better and better and better. But if you went outside of yourself and just saw the prize at the end, you would be blindsided by that hook that you didn't see coming.

People say you have to be angry to be a successful boxer. Is that true?

No. I had some anger in me because of the way I'd been raised, because of discrimination, because in the automotive industry everybody is angry. They are building these cars that they know they can't afford themselves, and there is a sense of injustice in the whole thing, so there is an anger there. I sometimes used some of those feelings to go after something, but very seriously, I saw my opponent just as someone who was trying to beat the heck out of me, and if I didn't maintain my technique and go after him, he was going to succeed.

Many people view boxing as a negative or evil profession. Others see it as a test of human endurance and physical courage. Now that you are back Home, can you tell us what the lessons are that must be learned by boxers?

There are a lot of lessons that come out of boxing. For me the lesson was a sense of faith and conviction that I could do something I set out to do. It was a molding of self-image. For other people a lot of times it was anger—they had been so put down by society that they were going to teach their opponent that they were not to be messed with. That was where the anger came in boxing. I never was trying to prove that I was better than somebody else; I was just trying to prove to myself that I was better than I had been taught.

Was that the secret of your success, that you had a different attitude from that of most boxers?

It was a combination of that and, again, that I didn't look toward an ultimate prize, that I just looked toward each match as using everything I learned to accomplish what I wanted to accomplish. There was a degree of prowess in it—you had to be trained the way you should be. You had to run to build up your stamina; you had to jump rope to get your feet coordinated; you had to work long and hard on the heavy bag to get power in your hands so they wouldn't bruise easily; you had to work on the fast bag to be able to get the jabs in. It was all a matter of technique, and each time I went into the ring, I went in to test and see if I had accomplished what I had put my energy into.

Who gave you the nickname "the Brown Bomber"?

The news media. At that time there were a lot of very famous white boxers, then here comes this black kid, brown kid, whatever you wanted to call me, and within my fists I held a bomb that could explode in somebody's face.

How did your mother, Lillie, react to your being bashed in the ring? You said she was pretty tough herself.

She was tough, but not when it came to physical punishment. She was not really too happy the first time she saw me all bloody. She thought that the discipline I was learning, the self-respect I was getting out of the ring was excellent, but she was still Mom and she wanted to take care of me.

In fact you took a few falls in the beginning, didn't you?

Absolutely, because I didn't go into the ring and immediately have that confidence in myself. I went in with the idea that ... well, maybe this is something I can do, but I don't know because I'm not really that good, etc., etc. ... so it took a while.

Tell us about the routines you had in your training.

I don't think I went totally into a good conditioning routine in the beginning, because I didn't have full faith in myself, and I didn't really know if I liked this boxing thing, because everybody who talked about it talked about the anger, just getting into the ring and beating the snot out of his opponent. I didn't do it for that. I did it as a sports activity, more or less. I was trying to prove something to myself, but I didn't think I had to put in as much effort as I learned I had to in order to have those reflexes, to have that stamina. So in the beginning, I didn't do so well.

Then you learned to train rather harder.

Then I learned that the training was everything. First having faith in yourself was everything—that made the training possible, and that also gave me an idea of what training I needed. I could tell when I was doing a particular type of training whether or not I was at my peak in that area. When I was running, did I have the stamina, or did I exhaust very easily? When I was doing the heavy bag, did my hands hurt at the end of the day? Different things like that told me what I needed to concentrate on in order to be in top condition.

In fact you had a particularly vicious punch, didn't you?

That's what my opponents told me. I just looked upon it as applying—as the physicists would say—inertia with mass.

So in 1934 you started work as a professional boxer. You, the new boy in the ring in Chicago, fought an Independence Day match, and darn it, you knocked out your opponent, Jack Kracken, in the first round. Tell us about that match.

I was so excited at that match because some of my family was there, and this was the first time it really hit me that if I was good at this I could make some money at it. I loved doing it, so it was being able to marry my love with a good job. I just figured the best thing to do was to go full blast from the very beginning, and that's when Kracken hit the floor.

"Full blast" meant that you had twelve fights that year. You won the lot, and ten of them were won by a knockout.

That's the way it went, and with each one, I didn't get cocky. I saw other fighters getting cocky, and I continued to train. People said, "Oh, you don't have to train so hard because you're going to knock them out in the first round." My response was the only way I could knock them out in the first round was to train.

Did you owe any of that to your trainer, Jack Blackburn? Was he the one who helped you perfect your incredible punches?

When I got to the point of really starting to win, he honed my technique and showed me the things that went together. He showed me the combinations and what spending all that time on that body bag could do, how it could wear a person down so that he would stand up straighter and I could hit him with a hook or a jab and knock him out. He was an artist on the entire fight, not just the knockout.

In two years you collected no fewer than 27 victories and no losses. Most of the fights you won by a knockout. Then came June 19, 1936. The fight was at Yankee Stadium, New York. Your opponent was the German boxer Max Schmeling, a former world heavyweight champion. He knocked you out in the 12th round. What went wrong?

Nothing went wrong, except my losing. What went right was that I finally met somebody who trained as hard as I did. Up until that time, I was fighting people who didn't look at boxing as something you had to live. They looked at it as just a job that they had to do. Schmeling was adamant about everything he did, as I learned later: he was particular about what he ate, about how much he slept, about his training schedule. He had an endurance unmatched by anybody else I had faced up to that time.

He also looked at the film records of what you were doing to find out where you were going wrong.

I never had the experience of going that long in a good fight because I would knock out my opponent. I later found out that he saw certain deficiencies in what I was doing: I was apparently expending so much energy trying to knock the person out—even though I didn't see it that way—that I was wearing myself down instead of pacing myself, so he latched onto that as the way to beat me.

Then, after you knocked out former champion Jack Sharkey, the soon-to-retire world heavyweight champion James J. Braddock agreed to let you have a shot at the title. Schmeling objected and took you to court, claiming he deserved to fight Braddock. That was all about money, wasn't it?

Money and fame. Boxers at that time were kings; they were lords; they were rulers within the blue-collar arena and beyond. There could be a lot of money if the promoters wanted to see a particular fight, and it was all about money for him. I wasn't that interested in the money. I was interested in having a good fight.

The court allowed you to fight Braddock for the NBA World Heavyweight title. You met in the place of your earliest successes, Chicago, and you knocked him out in the eighth round. What took you so long?

Well, there were a lot of people who said they wanted to see a good fight. I also was a little gun-shy after my fight with Schmeling, because I was fighting somebody allegedly of the same competence as Schmeling, so I went into that fight pacing myself.

You were knocked down in the first round, I think.

Yes, but I didn't go in there like a steam engine like I always had. It was good that I was knocked down in the first round, because that made me pace myself even more. But I was more aware of what he was doing and what he was going to do. It was a very even match for about the first six rounds, and then it got to the point where my endurance was better than his.

He was getting old, wasn't he?

He was getting old, he was getting tired, his reflexes weren't as good, but he was in superb shape. It was not an easy match.

So you won the heavyweight title, and you held it for almost 12 years, defending it successfully 25 times. Nearly all of your opponents were knocked out. What did your fame and fortune mean to you?

The main thing was security. I didn't have to worry about where my next meal was coming from or if I was going to be able to have employment, because people came looking for me. It also was a sense of accomplishment. For a while I did almost buy into the "greatness" of what a prizefighter was, and went a little outside of myself and got a little flamboyant and everything else, but then I was sort of beaten back in by my family when they said, "What are you doing? This isn't you!" So they were my fail-safe.

What did you spend your money on? You earned $5 million during your career, which was a huge amount of money, worth much more than it is today.

I gave a lot to the family. I traveled a lot. I helped a lot of little kids start into boxing, because I knew that if they got into boxing, if they got into the discipline, they wouldn't be out there on the streets running around. My siblings had a fair-sized family that I helped take care of. I didn't have big expectations of what I could do with the money. I just used it where it was needed.

Except for the government—you owed the government $1 million in back taxes, I believe.

I didn't have very good financial advisors, that is definite, and money coming to you from a prizefight didn't pass by the government. It came straight to you, and then you were obligated to the government. That's been changed. Now they keep better track of it. I was very unconcerned about things like that and thought that it would just take care of itself. When I didn't have money it was definitely no problem.

One of your most important matches was in 1938 when you met Max Schmeling again. This time Nazi politics played a big part. Tell us about it.

He was billed as the superior human. He was a publicity piece for the Nazi government to prove Aryan supremacy, particularly over the insignificant little black person. There were many things going on in the background. He had a support team that monitored everything he did, beyond what he put himself through, to make sure that he was in tip-top condition. There were spies everywhere trying to check and see what I was doing and if I had any little weaknesses that could be exploited so that they could use them as a propaganda tool. I was unaware of a lot of this until after the fact.

President Roosevelt said, "Joe, we need muscles like yours to beat Germany." You had the whole country breathing down your neck, wanting you to win.

I thought that it was just a matter of what was happening in Europe. I didn't realize it was as extensive as it was. Even the comment from the President—I thought it was just a rah-rah, nationalism-type thing.

Well, you knocked him out in two minutes, but the Germans claimed it was an illegal kidney punch. What's your response?

There wasn't anything illegal about it at all. If you talk to anybody who was there, they will tell you that he was so cocky coming into the ring—he had so much information at his disposal that he was going to sit back and exploit my weaknesses—that I just blindsided him.

Then came a change of pace altogether: wartime service in the US Army. You didn't see any action, did you?

No, I was more a publicity tool for the government, like a lot of the actors who went into the service. Great for the morale of the troops, though.

You got around in France after D-Day?

I went around and talked to the troops as sort of an ambassador—that was more what you could call my role than a grunt.

Did you knock any of the soldiers out?

Well, a couple of them sparred with me, but I was gentle on them.

After the war you went on defending your title, retiring in 1949. Are there any fights you won as champion that stand out for you now that you are back Home?

No, that was just a lifetime of experience in getting to know who I was, getting to know that we can take all of our physical attributes and hone them if we have faith in ourselves, that with discipline and understanding we can accomplish whatever we set out to do. Each fight showed me something different, showed me a different way that I could approach my adversary. They all had different techniques; they all had different ambitions; they all had different energies in them—some were angry, some were lackadaisical, some were full of pride. I learned to be able to deal with all those things, but none was more important than any other from the perspective of Home.

How does the spirit world view violent sports like prize-fighting and wrestling?

The question first is what is violence? Any sport that is a contact sport has violence in it, or the result can be viewed as being violent, but it is something that is needed by the participants to prove something to themselves. We don't judge violence any more than we judge cruelty. It is just a life lesson.

When you had finally left the ring, things became very difficult for you. Financial problems and tax debts crippled you. You had earned millions, but you hadn't a dollar to your name. You got work as a casino host in Las Vegas, and you were the first African American to play golf in a PGA event. Max Schmeling (now a personal friend) and Frank Lucas (your friend the heroin dealer) looked after your financial crises. You were a celebrity, but wasn't life out of the ring rather difficult?

Life out of the ring was difficult for me because it had no structure. When I was preparing for a fight, there were certain things I had to do. I had to run so many miles; I had to spend so much time jumping rope and on the bags; if I was trying to get rid of extra water I had to spend time in the sauna; there was the sparring with people; there was always something that had to be done. Once I stopped fighting, there were no requirements to do anything other than just be—except that after the government took all my money, there was the need to find some way to get funds, and since I was ill-equipped to do anything other than fighting, I had to rely upon what was then considered my fame to have people use me for one thing or another.

You were a man's man, a tough fighter. Did women play any great part in your life?

I was aware of women, but most of the time they were just a distraction from my fights. When I was fighting ten to fourteen times in a 12-month period, I was always in training, which generally meant being out in the country where there were no distractions, and there weren't too many people who wanted to come out there to see me.

Frank Sinatra paid for your heart surgery. Who else looked after you when you were in a wheelchair, before your death?

There were a number of what I call angels who looked after me. One was a niece who came in. There also were some people who were just astounded at what I'd been able to accomplish, and they had a little bit of hero worship. Some of the old promoters would pop in from time to time, people who had succeeded in making a lot of money based on what I had done.

Are you planning to come back to Earth anytime soon?

I've recently been looking at the prospects of coming back to go into teaching, and I think I probably will do that in a female body.

Thank you, Joe Louis, for talking with us.

Commentary

Toni: Although there was strength and a depth to this conversation, my biggest impression of Joe Louis was that he was a sweetheart. He didn't take himself too seriously. He really wasn't overly impressed with any of his human achievements—neither the streak of wins nor the ease of some of those wins, nor was he concerned about the politics behind his fights with Schmeling or about his financial misunderstanding with the government. He didn't have the dangerous razor edge that an angry person has.

When he proclaimed that he wasn't angry—boxing was just a job and a discipline to him—I truly got the feeling through the whole interview that this was, in fact, quite right. The main thing he was fighting was not other people but rather his own physical, psychological, and emotional impressions of himself, initially feeling a total lack of self-worth. His life became a concern to be able to accomplish whatever he wanted to accomplish, to finish whatever he began, and succeed.

Peter: Joe's career record as a professional boxer speaks for itself. He had 69 wins (55 knockouts, 13 decisions, 1 disqualification) and 3 losses (2 knockouts, 1 decision).

It is difficult to assess whether his power as a boxer was inherited at all from his natural father because Munroe Barrow was committed to an asylum when Joe was two and died two years later. When Joe was seven, Lillie Barrow married Patrick Brooks. His new stepfather added his eight children to Lillie's eight, so there were plenty of kids to fight!

In our dialogue, Joe's soul clearly enjoyed reliving the high spots of his career, and at times his personal recollections seemed almost like a pep talk for aspiring boxers. His soul's lofty attitude, which ostensibly excluded anger as a necessary element in a pugilist's armory, seemed a bit unbelievable. Perhaps sporting intention mattered more to Joe. What quite certainly did mean a lot to him was self-discipline and daily, rigorous, unremitting training, which was the open secret of Joe's 12 years as the world heavyweight champ. It also didn't hurt that he was able to make an intuitive appraisal of his opponents before he beat the living daylights out of them.

When it came to recalling his women, an informative amnesia set in. Actually, Joe was married four times—twice to Marva Trotter, whom he first wed just two hours before knocking out former heavyweight champ

Max Baer in 1935. (No doubt the honeymoon was spent with the blushing bride gently bathing his bloody bruises!) A girl, Jacqueline, was born to the couple after several years, but they divorced in 1945. Remarried one year later, Marva added a son, Joe, Jr. to their family, but the marriage was finally knocked down and out in 1949. Six years later Joe married businesswoman Rose Morgan. The union was annulled after three years in 1958. Finally, that same year, Joe married Martha Malone Jefferson, an attorney. Joe adopted her children, and this wife survived him.

In our dialogue he said about women, "...most of the time they were just a distraction from my fights." In fact it's quite amazing that he had time to fight at all, considering his affairs with Lena Horne, Sonja Henie, and Lana Turner, and his dalliances with showgirls and other "distractions." But I guess there's no point in arguing with him about all of them. Not if you want to avoid a black eye.

"I like anything that puts a smile on a person's face...
that can take the love from your heart
and let someone else feel it."

Frank Sinatra

1915-1998

Francis Albert Sinatra, you were the only child of Italian immigrant parents who lived in Hoboken, a town full of people who had recently settled on the New Jersey bank of the Hudson river across from New York City. Did your father work in New York?

My father worked wherever he could work. He went through a series of jobs when he first came over. Nothing seemed to last more than six months. He was very hard working and sometimes worked more than one job to make sure that we could afford the rent and the necessities.

What was your relationship with him?

It varied. When he was in times of anguish and concern, he had very little time for me. When things were going well, he liked to just sit and talk.

Your mother, Dolly Sinatra, was a ward boss for the Democratic party. What sort of a person was she?

Mom was a force to be reckoned with! She was what you'd call the power behind the throne. It was still not too seemly for a woman to have a lot of power, but Mom sure knew how to wheedle things out of people, and if she wanted something done, she could get it done. The neighbors would come and say, "We need a pothole fixed," or "Our sewer isn't draining right," and she'd get right on it and there'd be somebody right out there.

Did she object to your dropping out of school?

Quite strenuously.

But then you got work in a local newspaper, and finally a tough job as a shipyard riveter. Tough or not, you were great at singing. Where did you learn to sing?

I sang almost as far back as I could remember. Mom was always humming things, and I would try to verbalize along with her. It was quite hysterical in the beginning.

You never read music, did you?

No, I never studied at all, because I dropped out of school. I liked to go to dance clubs and listen to the latest songs on the radio.

And you had a good memory.

I had perfect pitch when it came to music.

Your mother got you a gig with a singing trio. After you joined they became the "Hoboken Four." They won a radio contest with 40,000 votes. How did you get so many?

Remember what my mother was doing—connected with politics? When she wanted to get out the vote, since she was the one behind attaching me to the trio, she got out the vote!

In 1938 you were sued for breach of promise. You won the lawsuit and shortly afterward married someone else, your long-time sweetheart Nancy Barbato. That year also saw your first record, "Our Love," followed by your first recording contract. Tell me about that time.

That period in my life was just full of ups and downs. I was experimenting with what I could do. I had a lack of faith in myself in the beginning because I had never been tested in any way through regular, musical channels. I thought I was good, and people told me I was good, but then somebody would come along and criticize me, and I believed what they said. There were some times I was so full of myself that I thought I could do whatever I wanted and not have to be concerned about the repercussions—which, of course, I found out was not true, but dear Nancy was right there and offered me a sense of stability that I grasped onto like a lifesaver.

You'd known her since she was 14, I think?

She'd always been there. She was one of the pushers in getting me to recognize my talent.

There was one important element in your background. Your mother's brother, Uncle Babe Gavarante, was sentenced to 15 years' hard labor for murder and armed robbery. You had an early friendship with Joseph and Rocco Fischetti, who were gangsters and cousins of Al Capone. You also had a long friendship with Sam "Momo" Giancana. When did your involvement with the mob begin?

[Chuckles] It began at family picnics. You can't choose who your cousins are. You can't choose your relatives or the friends your relatives have.

Were you actually a cousin of Al Capone's?

A "kissing cousin"—I don't wish to explain that right now. There was a relationship there, but we would just get together at family gatherings. They were very strongly supporting my singing career, and they would make sure that when there was an affair going on, my group would get a gig, so they sort of provided my income for a period of time.

Your promoters?

To a large degree, my promoters, yes.

Then in 1940 you joined Tommy Dorsey's band and made 40 records, including your first hit, "I'll Never Smile Again," and also your first movie, Las Vegas Nights. *What effect did such success have on you?*

I felt like I was in the midst of a tornado. Everything was happening; everything was coming at me; everything was swirling around. I got into a period when I thought that whatever I touched would turn to gold, and I became a little insufferable because of it.

Did you have an affair with Dorothy Bunocelli on a trip to Cuba in 1942, and was her baby girl, Julie, your daughter?

Yes, and yes.

There were several Frank Sinatras: the blue-eyed Italian boy who melted girls' hearts with a rugged glance and a beautiful song—from teenage bobby-soxers to Ava Gardner; the savvy singer who made a huge fortune; the tough gambling casino owner with connections to the mob and to political heavyweights from Kennedy to Reagan; and the poor boy who got rich but never forgot the poor and gave his time in charitable fundraising. Who was the real Frank Sinatra?

All of them. I had many different chapters in my book, and whenever I was in a situation, I fully lived what it called for. I enjoyed every aspect of my life—the whirlwind successes, pleasuring people, being on the edge with the excitement of what society thought was good and bad. But I did remember the humble beginnings of my parents and how hard they worked, and I tried to provide for people so that they could have the same opportunities that I had been given. When it came down to my interest in various nightclubs, casinos, and things of that nature, that was what I considered my retirement fund. That was my security so that I wouldn't have to worry in the future.

Before we come down to Earth, we choose experiences from which we will have to learn our lessons. There seems to be a dichotomy here—some of your experiences were highly positive, others very negative. Was it all pre-planned, or was it freedom of choice on your part that led you into things?

It was really both. I had pre-planned to examine all of the strata of human existence, from the poorest of the poor to the rich and privileged; from the meek, mild, church-going life to the raucous outlaw. I wanted a touch of everything, a taste of everything. I had set out to have a smorgasbord. I accomplished each of the goals I had set for myself by my free choice. Sometimes I chose to immerse myself in an aspect of life, and sometimes I stayed on the outskirts—just observing friends, relatives, and others who were within the whirlpool while I remained on solid ground.

So you wouldn't say that you were insincere or politically opportunist by doing something that was both right and wrong at the same time. It was a mixture that you had already decided upon.

I wasn't insincere in anything that I did. I was very "in your face" with my experiences. I was not someone who stood on the sidelines and let life pass him by. I wanted to be a part of what was occurring. If I couldn't be a direct participant in an event I would be right there as the event transpired, cheering on the participants and feeling the sweat as they went by. I was never completely an observer from afar. Judgment didn't figure into my choices; I didn't ask whether society liked or didn't like what was going on.

These were great days for you. You signed with Columbia Records and RKO Pictures. You were mobbed by 30,000 teenage girls at a concert. You starred with Gene Kelly in Anchors Aweigh. *Your wife gave birth to Nancy and Frank, Jr. Then everything began to collapse. You had affairs with Lana Turner and Marilyn Maxwell. Your angry wife chose an abortion, then gave birth to Tina, but you left her for Ava Gardner. And finally your career slumped and your voice gave out. Tell us about that time.*

Well, part of the smorgasbord that I was engaged in was the dregs of what could happen to a person if he went to extremes. I became very much impressed with myself. I became insufferable with others, thinking that I could do whatever I wanted to do and there would be no repercussions. So as I indulged myself with my physical wants and desires, those close to me suffered—something that I am not proud of, but it was part of the life lessons that I was learning. The entire situation between Nancy and me? Nancy is a soul mate of mine. We have incarnated together in other lifetimes, and in those, we generally just had one issue that we were dealing with. This particular lifetime we were dealing with the extremes that could exist, from being in a state of bliss to being in a state of chaos.

Your relationship with Ava Gardner was passionate but stormy. You both had many affairs. She had an abortion. The relationship only lasted for four years. Was sex just too easy to come by to maintain a real relationship with anyone?

There was a little bit more involved with it than that. I was in a turmoil in that I could get sex, if you will, whenever I wanted it, from whomever I wanted, just because of who I had become, but deep inside of me it did not make me feel good. It was a physical release, but I would despise myself afterward, so there was a constant sense of betrayal of who I was. It was very easy to come by, but never satisfying.

Commercial failure followed. You lost a recording contract with Columbia. Then things began to change. In 1953 you won an Oscar for the movie From Here to Eternity. *Your albums included the highly prized* Come Fly with Me, Songs for Swingin' Lovers, *and the award winning* Swing Easy! *There was a change in your approach, a greater emotional drive—was this a deliberate evolution in your style?*

It was an evolutionary process in a lot of respects. It was in the style of my performance, but more so in a recognition of who I was. I was getting an awareness of some of the reasons I was incarnate at that time, some of the reasons I was experiencing the things that I had put myself into. There was a greater depth to me then. I was no longer a superficial person. I had begun to realize how far some of my portrayals carried beyond the screen, how they affected people, and I was very conscious for a brief period of time of how I could affect people and influence their lives.

You joined the Rat Pack, a group of independent-minded actors including your friend Dean Martin, and Lauren Bacall, to whom you unsuccessfully proposed. Then your engagement to the actress Juliet Prowse came to naught. Your personal friends included President John F. Kennedy. Tell me what all these friendships meant to you.

There is a lot of confusion about the word "friendship." Friendship, to be true, has to come from both sides. It has to be totally giving, and it has to be without a sense of reward on either side. None of those you mentioned as friendships, with the exception of some of the people in the Rat Pack, was of a true friendship variety. In each case, one party or the other was attempting to curry some favor from the person who was their "friend"—such as my dabbling in the political arena and the dabbling of others in the entertainment arena. Either they were seeking to be known as a friend of Frank Sinatra, or I was seeking to be known as a friend of a president.

But Dean Martin was a real friend, wasn't he?

Dean Martin was a true friend.

You performed at a benefit in Carnegie Hall in 1961 for Dr. Martin Luther King, Jr., and with your acting friends you campaigned vigorously against segregation, especially that directed against black entertainers. Was your motivation religious?

[laughs] I don't think you could call it religious, because it wasn't based on the tenets of any organized religion. It was a feeling on a spiritual level that we were all the same, and everybody should be given the same opportunities. But it was also on a physical, emotional level, because I saw some of the same discrimination that my immigrant family put up with when we were first in the country and I was very young. There were always negative comments about the Italian Americans.

Religion was your mother's bailiwick early on, and when she died tragically in 1977 in a plane crash, you embraced Catholicism again fairly strongly. Was that a reaction to her death?

It was both a reaction to her death and a reaching out to find some firmament, something to hang onto and give me a sense of identity and belonging. It came at a period of time when nothing seemed to mean anything, to go beyond the next day or the next week. I had to feel at that time that my mother was still in some form, somewhere, and I had remembered back to my early days within the religion that they talked about salvation and heaven, and I wanted to sign myself up and put myself in line, so that I could at some time rejoin her.

How do you view religion today, particularly Catholicism?

I view all religions about the same from here, and that is that they are a set of physical laws and guidelines delineated so that people don't have to think for themselves and don't have to feel. They can give their responsibilities to someone on high to take care of them and direct them, and they don't have to feel, to connect with their soul and see where they're going.

Acting in the 1962 movie The Manchurian Candidate *had a big impact on you, didn't it?*

Yes, it did. I began to realize that my existence up to that time had consisted of mini-plays, but then with *The Manchurian Candidate* I realized the far-reaching implications that one person or one series of activities set in motion can have for a large number of persons. It was sort of like an education for me in the depth to which one action can ripple throughout an entire people.

You married wife number three. You were then 50 and Mia Farrow only 21. The marriage lasted two years. You hated personal criticism, and the mob turned on Jackie Mason, who was making jokes about your age difference with Mia. He got phone calls, then bullets through the door of his Las Vegas hotel room. Finally a man with a knuckle duster told him to stop making jokes about you and broke his nose. Okay, Frank, come clean: What do you feel now about your temper and your violent mob connections?

I don't think it was a very good way to go, but I did learn some things from it. I learned that physical force only has an impact upon the body; it has no impact upon who the person is inside. I learned that intimidation can change a person's immediate reaction to things, but it can't change their life's lessons or who they truly are.

In 1965 you celebrated your 50th birthday. You sang Paul Anka's "My Way," and then your most commercially successful album, Strangers in the Night, *appeared. You didn't actually like the "Strangers" song, but made "My Way" your own. Which of all your many songs were your favorites?*

It's a very difficult question to answer, because my favorites varied, depending on what I was going through at the time.

What are they now?

Now they're immaterial to me. I like anything that puts a smile on a person's face. That is one of the basic ideas and ideals for music as a form of communication—something that can take the love from your heart and let someone else feel it, and in feeling it, change their day or their week or their life.

Your career slumped a bit and you retired in 1971, only to return two years later with the hit "New York, New York." Your fourth and last wife was Barbara Marx, who survived you. Tell us about that marriage.

That was almost a marriage securing a caregiver for myself. I needed somebody to give me some stability in life, and Barbara was one of the most unflappable people I have ever known. She could defuse my firestorms. She could comfort my insecurities. She was just the perfect fit to give me a safe dock to prepare to transition.

Looking back now from Home on your successful but controversial life, what are the main lessons you learned?

There were many small lessons that all fit together to give me a true sense of what is inside of a person and what can come out, and how what we do gives us only a small idea of what we really can do. Mainly I learned that with each Earth incarnation we have the opportunity to experience one lesson or to have a free-for-all in which we can categorize all the things we have learned in our many lifetimes and put them into perspective.

When I referred earlier to this life as providing a smorgasbord of experiences, that was exactly what it allowed me to do. It allowed me to deal with issues of control, of the ego, of the third-dimensional [human] judgment systems for what was right and what was wrong. It allowed me to take each one of those lessons and know exactly how it could impact me as an individual and, much more, how it could impact other people.

In most of my previous lifetimes, I had not been particularly concerned with effects on other people, but as I went through the life review from this life as Frank Sinatra, it really came home to me how my actions influenced and affected others. I had a little sense of that when I was in the body, and tried to do something about it (as when I helped others), but during the life review I really saw that it went beyond the physical; it went into the emotional and mental aspect of life.

The Manchurian Candidate *was pivotal for you?*

In the perspective of the life, yes, it was.

As a result of these experiences we gain wisdom. What is the end point of your life as a soul?

Well, the soul never ends. What was the end point of me ...

Your soul's destiny.

Oh, destiny? I am very near to the point of being able to be a guide because of all of the experiences I have had, not only in this lifetime but in others. I can hear some of the critics out there now saying, "That son of a bitch is going to be a *guide* for somebody!" And I laugh because that would have been my response, were I in physical form. However, the wisdom that I got from all of those experiences allows me to see all of the implications, all of the perspectives, so that I *can* be in a position to assist others.

Thank you, Frank Sinatra, for talking with us.

It has been my pleasure.

Commentary

Toni: Energetically, Frank's soul was an extremely strong force. There was almost a sense of whimsy when he talked about some of the things he had experienced and done. Although it didn't really come out in the words, it was there energetically when he was thinking, "Oh yeah—I know that Joe Public really thought that I should be either venerated or hanged for what I had done, when all I was doing was just learning." He knows that parts of his life were misunderstood by people, but that means nothing to him, because it was his vehicle for learning what he had to learn. So the soul had a very strong sense of having accomplished what it set out to do.

Peter: At the very end of our conversation Frank Sinatra's soul gave a strong clue to the way all souls progress in their journey to maturity. It told us, with characteristic celestial humor, that—despite appearances—it was on the point of moving up to become a guide for other souls. This is not simply a matter of having a successful life, or just a varied life. Success, if it is measured at all in Home's non-judgmental environment, is a matter of readiness for the job. In Frank's earthly existence, his soul appears to have had a life that brought together themes from past lives in a kind of "wrapping up" of human experiences. Once more well illustrated, we see the way in which souls progress spiritually by learning lessons of all kinds, good, bad, and mixed.

So Frank had experienced the satisfaction and the power of the music (in which he had perfect pitch and excellent recall) that created his reputation and drove his career. He enjoyed true friendships but also used other people and allowed them to use him on occasion. He was aware of the difference, or said so, but one wonders if in his four marriages the boundaries between loving and using might have become somewhat blurred. As the brutal Jackie Mason incident implies, his sensitivity about his and Mia Farrow's 29-year age gap suggests that his motives were at least mixed.

But whether in his inherited connection with the mob (remember as this link was inherited, it was definitely taken into account before incarnation), or in his use of political connections (going back to his mother's own involvement as a political organizer), his reputation scraped by, and his magical voice remained triumphant. Although the heady availability of sexual favors failed to satisfy his spirit, from what we were told, he learned his Earth lessons well.

All this may be slightly surprising to our human minds but I guess it is: *just one of those things.*

"As limber as I kept my hands, I had trouble
with arthritis, particularly in my shoulders.
It was a very well-kept secret."

Yehudi Menuhin

1916-1999

Yehudi Menuhin, you were born in New York. Moshe, your Russian-Jewish father, had been a rabbinical student and was keenly anti-Zionist. Your sister Hephzibah was named after a queen in the Bible, but your name simply meant "a Jew." Was there a special reason for that name?

It wasn't the first name my parents chose. It started out as kind of a label and just stuck. It was put down on some documentation in the very beginning as "Yehudi."

Was your family devout?

My family went more or less with convenience. If it was convenient within the realm of who was available and what was available, they were devout. If there were other things that took precedence in survival, that was where we went.

Would you regard yourself as a secular Jew or a religious Jew in those days?

In the beginning I was a religious Jew. I was very interested in everything that had to do with Judaism, and I found that there was a mystery to it, a rhythm to it. It sang to my heart, and it seemed to encompass much more than I as a small lad could possibly be.

You and your two sisters were excellent musicians. Were your parents musical?

My parents wanted to be musical but never had the opportunity to really study and go anywhere with it, so they indulged us even to the extent of not having things for themselves at times.

You performed with your sisters from time to time. Would you describe them as soul mates?

They weren't soul mates, but we definitely had made contracts out of our soul group to be together, to begin the journey that I was on musically.

Did you have past lives as a musician?

I did have past lives as a musician, but nothing to this degree. This was a culmination of all of the beginning phases. It was as if, in other lifetimes, I were just learning to read music and play scales, and this was the lifetime of feeling it and performing it. The past lives were not where I was a professional musician. They were all lives where it was for entertainment, sometimes for a kopeck on the side or something like that, but nothing where I made my living as a musician.

You started learning to play the violin when you were only three. Your teacher was Sigmund Anker. Tell us about that experience.

From the cradle, I'm told, my toes would tap and my arms would move as if I were playing, so it was decided that if I could coordinate myself that well that early, I certainly should be able to pick up "the wood," as they called it then, and make some music with it. My dear teacher Sigmund was so patient, and he saw within me even at my early age that there was something different, that I could feel the music, that I could become a part of the music, and that what I brought forth from the wood was a song that could be felt by others.

Just four years later, in 1923, you performed with the San Francisco Symphony Orchestra. Did you understand what people meant when they called you a prodigy?

To me it just meant that they were giving me the opportunity to do what I chose to do. It didn't mean anything more to me than that at the time. My parents kept everything in perspective for me; I was still to learn other things and not live my whole life through my violin—although I did later.

It must have been difficult to have a normal childhood within that experience.

It was difficult because there was a lot of teasing. Even at that time it was considered sissy to get out there (unless it was a fiddle at a dance) and make beautiful music with—as the boys used to call it—my "box."

There seem to be many musical geniuses in history; why is that?

Music is a form of communication. As you have learned in your interviews, going back all the way to Ella Fitzgerald, who was one of the original angels who helped form communication as you use it now and as you are using it today to understand me, it is a way in which, instead of words, you can use the vibration created by the words or by the music as a way to convey your feeling, your intention, your love, even your disappointment to others.

Have you listened to the new violin concerto by the teenage composer Jay Greenberg?

I'm aware of it, yes. There has been much criticism and much laudation of that composition, and if you sit back and just go into the musical vibrations, he paints a picture for you in which he wants you to be totally absorbed.

Albert Einstein said he had downloaded physics information from the universe. Do kids like Jay do the same with music?

They are very connected with the celestial records, their Akashic records, and with forms of communication they engage in when not in body form. So when it comes to music it's very easy to tap into the bit stream of information drifting by. With Albert it was a little more difficult because he had to fine-tune what he took out of that constant flow of vibration through the universe.

At 13 you gave a concert in Berlin where an ecstatic Einstein said, "Now I know there is a God!" Which of your teachers, Louis Persinger, George Enescu, or, later, Adolph Busch, did the most to inspire your playing?

I don't think that I can say one did any more than another, because each taught me variations of techniques that would allow me to change the phraseology of my communication, of the way that the vibration came out of my instrument. It was as if I needed to tune up on my mathematics, or I needed to tune up on my social studies, or on my religious affiliations, or my connection to the Source. Each one provided tiny little pieces that together made a whole. So was one more important than another? No. Each one formed a complete piece of the whole that I became.

You said you wanted to meld "Kreisler's elegance, Elman's sonority, and Heifetz's technique." You had an individual style—can you describe what was different about it?

What you probably could say was that I brought the love that was inside of me, didn't reproduce or try to duplicate what anyone else had done but added my own particular accent to what came out of me. It is very easy in music to mimic another individual, but in mimicking another individual you don't add anything to the body of communication that is what music is. With me, I wanted to add my own contribution, my own joy of life and the living that I was doing, and that was what I presented in my technique, as you call it.

Three years later, at age 16, you played the first recording of Elgar's violin concerto, with the composer conducting. You seem to have forged a special bond with him.

I could feel the undertones, the secret whisperings beneath the surface of the music that he wanted reserved for those who could appreciate and could understand what a composition can convey to you. He told me that most musicians simply read what was there and never felt what the depth meant within the notes. I was attuned to his feelings when he had written the composition. I knew not only what he wrote, but what his inner feelings were at the time of the writing.

Was it Elgar, or your musical colleague Benjamin Britten, or the British musical scene in general that drew you to live in Britain and finally seek citizenship there?

It was a mixture of things. The biggest influence on me was the lack of pressure that I felt there. Whenever I was in the United States it was as if I were a puppet with somebody else directing me, somebody else was telling me what I had to do, where I had to be, how I had to do this. When I got to Britain they said, "Be yourself. Play as you want to play. We want to hear you. We want to hear the inner self portrayed in the songs that come from your strings." That, to me, was freedom, and that was why I sought to stay.

During World War II you gave 500 performances to the Allied troops, and then you went with Benjamin Britten to play to the Bergen-Belsen concentration camp survivors. Reconciliation was important—you were the first Jew to perform postwar with the Berlin Philharmonic, am I right?

Yes, I was the first one, and it was not because of my religion or my nationality; it was because of who they thought I was. They were not intimidated by the fact that I could move them with my music. They saw it as a way to bridge many of the things they had had no part in whatsoever; they were as aghast at what had occurred as the rest of the world was. They saw music as a salve to start the healing process between those who had been the harshest of enemies.

You had a clear understanding of Beethoven, Brahms, and the German musical scene early on in your career. After World War II you were able to help Wilhelm Furtwängler. Tell us about that relationship.

There are times when a person tries and tries to get the hang of something, accomplish something, and in the pressure to get it perfect, misses the heart of what is there. I was able to show Furtwängler what was within the music that he was missing, that the things he sought to play were not scientific or mathematical progressions on their own. They appeared to be that way, but when you added your heart to them, they became the communicator that people needed to be able to feel and to be able to be transported out of the difficulties, out of the mundane world, into a place of peace and joy and love.

You owned several violins, including the 1742 "Lord Wilton" Guarneri del Gesù violin. What was the special quality that you looked for in an instrument?

I looked for a resonance. Just as when a person carries on a conversation and changes the tone of voice or pitch or speed of communication, changing the resonance of various types of music with a different violin changes the appearance to the listener. The same piece of music played on two different violins with totally different resonances will affect the listener with different moods and create different visualizations. I would choose the instrument that was light or medium or heavy based on what I was trying to give to the audience.

When you were 19 you had cancelled concerts, and in your forties many people felt that your playing had gone into decline. You re-grouped, but seem to have felt more comfortable as a conductor after that. What went wrong?

In a word, arthritis. As limber as I kept my hands, I had trouble with arthritis, particularly in my shoulders. It was a very well-kept secret. The stiffness prevented some movement, and just a very minute change in the position of holding the violin changed the sound that I got out of the instrument, and it was not giving what I thought people deserved.

That affected you as early on as when you were 19, then?

I suffered a type of influenza at 19 that got into the muscles and the joints and had the same effect as when arthritis comes on in mid-life.

Tell us about Bartók's Sonata for solo violin, which you commissioned.

I had an idea of a way to introduce people to the variety of influences that could be wrought upon a human body by the variances in a musical composition. My intent was to have this appear as a beautiful piece of music but yet be a primer to take people to different states of sensation throughout the piece of music.

How well did you know Béla Bartók?

I knew of his work—we had done some work together, we had consulted. Were we the best of friends? No, but there was an immediate feeling that I had with him that this was the person who could be my translator.

You were proud to be a vegetarian, warning people about the dangers of meat and processed grains. How do you view vegetarianism now from where you are at Home?

[laughs] For me and for my body at that time, it was what I needed to keep myself in the trim that I wanted to have with the energy flowing through my body the way I wanted it to. I was so very sensitive to vibrations of any kind that when (early on) I consumed animal flesh, I could feel the energy of the animal within it. I didn't want my body to be contaminated by feelings other than my own, so anything that was altered, anything that was killed or mistreated, I could sense the pain within it, which made it imperative that I be as pure and as unaffected by those vibrations as possible. I did at times, when I was sensing things, become a little fanatical with people, trying to say that what was good for me must be good for them. I now know everybody is individual and that some human machines just will not function without animal flesh.

In 1952, you met the Indian yogi B.K.S. Iyengar and through him introduced hatha yoga to the West. What did the discipline of yoga do for you?

Yoga allowed me to be totally in tune with my body and all of the energy transferred and transferring through my body, which allowed me to have a kind of sound chamber within which the music I played resonated, so I could test and see if I had the right phraseology to create the energy that I wished to give to others.

Did it help you with the arthritis?

At first it helped me keep my muscles and bones limber so that I was able to continue as long as I did. After the changes began within the joints, it made me totally aware of the restrictions that were gradually being placed upon my body.

You also met Ravi Shankar, the Indian sitar master, and played with him at the Bath Festival, for which you were the musical director. How much did Hindu culture change your life?

I don't know if it could be said that it actually changed my life. It enriched my life by giving me the opportunity to take these wonderful practices that were very prevalent within their community and to practice them myself. I was not, during my physical incarnation, a total devotee of anything. I was very open to all of the things that could impact the way I perceived that I played the music, that I conveyed the music, and that I helped others to comprehend that form of communication.

So you wouldn't regard yourself as a reincarnationist in the Hindu mode?

[laughs] I'm well aware of the fact that I have been reincarnated a number of times, but within their realm of saying that what occurs in one lifetime affects what you come back as in the next lifetime, definitely not.

You married twice and had four children. Would you describe yourself as a family man?

Family was very important to me because of the family life that I had as a child. It was what gave me the first sense of steering others and helping them develop their potential. I wanted to be able to do that with my children. I also saw the close ties between my parents and wished to have that same sense of completion.

In your later career you raised money for charity and did a lot of conducting and musical directing. You founded a school for musically gifted children in England, a musical academy in Switzerland, and Live Music Now, a charity helping young musicians to perform in hospitals, schools, and prisons. You were knighted and, later, given a life peerage. Was this the most enjoyable time, or did you long for the glorious days of your youth?

I was always very content wherever I was. I don't think that any particular part of my life seemed more important to me than any other. The enjoyment of performing was grand, but just as grand was seeing my "devotees" going through the hospital wards and bringing that sense of hope and love to those who were there. I had planned a very complex and integrated sense of experiences for that lifetime.

Did you achieve the lessons you came down to learn?

Yes, I did. I was very, very satisfied with what I learned.

And now that you are Home, how do you view your achievements?

I view my achievement as having a very successful life—having chosen lessons before I went there and having accomplished them, having learned from them, and having the opportunity to go beyond the lessons as part of my pathway of enriching others with the particular talents that I had within that lifetime.

Since you are honored and remembered almost as much for your humanitarian efforts as for your musicianship, what sparked the drive to help humanity in the ways that you did?

Well, first off, as I was planning to come down here, there were certain things I wished to accomplish in the form of communication with music. Those were the lessons I came down with. The secondary lesson was dealing with the medical problems I had, and doing it in such a way that it did not define who I was—that, as a matter of fact, it was very much unknown by so many people, because to me it wasn't important. It was the sign that if I dealt with that, that was the last of the big lessons I had to accomplish while in physical form. My life's purpose, then, became to instill in others the joy and the love and the importance of musical communication. The way for me to do that was with the various programs that I became involved in, so it was my life's purpose that continued; I was one of the fortunate souls who had about a fifty-fifty life: 50% of lessons and 50% of life purpose.

Thank you, Yehudi Menuhin, for coming and talking with us.

Commentary

Toni: During the whole of the interview there was music playing constantly in the background. It was changing and the vibrations were just absolutely phenomenal. It got intense, and there were counter plays of things in the background, and as it got more intense, that was when it was almost as if he were trying to reach for the right word. There were a lot of times when it seemed that he wasn't totally comfortable with conveying things to us in English, that there would be like a burst of music or vibration whenever he had trouble finding a word. It was like he was trying to give it to me in the way in which he felt comfortable communicating, which was through music and vibration. It was an extremely fascinating interview.

Peter: There was a stilted, almost disjointed element in this dialogue, to which Toni refers, which surprised me. The last question, asked by my musician wife, Sonia, who was present in the room, brought forth Yehudi's warmest, most relaxed response. My sense is that the musical spectrum of celestial vibratory language is where this soul finds greatest comfort.

The early-onset arthritis that afflicted the great violinist, who confessed that it affected the quality of his playing, is seen now by him as an important physical lesson he had chosen to learn. I wonder now if any musical historian will be brave enough to take the evidence of this statement by his soul and dare to include it as an historical fact.

The big joy to me in this dialogue was the way Menuhin expressed the depth of his musical understanding. He "could feel the undertones, the secret whisperings beneath the surface of the music" of Elgar's violin concerto. With Furtwängler he had been able to lead the great conductor away from the perfection of his interpretations to a depth of feeling he had missed before. His violins were selected for their personality, the Bartok commission chosen for its ability to open new vistas of understanding. There was a resonance in all that he had done that was in harmony with his musical nature, including his espousal of Hatha Yoga and his great educational work with gifted children. Souls I have interviewed have rarely expressed as clearly as he did the sense of satisfaction at lessons well learned and a life well lived.

"My plan for my business was not to drive people out of business. My plan was to benefit and to provide for the needs of thousands."

Sam Walton

1918-1992

Sam Walton, your father was a struggling midwestern farmer who became a mortgage broker. Your family moved homes a lot when you were a boy. You had to work hard at earning money as times were hard. Was it that experience that instilled your entrepreneurial drive?

Not only did it quite certainly instill a drive in me, but it also gave me a firm feeling for what other people were going through, particularly those who did not have the initiative that I had, and it allowed me to move forward on my own.

At high school you played team sports, and became an honors student who was well respected by your peers who voted you the "Most Versatile Boy" when you graduated. But you had another, lifelong passion. You were Missouri's youngest-ever Eagle Scout. What did scouting mean to you?

Scouting to me meant finding out about myself, being able to integrate life into my persona. It forced me to look at things that I possibly wouldn't have looked at, different crafts, and different ways of doing business. It also promoted a very strong loyalty to the idea of service to others. That was something that I took to heart. I saw that the reason why Eagle Scouts had to do service projects before they could be awarded their badge was so they could feel the importance one person can have in a large group of people, and so they could learn to organize others in helping toward the completion of their project. I used that formula to start developing—I guess what you would call—my empire.

Studying economics at the University of Missouri-Columbia, you joined a fraternity (Beta Theta Pi) and QEBH, a secret campus society, and then, after college, a professional business fraternity (Alpha Kappa Psi). What did all these societies mean to you? Were they a fast-track to wealth and power?

Alpha Kappa Psi definitely was. The other ones? Within the groups I had the sense of being a part of something. It started when I was in grade school and high school and I belonged to all the associations. I needed a large group of people around me to try out my ideas on, to see how they worked. What better way to do it than in the fraternity, a group contained inside one building. It was a training ground for me which definitely allowed me to hone my people skills. I found from my study of economics that if you didn't have people skills, you could be excellent on paper but you would be somebody else's boy. You would not be your own person unless, in addition to having the knowledge of how to make money, create a business, and be successful, you had people skills to carry it out. Then you could be your own person.

Were you at that time convinced that you would make a lot of money?

No. I just didn't want to be in the nickel-and-dime jobs I had had in my youth. I wanted to be comfortable and to provide for a family. It wasn't until I had started in business that I developed all the ideals which came to me, and the boy scouts' ideas popped back that I could be of service to others while filling my pockets.

You worked for JCPenney as a management trainee until World War II when you joined the US Army Intelligence Corps. Before joining the Army you married Helen Robson, a successful business graduate from a wealthy banking family. Tell us about your relationship with Helen and with your four children.

Family was very important to me; all people were, but particularly my family. Growing up, my own life had been difficult. My father was very hard working and we didn't see much of him. So I had as a role model this person who was always busy, who was always concerned with where the next dollar was going to come from and how he was going to fill our mouths. I wanted to give my children a broader experience. My darling wife understood exactly where I was when it came my time to stumble out to the business world, and she was a terrific confidante to me when I started to create my empire. But to me everything was about family.

Have you had many lifetimes with Helen?

We had had one previous lifetime that we both knew of. I have since learned we had a number of lifetimes together.

So you had an understanding while you were on Earth of the previous lifetime?

Although we didn't believe in reincarnation at the time very much, we had a number of joint déjà vu feelings, where we would talk about having done things together. It started out as a sort of a game of imagination—you know, "remember when we did this!"—but then we realized that it wasn't coming from imagination, it was coming from true memories. We were blessed to share that, and it brought us closer together because we knew that we were connected at a depth beyond the rings on our fingers, and the church ceremony.

Did your souls have a contract to marry before coming down?

We had made an agreement that we would probably marry. There are choices we all have when we come down here. We two were on a planned collision course to meet, and then the sparks just flew so there was a 98% chance we were going to get married when we came down here, but freedom of choice still prevailed.

Your son John transitioned recently. Have your souls been in contact since he came Home?

Oh yes! It's been a very nice reunion. I had the occasion to meet him at the cross-over and it was—there's such a closeness between us—it was like a family reunion in more ways than being around the table and sharing a turkey; it was an energetic reunion. Of course, he's been aware that I have been looking over his shoulder since I've been up here. [laughs]

Did your work as a military Intelligence officer teach you anything that was useful in your later career?

To some degree. Intelligence is knowing what the other person is doing, knowing how to infiltrate to learn their plans, learning how nothing is truly secret, so if you try to deceive somebody it is going to get out. Different "subversive" ideas—things that I had never thought of—came into my knowingness, so that I knew things that I could do to find out the direction to go in, as well as to be watchful that others did not come in and undermine what I was trying to do. It was like studying military games in the business world. I learned the ground rules in the military and the application of them while in business.

How do you feel about recent developments where nations increase the surveillance of their own people?

Well, of course, up here we don't have any judgments, one way or another, that it's right or wrong. It is what leaders truly feel they need to do to have a degree of control over their people. I can't say it's wrong, if that is the basis of their ideology. It is not something I would have chosen to do were I still in human form. So I watch it as a comic relief.

But you were a fierce opponent of communism. Doesn't that smack of communist control?

That was while I was in body form. That's judgment that one ideology is better than another ideology. I don't have those judgments now. I guess you would say that I am tolerant of other people's pathways.

You remind me of living in an Ivory Tower! Shouldn't we have any judgment about surveillance, and liberty, and that kind of issue?

Depending upon where you are in your pathway, yes, judgment is very important. In order to be successful in the [Earth's] third-dimensional world of polarities you have to make those decisions to get ahead. You have to know, in order to stoke up the ego, what makes the big bucks in the third dimensional world, what moves things along, and what is right (and wrong) for your agenda. To be under the watchful eye of someone else restricts not only your freedom of choice but also the extent of the experimentation you might engage in to change your situation. So if your path on Earth is to be able to create change, then surveillance would be wrong for you. If you are on a spiritual, rather than a physical path, the amount of surveillance is immaterial to you, because it is something you don't choose to deal with. It's part of life. You don't make a judgment about it. In your social and your private life you just go by standards that society wants you to adopt. In your spiritual life, however, you are just an observer.

With money that you and Helen had saved, and a loan from her father, you purchased a Ben Franklin variety store franchise in Newport, Arkansas. You were very successful there. What was it you had discovered that led to your store's being the best of the six-state franchise?

Again, people skills—not only with the employees but in particular with the customers. The phrase that people tout but do not always live by, that "the customer is always right," was something we firmly believed in. The definition of "right" might vary a little bit, but you could always make the customer happy. That was what we endeavored to do. Any of the employees who were not willing to go that extra step to satisfy a customer did not stay around very long. People who came to the stores felt they were dealing with family, and that's the way we treated them. We did not let them walk all over us, but we were willing to see their point of view on things.

You opened a second store which didn't do very well, then your landlord refused to renew the lease on the first store. You sold him your inventory at a fair price, but wasn't being put out of business a severe lesson?

It was a two-fold lesson because I had become too complacent in what I was doing, and I was not using my full potential. I was sitting back, everything was working well, and I was able to take care of my needs but was not using all of my abilities. So it was what we call here "a spiritual two-by-four," a little whack over the head to make me take a look at my life, evaluate it, and see what I could do with the abilities I had. In physical terms it was a setback because I was starting over. In spiritual terms it was one of the starting points which allowed me to really step into my potential.

You opened a replacement variety store in Bentonville, Arkansas, called "Walton's Five and Dime." There you and Helen became leaders in the local Bentonville community. At that time did you intend to settle down there as a family?

That's difficult to explain. Wherever we were as a family was home. I don't know if we felt consciously that this was where we needed to be, but at the moment it was the right place for us and we practiced the principles we already had of providing for the community. Between us, we had extraordinary human talents to help people. Going back to the scouting principle, we gave of ourselves in service to the community, and that occurred wherever we were.

This community service was given by your whole family?

It grew into the family. It was not that I demanded anything of anybody, but I showed them by my example what I had learned, and how I truly felt that this was part of my purpose in that physical lifetime, and that it was a beautiful way to share with other souls. The family sort of jumped on the bandwagon.

Do you feel that large corporations, like Wal-Mart, that tout their involvement in society are doing it more for self-interest than for a real interest?

Some of them do. Truly many of my principles are being adhered to. Not at all levels, but it has become such a large corporation it is hard to control your extended, *extended* family members. The basic principles that I laid down were of service to all, to provide for the community. One of the things was that all products had to be made in America. A decent wage would be maintained. We were going to make people feel comfortable as they entered our stores. We were going to provide for some of the less fortunate but employable, such as the mentally retarded and the handicapped. We tried to work that into our corporate picture.

Soon after opening at Bentonville, you started developing a chain of local stores and after that the Wal-Mart empire. What is it that drives the entrepreneur to go on and on expanding a business—is it fear of failure or hunger for more wealth and power?

With me I don't know that it was either. I cannot speak for all entrepreneurs. I know some run on fear and some run on the power that money can bring. For me it was just expanding my Eagle Scout project. [laughs] Taking that degree of service to others and putting it into practice. Trying to provide goods at a price people in the local community could afford. Our first starts were in the poorest communities where people had not had the opportunity to purchase new things. Everything had been hand-me-downs, but then we put them into a reasonable price bracket so that everybody might aspire to have their own things. For me it was that I had these abilities and wanted to watch them sprout and see my garden grow. As for the money that came in—I had nowhere near the ability to spend it. So it wasn't for the money, or through fear. It was for the fun of doing it.

You enticed talented managers to join your company, as you said, "without any shame or embarrassment." Wal-Mart's massive growth resulted in siphoning off good staff and so deeply undercutting prices that lots of small retail stores were put out of business, and their hardworking owners' and workers' hopes dashed. Now, back Home, do you see any social consequences to company growth that should be avoided? If growth puts the competition out of business, won't a price be paid by the customer?

Within any situation, if you provide lower-price items to people who have a choice between buying something affordable or not purchasing it—buying a good set of clothes plus a work set of clothes, say, instead of only buying a good set of clothes at a more exclusive personal store—they are going to go for the two sets of clothes. My plan for my business was not to drive people out of business. My plan was to benefit and to provide for the needs of thousands. Within that (as it is in military maneuvers) there is a cost, and that cost was the failure of some of the small stores that had to pay premium prices for their stock. But they had never serviced a fraction of the people who were financially able to shop at my stores.

So Sam Walton, who went around quite incidentally closing lots of businesses, was actually performing a "public service"?

That was the intent. It was not the intent to close stores. There really was no competition with what I was providing and what they were providing. They were also in the goods business, but I was providing for the majority of the population and not a small section of the population. Because my prices were so good, they did lure people, who had been paying twice as much for a similar item at a small store, into my larger stores. But my basic concern at that time was for the majority of society.

In Wal-Mart's drive to bring down prices for Western consumers, unscrupulous suppliers linked to the Third World have paid their workers slave wages, and many have also complained that Wal-Mart takes advantage of employees, who have historically been paid badly. Should there be standards set of "fair trade" and "fair pay" for big business?

From the standpoint of economics, no! [laughs] This may sound a little heretical because it sounds contrary to everything I have said up to this point, but if you are asking me as a business-trained individual, the concern is the bottom line. "Business" is not concerned with the entirety of society but rather what return is available for the investment and work put out.

I'm asking you as a spirit.

As a spirit: no one has the right to use another soul unless that soul has contracted for that experience. So that would be my answer from this side. The souls who are in the positions of slavery are there to learn something about themselves, to experience being controlled by another, but also, hopefully, to experience that they can think better of themselves and find an alternative.

But isn't that the whole point about slavery, whether it is economic or physical, that you don't have the opportunity to change your status?

There's a large perspective of what slavery is, and from here I can see that what some people interpret as slavery, some of the "slaves" interpret as salvation, because it is so much better for them than the alternative.

Which is starvation!

Which is starvation. So, again, we are talking about the spiritual perspective, the lessons the soul is seeking to learn which result in your spiritual path during your physical experience. In the body I tried to guard against slavery-type situations when I became aware how goods were produced in foreign countries. That was part of the decision when I established the policy that our products must be made in the United States. The secondary reason for that was to help the economy of people in the United States who would then have employment. My soul's intention was not always visible to me or to others.

Do you feel that Wal-Mart has moved away from that stand?

As a corporation, yes.

You and Helen put up nearly all of the money needed for the first Wal-Mart. There was risk involved but you won big. Andrew Carnegie gave most of his wealth away. Bill and Melissa Gates are following suit, and so is Warren Buffet. How do you feel about their drive to return most of their wealth to the world community?

[laughs] You have to consider their position, and my position when I was down there. Their position is that they make money at any cost. They did not make money with the intention of providing benefits for society by their products or by what they did. Their money was all self-aggrandizing. So they had to assuage the guilt, which came with the gathering of wealth, in other ways. I truly felt that I helped people by the very business itself, so therefore, I did not have any guilt to assuage by further giving away my money. I left that up to my family—to feel guilty or to carry on their own dreams.

I guess you've also learned that "you can't take it with you."

The motivation for what I was doing was to provide for my family and make them very comfortable, but also to provide a source of employment for people, and a source of goods that were reasonably available to people, particularly in areas outside the range of the normal fancy dry goods stores.

If you were responsible for running Wal-Mart today, what would you do differently?

I would be true to the policies with which I began the store—making sure that people were not used, and that people were provided for. Toward the end of my life on Earth, I was not as aware of the day-to-day operations as I would have liked to be. That was in my retirement when I gave a lot of the operating duties over to various other family members. It appeared that I was the head, but I was just a rubber stamp at the head of the family. I was not totally aware until I got here that so much of my intention and my philosophy was being shifted and almost sullied by things that were going on. But that was the path of the people who were doing it.

You were a staunch Christian supporter of the Presbyterian Church and its outreach. Has your understanding of the nature of God changed in any way since your return Home?

Very much so. In physical form I was one of those believers in the old gentleman in the white beard and flowing robes and with fire and brimstone if you did not adhere to the principles as established by the hierarchy of the church, supposedly through the traditions of the religion and the Bible. Now I know that we all have a piece of that little beard inside of us. And it is for us to be tickled by those whiskers to know that each of us creates what we want to create. On the fire and brimstone theory, we don't have anybody else to blame for what we do to ourselves.

So there's no heaven and hell?

There's no heaven and hell but what you make of it.

Where do we go when we die?

We go into unconditional love. We go into a place where everybody is the same, has the same power. Some have more knowledge and more wisdom because they've been down to Earth more times and had more experiences. We're all the same. There is no right, there is no wrong;

there is nothing but total love and understanding shared by all.

So why would anyone want to leave?

You know, just like any good, rich food—you can only take so much of it, then you want to experience something else. Unconditional love is great. But then there's more unconditional love and more unconditional love. There's no excitement in creating an empire. There's no sharing with another individual on a physical level. There's (strange though it may seem) no negativity, no pain. Only when you have known negativity can you realize how magnificent is the opposite.

Thank you, Sam Walton, for talking with us.

My pleasure—and Wal-Mart's still good!

Commentary

Toni: There was deep sincerity in what he was saying about what his intentions and ideals were for the store. It wasn't to crush anybody but to provide for those who couldn't afford goods in any way, and to provide quality items. He learned a lot dealing with his stores, and when he was in the Ben Franklin franchise he was riding on someone else's horse and not using all his abilities. His wife was right beside him in his development. I did not feel any nasty dogmatic business approach in his presence. His soul still yearns for the beginning of it all and hopes that his original good intentions will eventually return to the Wal-Mart scene, where little people will still be able to afford good-quality goods. Sam's concern seems to be to provide the best available for the most people.

Peter: Unlike millionaire loner Andrew Carnegie, whom I interviewed in our first book of this series, *Talking with Leaders of the Past,* Sam Walton was the quintessential team player. Scouts, Eagle Scouts, sports teams, college and business fraternities, and lastly his own family, all shaped the familial response that was a hallmark of his adult life—a togetherness that was rose-hued by Sam's big brush. "Family" in his first store was created by his order, which if not acted upon by staff members could result in their dismissal. And wow—did the family concept work hugely in Sam's favor! It has been a way of life in his stores that has been branded by critics as a tool with which to gain maximum return on investment from overworked and underpaid workers.

As with Carnegie, however, the experience of being wealthy and successful left a spiritual mark. Sam's soul was a bit troubled by changes in corporate attitudes and policies at Wal-Mart, but it always measured human issues in business terms. Little retailers who went out of business because of the new local "big box" store did so, we were told, because of *their* inefficiency. There were no regrets. Nor was his huge wealth a problem for him (he had earned it), though it might just be a lesson for his family to learn.

Everything in the beautiful Home we all came from is unconditionally loving—with no judgment calls made in human ethical terms of right and wrong. All is very pleasant and fulfilling there, but it affords nothing like the sheer excitement of building the largest, most successful retail empire in the world. Or should I have said "retail *family*"?

"I was the one who said you cannot forget me. You cannot escape me. I will make you face who you are and what you believe."

James Baldwin

1924 - 1987

James Arthur Baldwin, I heard you address the World Council of Churches in Uppsala when you took over from the late Dr. Martin Luther King, Jr. The audience there really appreciated you.

Well, thank you for the kind comment.

There were more press people there, like me, than delegates.

Yes, we could have used a few more people who were really interested in what we were doing, what we were trying to accomplish.

You were the oldest in your mother's family of nine children. Your own father didn't stay around. You took the name of your stepfather, David Baldwin. Did you choose that family situation in advance of incarnating?

We always choose where we're coming to and it can be for a number of reasons. It can be for the turmoil expected within the family. It can be because of the genetics that are running through a particular family line so that we will experience disabilities, diseases, addiction tendencies—things of that nature, or because we have contracts with some of the parties who are also going to be in that family.

Did you know who your biological father was?

I knew who he was, but he was not playing a part in that particular life for me.

How did that situation affect you?

Psychologically it gave me certain feelings of abandonment later in life. You know—what was wrong with me that he didn't want to be a part of my life? I had planned to experience these feelings, but it also put into perspective the graciousness and the kindness and the lovingness of my step father, and how he brought the family together as a family.

I'm interested you call him gracious and kind because he is reputed to have been quite a brutal man.

He had his ways. [laughs] He had his ways that most would consider brutal, but it was what I had got myself into. I'm talking "graciousness" as a soul taking on such a position. In point of physical fact, and pardon my French, he was what most would call a "bastard." But that again, that cauldron, was something that I wanted to feel, to have the experience of the emotions that are fostered by being in such a situation.

What was your relationship like with your mother?

Through a lot of my life, I didn't think too highly of her because of the way she allowed herself to be treated by her spouse. I went through the whole range of emotions of feeling sorry for her, having disdain for her, having sympathy for her, wanting to help her. It was a roller coaster upon which I felt all the different things humans can feel in relationship to each other, and the way they are influenced by outside forces.

In your novels Another Country *and* Tell Me how Long the Train's been Gone, *the characters are straight, gay, and bisexual. How early on did you become aware of your homosexuality and how would you describe yourself?*

Very early on I became aware of homosexuality because my stepfather was a homophobe. One of the neighbors was gay, so it was a topic on which we were preached at concerning him. I would describe myself as an experimenter—sometimes just to see what was there, and sometimes being forced there out of rebellion.

How did your mother react to your gay lifestyle?

My mother had a certain fear that my stepfather would kill me, would beat me to death.

What is the soul seeking to achieve in the advance choice it makes of gender and sexual orientation?

Basically, with gender, the soul is trying to experience all the things that society envisions concerning a particular gender. With sexual leanings, if it is a heterosexual one, the idea is to be able to marry together all of the energies that are possible between two people of opposite sexes. You take together two people leaning toward totally different types of emotions and different types of ways to handle everyday situations.

When it comes to homosexual tendencies, this chosen experience can be for any of several different reasons. It can be selected to deal with all of society's reactions to what homosexuality means, or it can be chosen to be able to further identify oneself within that particular sex by having a partner who is like a role model for you. It's a very close relationship that allows you to compare notes, so to speak: "I'm having these problems; how do you solve them?" "What are your feelings when you get a reaction from outside a certain type?" There are all kinds of reactions and situations that come to you, and those are, or they encompass, the various reasons that you choose a particular sex, a particular lifestyle, a particular sexual orientation.

As a child you had a great appetite for books. That led early to self-expression. Your first story appeared in a church paper. Did anyone help you in your choice of books?

Some of my teachers and a friendly librarian helped me in my selection of books. Books for me, from an early age, were used as an escape. It was something to do or someplace that I could go to get out of the turmoil that surrounded me. And when I repeatedly would start talking about stories or books, the teachers would say, "Have you read this?" Or I would say to the librarian, "I need to go on a vacation," and she would bring me a book of someplace I had never been or possibly even heard of. If I needed an experience to help define myself, she would find me the book that would help me explain the human place. Her name was Alice Finerty.

Which books made the biggest impression?

Once I began to consume the books, at first I just read them for escapism, to transport me to someplace else. But then I changed to feeling the energy of the author that was in the book, or the energy of the place that the book was written about. Then I got the sense that I might be able to create a world, a reality, for someone within a book as it was being created for me.

Does that explain your choice of Paris later in life?

It's one of the places that had always seemed to me to be accepting of whatever you wanted to do, whoever you wanted to be.

You fell in love with it as a boy?

I did. From everything I read there was an openness about the way they, to some, tolerated differences, but to others embraced differences.

Were you a writer in a past life?

Not to the degree I was as James Baldwin. I had been a recorder keeping histories and documents for other people. I was involved in the compilation of some of the earliest encyclopedias as they were being produced. But to move the heart of a person with words in a novel, no, I had not done that before.

You knew how to move hearts. You were a fluent speaker and became a teenage preacher in the Far South Pentecostal Church in Harlem. Was this primarily your religious zeal? Or did you try to please your preacher stepfather, David?

I think that the best way to put it was that I was trying to survive. This was a way to get my stepfather to not scrutinize me as much as he did the other family members because I was doing something that was accepted by him. My success with the way I drew people, the way I touched people, he saw as *his* success. So there were some other things that I did that he just then totally overlooked.

How do you now view the message of the Pentecostalist Church?

As with every religion, there are people who need the messages. There is to us here at home no message that is right or wrong (except that we are *all* the same). The way the Church wraps the message is what brings people in to listen, to find what they need. This may be solace, it may be direction, it may be control. I will not get into a position of judging what is right and what is wrong. Just that everything has its place and its need within your world.

You said, "Those three years in the pulpit...turned me into a writer, really, dealing with all that anguish and that despair and that beauty." Would it be true to say that as a writer you remained a secular preacher?

To a degree that would be an accurate statement. But rather than preaching (because preaching seems as if you are making judgments and saying that "what I say is what you must believe"), I found my writing more to be: "Let me show you the options. Let me show you what is out there that you may not have seen, so that you may accept it, or deny it if it does not fit you, or take and modify it if it will further enrich your life." I did not, within my writing, attempt to say, "Everybody, this is the way it is. This is what you must believe." That had been my intention and it was what came out from my pulpit.

Some have called your writing "a gospel of recognition, responsibility and redemption." Is that fair?

I don't think that it's fair or unfair. It depends upon your perspective and location in life. It depends upon what you have as a guidepost within your life. If you are within a pattern of belief, whether it be from an organized religion or some type of self-belief that you have to guide you, and you follow this guidance, then my books are merely seasoning for your meal. This seasoning then may or may not be used to help you enrich your current patterns, if you find it is to your taste. If you do not have, or did not have, a basis before coming to my books, a belief system, a firm, set way of perceiving things, then my books could be your Bible, providing you direction.

Your youth was spent in the black areas of Harlem and the Bronx. What were the chief experiences in your youth that made you such a furiously dedicated opponent of racism?

There were so many things that contributed to my opposition to racism. From the time I could first remember, there was a very definite black and white in the world. In the beginning I did not venture much out of the black from fear, and felt there was protection among my own kind. But then, as I began reading, began exploring the world, I realized that I was confining myself and limiting myself by staying within what I thought was comfortable.

As I began to venture out it was like being slapped down. I was very conscious of the energies that existed between the races. And of course, because I was in fear of conflict, racial incidents were drawn to me so that I might experience them. In being concerned about them I was broadcasting to the universe, "Let me experience that which I fear, that which I have not experienced." Then I was able sit back and realize, particularly from my readings, that there were parts of the world that were not racist. I began to let everybody know, through my writings, through my talks, that there was another way to live—that there was no difference between the colors of our skins.

Tell me about your friendship with Richard Wright. He had similar experiences himself, and he ended up in Paris before you. Your book of essays Notes of a Native Son *was clearly a tribute to his great novel* Native Son. *Did you then accuse him of being a poor writer?*

That was very much blown out of proportion. There were certain things that we stimulated within each other. We would sit down and have discussions about the importance of words and how words could direct the emotions of people, how words could direct the flow of the energy of people. In point of fact, if you had to grade things within the human plane by good, better, and best, I had a better turn of words than he. And it was something that he even acknowledged. To say that I made accusations about him was not actually true. Things were taken out of context. It was more that we were trying again to push each other.

But your friendship came to an end at that time.

He started taking very seriously everything that was going on. He did not like the way my material was being accepted. At one point, he tried to get me to go into collaboration with him on a work, and I was not ready to do that, and he thought that I was depriving him of a great opportunity.

Why were you an alcoholic?

There were some pressures that I just could not deal with. Once I was out of a safe, seemingly protected space where I didn't have to fight my way upstream, and then found myself thrown into a place where I had to worry about what was going on, I sought help. As a boy I was able to escape into the novel; as I got older I escaped into the bottle. It was a way of numbing the turmoil I felt.

Two of your friends were the musician and civil rights worker Nina Simone and the painter Beaufort Delaney. Tell me about your friendship with them.

I loved them dearly because they were both visionaries—visionaries to the extent that, while so many of my people at that time saw imaginary chains that held them back, my friends saw instead that with their talents they could cut those chains, and they could fly; just as I did with my writing, they did with their music and their art. Well, it was more than simply the art—it was in the whole creative production of what they could do. It was like they were presenting possibilities.

[At this point in the conversation Baldwin transmitted a picture to the Channel. Toni reported: "The image I am getting now is of one of those Easter eggs that you look into and there is a whole elaborate village inside. From the outside the shell is plain and boring. But look inside the egg and you are transported into a whole new world. So he is saying that is what all three of them could do."]

It didn't matter if your outside world was plain, if you were still living in the ghetto, if you were still in the place where you were being repressed. You could go into these arts, use those arts (whether it be music or painting or literature), become a part of that picturesque egg village and create your whole reality within the beauty while you were still in your plain wrapper.

You went from the plain wrapper into a very much more elegant one. In 1948 you went to Paris. Also during your life, you spent time in Turkey, Switzerland, and the South of France (where you died). What were the underlying reasons for your self-imposed exile?

I didn't consider it much of an exile. I considered it an escape and a reward. I was in an enviable position of being able to, at that time, afford what I had dreamed of having. I was in places where I was accepted, where the color of my skin didn't relegate me to the back of the bus. I could go into any café and sit down and havc a glass of wine, a beer, a cup of coffee, and be accepted. In trips back to the United States I found that very little had changed, regardless of whether I was recognized or not. I chose at that time to take the world I had created and live in it, not be incarcerated by where I had come from.

In 1953 you published your largely autobiographical novel, Go Tell It on the Mountain. *It looks at the good and bad qualities of the African American Christian Church, and it challenges racism in America. What was your purpose in writing the story?*

The main purpose I had was to take complacent people, particularly within the United States, put my hands on their shoulders, and shake them into awareness—into the realization that viewing their thoughts or how they lived as being the only way that things would or could happen was so near-sighted. They needed to know that there were good points in the way they had been brought up, but also that they didn't have to stay within the restrictions of those things. They didn't have to hang on to a cultural identity for the negativity that it encompassed. They could take the positive from that cultural identity and go outside and accept the positives of everything that was around them and create a new person, a new identity.

Your second novel, Giovanni's Room, *was explicitly sexual. Why did you choose a cast of white characters for that story?*

It was a little bit of fun, [laughs] and I chose whites because, had I chosen blacks, the entire race would have been typecast by the book. People who were white, or of other races that had not had much dealing with blacks, would have believed that all blacks were the same. Because whites come from so many different places—whether it be eastern Europe, the United States, Canada—readers could get the idea that I was discussing particular tendencies and yearnings that some people had, which were not specific to a race.

In your next two novels you showed a change of direction. In Another Country *and* Tell Me How Long the Train's Been Gone, *racial and sexual issues abound in a disturbing pair of stories. You thought such issues were always intertwined and said, "If Americans mature on the level of racism then they have to mature on the level of sexuality. I think Americans are terrified of feeling anything, and homophobia is simply an extreme example of American terror at growing up."*

I was hoping with those books (because I was using a fair amount of personal experience in writing them), to show to people who were reading them simply because they had read my former book [*Giovanni's Room*] that there were not a lot of differences between the races, except for the fact that blacks were truthful in what they did. They were not hypocritical. They did not take their sexuality and close the door and hide it. They lived the way they felt they needed to. They weren't puritanical because that's not the way the human animal is.

Do you now see the link between sexuality and racism quite as strongly as you did then?

No, not at all. I do see that blacks are still more truthful. Basically blacks, if they are not in positions where they are competing with whites, such as white collar workers, are true to themselves and their feelings in the way they express themselves in all matters including sexuality. Whereas the whites, if they are in higher echelons where they feel they are on a pedestal and must be honored and obeyed, keep their sexual tendencies hidden behind the closet door. More of the whites, the normal Joes, the ones who are not out there on pedestals, are beginning to have the same feeling and exhibit the same tendencies toward sexuality as the blacks. This is the normal, healthy human response to sexuality.

So then we had the disparity of the blacks being overtly sexual and the whites being repressed. We now have some of the blacks being repressed to fit into white society, and we have some of the whites finding they don't have to be repressed because of what they do or how their family is viewed within society. They relish being true to themselves and their feelings.

Then came the civil rights era. You were speaking at rallies in the South. The New Yorker published your essay "Down at the Cross." Your face was on the cover of Time *magazine. Then your friends Dr. King, Malcolm X, and Medgar Evers were all assassinated. Explain why you believed that America did not have a black problem but a white problem.*

[laughs] That's very simple—we were not trying to assassinate everybody. The problem was in the white population feeling that they should be superior just because they had always been the owners. And how could their possessions be better then they?

They were locked into history?

They were locked into history. They were locked into the stories that were passed from generation to generation. They were locked into the societal beliefs that had always been preached. When they saw these great, great people who far outshone some of their best and brightest politicians and world speakers and motivational speakers, there was such a fear that their response was, "Let's erase the trace!" And in deciding that, their only possible course was to kill them all.

How do you now view the relationship of black Muslims with the rest of American society today?

Black Muslims are trying to take a religion and a way of life and use it to enrich a life that, within the United States, was splintered off from their homelands. When you are born in a family and you always belong to the same group, whether it be a religion or a political party or some type of community organization, you have a basis of identity for yourself. When your history encompasses coming from different continents, such as the mixture of African, Caribbean, South American, and all the coloreds that were brought together into the United States, you don't have a sense of a shared identity.

The black Muslims have clung to a feeling that their religion will give the people an identity that can bridge all of their differences. They also, to a small extent, are connecting with some of their ancestors of color who were in the Muslim countries, even though these people were never brought into slavery, as the majority of the people now in the United States were. They are looking to religion for a sense of identity, creating almost an elitism of these people who were never possessions. When the energy of the free man permeates you, you know to the roots of your being that you cannot be called less than, nor the property of, another.

To parts of American society the black Muslims are being perceived as a threat, just like the civil rights leaders. Whenever a strong faith in self is seen, society knows that you will not have willing followers blindly heeding your instructions. Their only fight is for self-recognition and peace of mind.

By being Muslim they can, in a religious sense, go home.

They have that identity, they have that home, they have cousins, they have uncles that are all part of this immense group that was at no time ever controlled by another.

Your supporters came to expect incisive social and political commentary from your pen. Your detractors said that you were too angry, too political, too sexual. Now that there is a space for balance in you, how do you see the part you played in the mid-century movement for gay rights and civil rights?

I was that klaxon that was constantly sounding off to let people know that they could not shove either me or the issues under the rug. I was that beacon that says when the light swings around, you will be identified. Whether or not when it makes its rotation the rest of the way around you can be seen, you cannot completely hide from the truth. I was consciousness and the conscience of a lot of society during my time. I was the one who said you cannot forget me. You cannot escape me. I will make you face who you are and what you believe.

Thank you, James Baldwin, for talking with us.

I hope I have been able to bring some more light to the subject.

Commentary

Toni: Wow! That was a very dynamic interview. There were times when I felt what I could only call a sense of residual outrage at some of the things James had to go through in his time on Earth. But then there was his calmness. Whatever obstacle they put in front of him, he found a way to get over it. Whatever things people wanted to hide, he found a way to bring them to light for analysis and discussion. I had a sense that his energy went across all time, not just the time that he was here; that he brought together the past, the present, and the future; that he sought to make this cohesive package that would provide people choices with which to have additional experiences. It was as if he were always on a soap box during the whole interview. His oratory wasn't tinged with bitterness or malice or anything else—it almost had a little bit of glee: "Ha, ha—you've caught me with what I was trying to do." A number of times he was openly laughing in the background.

Peter: Once again we discover that when a soul wants a human stimulus beyond the ordinary it will most likely be achieved in a childhood of challenge, abandonment, brutality, and disaster. Unlike some souls whom I have interviewed, who had powerful past lives or were more than usually able to tap into the universal knowledge database, James Baldwin had chosen the rocky road to success. He was abandoned by his biological father and brutalized by his stepfather, found scant solace in his weak mother, was small in stature, black in color, and homosexual in orientation. In one aspect (as he pointed out tellingly) he was not disadvantaged: all souls are equal. Unstated, perhaps, was that this very equality of all souls in the God-Force is the basis for all claims of human equality. And the call for equality came trippingly off his tongue in this dialogue. This, his earthly passion, seemed virtually undimmed by the fact of his transition Home.

In life, James Baldwin was openly and aggressively homosexual. No doubt the forcefulness which he put into his most sexual novels bore witness to the heavy hand of David Baldwin, whose very presence threatened physical annihilation when James was a youth. This was the side of black culture he did not want to betray when he chose white characters for his novel *Giovanni's Room*. But if African Americans contained a truth-telling mixture of normally straight, homophobic, and gay people, there is no longer for him now a direct connection between sexual orientation and race. I was a little surprised at this remark because, historically, the powerful idea of equality has brought together such causes as universal suffrage and emancipation, the right to choose and lesbian freedom, and so on. What James did not leave out was the clear reminder that sexual orientation is an issue decided upon before incarnation and is, therefore, a natural human condition, albeit a challenging one.

In one regard James Baldwin did not let us off the racism hook: White people are basically afraid of black people. We have a "white problem," not a black one. In some respects, given the rise of the number of African Americans in the middle class of America, and a small but truly influential rise in black political leadership (to say nothing of the long list of black sports multi-millionaires), his argument might be seen a little dated.

As an immigrant from Britain, where slavery on its shores is virtually forgotten, I see his "white problem" in the USA as being all too true, especially (but not solely) among fearful, older, working-class Americans. The light from Baldwin's beacon continues to rotate and illuminate our hostility and fear. Perhaps it would be all the brighter if it were seen for what it is, a beam of unconditional love.

"If you take yourself too seriously,
you're missing the experience, and that experience is
we are something more than what we appear to be."

Peter Sellers

1925-1980

[Before the session we had some good-natured banter with Peter Sellers in the style of the *Goon Show*. In the first question the word "deaded" is Goonspeak for "killed."]

Peter, when you were actually "deaded" by a heart attack in 1980 you played a posthumous joke by willing that "In the Mood," a piece of music you thoroughly disliked, would be played at your funeral. Did you attend the service or couldn't you stand the music?

[laughs] Well, there was a bit of curiosity to see who would actually show up and to learn what people really thought about me by what they would say, so of course, I was there.

You are known as a superb comic actor, but in fact you were often depressed and anxious about failure. You had poor relations with directors and fellow actors. A perfectionist, you abused your wives, and you drank heavily and took drugs in quantity. How much of this had to do with your family background?

A lot. It was what I had come down to experience. I wanted to take the immensity of what a person could put up with and yet portray or create something that was totally different as recognized by other people. I wanted to have these human experiences that would be the antithesis of what I'd projected in my professional life. Of course, I was only able to do that because of the good writers, but my timing was impeccable based upon the jokes I used to play on myself to decide whether I wished to remain in human form.

You had suicidal tendencies?

That's about the sum of it, yes.

For how long a period?

For a time the depression deepened to the degree that I did not think I would be able to climb out of the hole I was in. It was a totally self-destructive phase, and I struck out at those around me to see if I could get a reaction from them to help end where I was going.

Your mother, Peg, was very dominant, wasn't she?

As in our script [see note above], a little like Hitler, yes. She had those tendencies of being completely in control, being maniacal about little things, even where her thimble was or where the dish towel was in the cupboard. It was as if our moving anything in the house would create a firestorm.

You were not, in fact, Peter. The first, stillborn, child was Peter. You were Richard Henry, but they called you "Peter." Did that leave a mark on you?

It was very difficult to try to be something I was not. The only thing that it allowed me to do was project outward. That was what led to my acting, because my entire life was acting the part of my brother, the child who was wanted, who was anticipated. I was the one who came along and was the disappointment.

Was Peter another soul, or was no soul assigned to the body?

It was not assigned a soul. I was that Peter.

You had a number of heart attacks, one massive one shortly after you married Britt Ekland. Were they pre-planned physical lessons or did they have a spiritual cause?

The physical cause was the substances I subjected myself to. The spiritual cause was being responsible for the actions that I was creating in my world at that time. The life lesson was to know that everything we do has an impact on the way we can learn lessons, and if we go to the extreme, it can terminate that which we sought so dearly to be able to encounter, endure, and complete.

You sought help from psychic healers. Did they help?

They were of assistance when I allowed them to be. It was like so many things in my life: I tried to make somebody else responsible for what I was going through, make somebody else the fall guy if it didn't work, but I now know it was completely my own energy that directed where I went, what happened to me, and to whom I turned for assistance.

You also sought advice from Maurice Woodruff, the astrologer. In what ways did he help you? He was with you for some time, wasn't he?

Maurice was as much a friend as anything else, but he had the knack of being able to help me excuse some of my behaviors by finding planetary "transits" that would cause a disturbance in my field, which might have caused the reactions and overreactions that I had perpetrated physically.

The way you say that suggests to me that you don't now have much trust in astrology.

Astrology, as with everything else upon the planet, is about forces that have an impact or set a stage for what bombards the particular body in which a soul is incarnate. What it doesn't do is make the decisions as to what you should do once you are in that scene.

So is it an imprint made on you at birth rather than guidance for you now?

It's an imprint and it's a background. It is not a moving factor.

So horoscopes are not worth the paper they're written on?

Unless people need a motivation or something to help build up their self-esteem to know they can do something. If they think that there is an outside source that is helping them do something, or has created a scenario for them to be able to do something, then they have more confidence in the outcome and may undertake something that they wouldn't normally have undertaken. But it's all part of that wanting someone else to be responsible for your actions and for what's happening to you.

When you had that heart attack, did you have a near-death experience?

[laughs] I had a near-death experience, which I put immediately out of my mind as being too ridiculous—just something a script writer had decided would be a cute play or something that I could do as a movie, being caught in between reality in the physical and reality in the spiritual.

From your position now, how do you view what happens in a near-death experience?

It can be a very beautiful, awakening, life-changing activity for the human. It is one of the times when a soul who is unaware of its essence, its connection, its being a piece of Source, can have an experience that either allows it to know of its magnificence or opens a door through which it can explore to connect with the essence of who it is. Or the person can slam the door and ignore it as a dream, as I did.

The Masters and others I've interviewed have explained that much is pre-planned before we come down. Is a near-death experience a pre-planned event?

Not generally. You don't generally say, "At this stage in my life I'm going to have a near-death experience." It is usually the result of some over-stimulus that you have created in your life: it can be from having the accident that you had planned to change your life affect your spiritual life as well as your physical life; or it can be that in wanting to abuse your life and be addicted, you take so many chemicals that you reach the state of being able to open those doors beyond the physical. On rare occasions it is planned for as a way to trigger your further path into connecting with your spiritual aspects. It also can be a planted key to see if you take the initiative to go beyond who you are as a human, to go back to that sense of feeling within yourself. So it could be for a number of reasons, but normally it's not definitely planned. We don't generally say: "I'm going to have a near-death experience on day 4,000 of my life." No.

You grew up dancing, drumming, playing the ukulele and banjo. Had you been a performer or a clown in past lives?

Let's just say I was very adept at being able to be what I was not.

Can you illustrate that, please?

I entered many lifetimes in which, for one reason or another, I had chosen a pathway that was clouded, where a façade was built around me, to accomplish something, but yet I tried to live with the core of who I was. There were times when I was a spy. There were times when I was completely encapsulated in my body by some physical disability that prevented my being able to move and interconnect with the outside world by anything other than, say, moving my eyes or moving one digit, so that I had to find a way to get my feelings across to others without their being able to interact with me in a normal way. I also did the—I guess you would call it—Vaudeville circuit, the gypsy, the matador, the troubadour, even the village idiot who with mental deficiencies was still able to whip the village together to save it from itself.

During wartime service in the Royal Air Force, where you were an entertainer with ENSA, you met Michael Bentine, Spike Milligan, and Harry Secombe, and, later, you all created the BBC radio show known as "The Goons," which lasted from 1951 to 1960. Tell me about them.

They were dear souls who had the desire to let others open up the feelings they had inside. The best way to do that was, of course, through laughter. Each had a particular talent, and when we strung them together we created an atmosphere wherein we could reach even the most staid of individuals. Nobody was able to resist at least a smile, if not outright belly laughter, and in reaching that expression, that release, people were able to know that it was all right to laugh, that it was healing to laugh, and that it put them in a place where they could sense what other people were trying to accomplish.

Did you draw from the experience of Tommy Handley and his show during the war?

I was aware of it. I think it probably did have an unconscious influence on me. It wasn't something that I sought to ape.

Then came your films. Early successes were The Ladykillers *in 1955, and* The Mouse that Roared *and* I'm all Right, Jack *in 1959. Did making films suit your talents better than radio or the stage?*

The one thing that films allowed me to do that the others didn't was have re-takes. I was able to put myself in the "mood" that I thought I needed to be in, and then if I overstepped it (like one too many pills or something), it was really easy to do a re-take. I had to watch what I did when I was doing it live because there were no re-takes, no way that I could say, "Oops, excuse me, I'm not ready for this," and I could do that with films. So if anything, the films allowed me a broader expression of who I was because I could dull down all of the physical things that were tormenting me to allow my inner essence to come out, and if I had dulled down the turmoil too much, I just did a re-take.

In 1960 you scored a hit in The Millionairess *with Sophia Loren. Did fascination for Sophia lead to the breakdown of your first marriage with Anne Howe?*

Let's just say it was a contributing factor. Up until that point I hadn't considered myself extremely glamorous. I was just this kid of a thousand faces. I didn't have the confidence in myself as desirable to beautiful women, and when Sophia expressed an interest in me as a person, my head began to swell to the extent that I thought I could do anything and fly above propriety.

Your next big movie was The Pink Panther *in 1963. How did you develop the character of Inspector Clouseau, which made the series of films so popular?*

It occurred to me, as I was struggling with my lack of self-worth and self-confidence, there must be people out there who tried so hard to do things but were totally incompetent at what they did, but they didn't know it because they had confidence in themselves. So I thought if we have a person who is so totally incompetent that he can't get anything right, but because of his faith in himself he wins the day, that would be a boost to so many people who needed to think that even though they didn't have that university degree they could be as important as everyone else.

I think you once said, "It won't be easy; that is why I have always failed where others have succeeded."

My point is made.

Less well known was your movie Heavens Above! *made the same year. You had a mixed religious background; were you religious?*

No, I wouldn't call myself religious. I will just say again: I played whatever part was needed to be played in order to be accepted by those around me and to keep from having the wrath of Mum come upon me.

She was Jewish, wasn't she?

She was Jewish by heritage and background, but she was whatever was convenient at the moment.

In 1964 came Dr. Strangelove. *You had three characters in the movie and broke your leg in one of the scenes. Tell me about it.*

It was probably, for me, the most madcap of the movies that I made because it was something in which I could be totally schizophrenic. I could take each part of me that was vested in strong emotions about things, even if it was diametrically opposed to another person I was playing in the movie, and be able to go full out in each one of the parts. It was fantastic for me.

Were you strongly opposed to nuclear weapons?

My feeling was that, knowing how destructive a single individual can be to self and community without having a finger on a weapon, we were all entirely barmy (stupid) to allow anybody to have a finger poised over a nuclear weapon.

How much do you now believe movies like Dr. Strangelove *affect social consciousness?*

Carried upon the back of comedy, more people get the message that we are putting forth concerning social consciousness than get it from an orator on his soapbox with his impassioned speech, because they are getting it from the common man. They are not getting it from somebody whom they potentially see as a demagogue.

You were good friends with Princess Margaret, and Prince Charles is said to have been a fan of the Goons. Tell me about your relationship with the royal family.

It was one of those times in my life when I kept pinching myself to ask, "Is this real?" Here was this kid—by their standards from the wrong side of the tracks—who was actually looked up to by them in some regards. I sensed from their reaction that we all really are the same, and someone of their greatness didn't have the pretensions that they could interact only with greatness. As my mother would say, they were true mensches.

You were quite versatile as an actor. Your part as Clare Quilty in Stanley Kubrick's Lolita *was acclaimed for its intensity, but did you have any qualms about subject matter of the movie itself?*

I really didn't care too much for the subject matter, but at that time I was trying to stretch myself to see how many different types of performances I could present as being totally believable. I judged that a success.

In 1979 you played the gardener, Chance, in Being There. *It brought your second Oscar nomination. Tell me about that.*

That was probably one of my most endearing and favorite performances, because it spoke to the very core of me, that you didn't need pretensions. Simplicity was the thing that was important. Being true to yourself, accepting yourself exactly as you are is very important. Not complicating your life was important. But at the same time, you had to know who you were. At the beginning of the movie, Chance didn't know who he was. He knew that he was a gardener, but he didn't know how to take care of himself. He knew that his meals would be provided, that his clothes would be taken care of. He just figured he had this connection with the Earth, and that was the important thing. But that education he had of the interconnection of himself with Earth, when told to another person, applied to every facet on the planet. I found it to be a magnificent example of the soul's interaction with the Universe.

Peter, your acting contained some stunning work. We are glad you make us laugh so heartily. What lessons did you learn during your life here?

If you take yourself too seriously, you're missing the experience, and that experience is we are something more than what we appear to be. We need to go into ourselves and explore how things impact us and how we in turn affect them. We can learn all kinds of lessons, and we can marry them with what we present to other people. My lessons of getting to understand myself, building up my self-worth and self-confidence, overcoming being controlled, experiencing what it is to be addicted to something (and not being able to get away from it), can all be played out and explained to others through the work we do, even if we ourselves don't get the point at that moment.

Are you planning to come down anytime soon?

As a matter of fact, I'm discussing a renewal at the present time.

That's the first time someone has used the word "renewal" as if it were a technical term.

[laughs] "Renewal" in that sense means reinventing what a human can do, and that's the trailer for the movie.

You're a man of many voices. Which voice are you going to be using this time, an Indian one?

Well, I can give you a tip: I think it's going to be female.

Thank you, Peter Sellers, for talking with us.

Commentary

Toni: That dialogue felt like being on a merry-go-round, a carousel. I was at an amusement park being bounced from one type of entertainment to another—getting the experience of the joke house, going through the tunnel of love where you didn't know what was around the next corner, whether it was going to be scary or loving, warmth or a blast of ice cold. He gave me a sense of the extremes of emotions that he went through during his lifetime, and underneath a lot of it was a sense of the lost little boy searching for security, searching for an understanding of who he was. I have the feeling that now he's well aware of who he was. He can look back at all the experiences he had as Peter Sellers, see all the roles he played, roles within which he gleaned a knowledge of his soul's essence—his off-stage life, so to speak. This was a very deep, moving, dynamic interchange, and there were a lot of times when he was laughing—at himself, the questions we were asking, and just the whole human experience in general.

Peter: His mother must have been a horror to live with, and he appears to have spent the rest of his life reacting to his childhood experience of her insane foibles. His colleagues in the acting profession were, doubtless, well aware of his continuing emotional struggles. His fans only saw his superb command of comic roles and read of his falling in love with Sophia Loren and mixing with British royalty. But the soul took us behind the scenes to the actor's inner doubts, depression, and despair. It is remarkable that, like his fellow Goon the bi-polar Spike Milligan, Peter was so able to turn inner pain into glorious and infinitely silly humor. He could be mildly funny as in his favorite character Chance; dotty as the bumbling Inspector Clouseau in *The Pink Panther*; or "totally schizophrenic" as in his multiple roles in Dr. Strangelove. Whatever role it was, there was an amazingly pointed excess, which was, perhaps, the main way he imitated his mother.

For me the whimsically earnest soul of Peter Sellers whom we encountered in our dialogue was best expressed in *Heavens Above!* as the Reverend John Smallwood. The priest having confounded the Church of England by actually taking the commandments of Jesus seriously, ends up at the Bishop of Outer Space, singing hymns lustily in a rocket going into the heavens. Now at last we know that Peter actually got there safely and is enjoying the view.

"If all of our efforts can be circumvented by importing people from other countries more cheaply, that is going to be done for purposes of profit by the farmers."

Cesar E. Chavez

1927-1993

Cesar Estrada Chavez, you were born in Yuma, Arizona, one of seven children of Librado and Juana Chavez who were Mexican-American farm workers. When you were young, your hard-working father agreed to clear a man's land so he might purchase the little farm you lived on. The deal fell through disastrously. Tell me what happened.

What happened was my father was taken advantage of. He worked so hard. He spent months and months clearing and moving stones. The biggest thing was tree roots—on some of the trees he had to dig down to get at the roots; he would chop out what he could, he would burn parts, he borrowed a team of horses from a neighbor to pull on some of them, but mostly it was brute force. With the boulders he removed he built a barrier between the different lands so that there would be a clear demarcation of our land from the majority of the rest of the land.

How big was the area he cleared?

The area was not only the small part that we were going to have, but also part of the adjoining land for the owner, which was the agreement—he would do that in exchange for being able to purchase the land.

That must have given you and your father a great sense of injustice.

It let me to see for the first time that there was such hatred—I would have preferred to say discrimination, and I started to say discrimination, but no, at that time it was a hatred—for people who were perceived not to be the same as oneself. The landowner, who was white, thought that my Latino father was uneducated—which, essentially, he was—and that he didn't understand about contracts, and the owner could therefore take advantage of him. My father, on the other hand, being a very upstanding person, thought that if he had the word of an individual and had shaken hands on the deal, that was all that was needed. The whole incident absolutely crushed my father. He had such high hopes for the work. He had at one point injured his back with some of the work that he did, and then he was told, "Show me where I made the agreement with you," which, of course, he couldn't.

Was this incident the starting point of your desire to seek justice for migrant farm workers, or were other experiences more motivating?

At the time, this was what started the fire burning, seeing how we were treated. When my father went to others to seek their advice and support in putting through this agreement he had made, he was laughed at as being a stupid Latino. That we could be treated as such insignificant beings simply because of our ancestry felt just like branding me with an iron—it did not allow me ever to forget.

Although you were all American citizens, weren't you?

We were born in the States, we were all citizens, but we were still second-class citizens to these people. I had seen the discrimination in some stores, and our education was not as good as that provided to a lot of the whites, and I had sort of just fluffed that off as being something that I was dreaming up, but this allowed me to see that, no, there was a double standard.

Because your father worked in many places, you attended more than 30 schools, and you had to leave school when you were 14 to go into the fields and help support the family. But you passionately believed in educating yourself, didn't you?

After the incident with my father and several other incidents, I knew that education was the first step to making a difference, to being able to come to the table with some degree of equality. I did everything I could to increase my education when I couldn't go formally to school. When children of the workers who lived in the same hovels that we did would come home from school at night, I would quiz them about what they had learned and would get them to help me with reading and mathematics so that I could continue to improve on the very basics that I had learned before leaving school.

What was life working in the fields and vineyards like in those days?

Very hot, very hard, very tedious.

The pay?

The pay was ridiculous. We had a quota set by the employer, and if you didn't fill your quota for whatever reason, you weren't paid.

Day labor, I suppose.

It was day labor, although it was termed day labor so they didn't feel they had to provide any commitment to us. We would work for a season or a period with the same farmers, so every day for weeks during the season we would go back to the same farm, and then we'd be shifted over to the next farm to do the same things, and then the next farm, and then come back to the first farm for the next phase.

Pesticides?

Pesticides were something that we just saw as a part of the job. There were no precautions whatsoever given us about the pesticides. We weren't told about any potential harm. We weren't provided with masks for our faces as we were spraying the pesticides or as we were working in the areas right after they were sprayed. If we were mixing them we weren't given gloves to prevent the chemicals from being absorbed through our skin. There were those for whom mixing became their regular job—they called them "buggers"—and I did notice that over the years the "buggers" seemed to be the ones who were ill the most and had all kinds of weird things happen to them, like problems with their teeth, their gums bleeding, and sores, but nobody ever told us that pesticides were harmful for anything other than the insects for which we were using them.

In the five years between losing your farm and 1942, when you were drafted into the Navy, were you involved in labor organizing, or were you too busy courting Helen Fabela?

I was too busy living. There was the compulsion to get the quota done every day. There was the need to get that money so that I could court Helen. I had to continue with my education, which I was doing on my own, and I just got into a routine and the years passed.

You served in the navy for two years. Did you enjoy Navy life?

There were some aspects of it that were nice, but there were other situations that reminded me of the way we were treated as second-class citizens. Now, the Latinos were not discriminated against as severely as the Blacks were, but we were still considered not to be as educated, not to be as technically capable of doing things, so we were limited in the positions we could have and in the things we could do. There were some good parts in that I had a place to sleep and I was always fed—there wasn't a worry about that—and we got our pay regardless of what we did, so it differed from the fields in that regard, but not in the energy of the way we were treated.

There was also the famous Navy discipline.

Yes, I didn't always do too well with the discipline. It was a little like having an overseer with free rein over every moment of your life.

Did you see any military action?

No.

Returning home, you married Helen, moved to California, and settled in a Latino ghetto, the East San Jose barrio of Sal Si Puedes ("get out if you can"). Tell me about your marriage.

My marriage was very delightful for me; it was very fulfilling. It also put stressors on me of always having to produce, of being able to come up with the money, of being able to find ways to go around the barriers that were put up for me. In the area there was a depression, always this oppressive energy coming from others of hopelessness and helplessness.

But I imagine there was a hopefulness in having a family—you had eight children, didn't you?

Yes, I did, and that provided for me not only a hopefulness but a pressure to see that they had what they needed, to see that they could go and get an education and not have to leave school and work to provide for their family—that they could to do whatever they wanted to do.

While you were in the Navy, CORE, the Congress of Racial Equality, was founded. CORE organized, with the Fellowship of Reconciliation, the first freedom ride on buses in the South. But then Congress passed the Taft-Hartley Act to limit labor organizing. You met with Fr. Donald McDonnell and talked about civil rights. Tell me about him.

Father McDonnell opened a door for me that I hadn't seen before, and that was that minorities could be heard, that they could get changes brought about by a massive concerted effort to let people know about what was happening within our communities. It gave me the hope that I would be able to somehow get the plight of the Latinos known to make a better world for my family.

Eventually in 1952 you were recruited by Fred Ross to be an organizer in the Community Services Organization, which was a civil rights, get-out-the-Latino-vote group. Tell me about Fred and the CSO.

Fred was a visionary, an organizer, the type of person who drew to him people like myself in whom he saw a burning ember for change. He knew how to fan that flame and get it into a blazing fire so that we could use it to get the word out. The whole organization knew that the way to start in the United States was through the democratic process, through voting, and since the majority of the Latinos were citizens who had never voted, we were a powerful wedge that could be used for change.

You became national director of the CSO in 1958. What made you decide four years later to leave and co-found the National Farm Workers Association (NFWA) with Dolores Huerta, who was also from the CSO?

I saw what was being done by the CSO nationwide, and it wasn't addressing the problems that I knew the most about. Those problems were what I had grown up with—the way that my family, my relatives, and my friends were being treated by the employers, by the farm owners. I wanted to take the power that I saw work on a national level and bring it down to the local stage and have an impact on something I knew needed to change.

Dolores, with her seven children, joined your family living in Delano, California. Tell me about those days. Was she a soul mate of yours?

Dolores was a soul mate of mine, and in prior lifetimes we had gone into battle together, so our energy was very compatible. When she moved in with the children and we formed this big, happy family, there was just such an energy and such a hopefulness that it inspired everyone.

Was Helen happy with that?

Helen was also a soul mate of mine, but we had never done battle together, and she embraced what was going on, what work we wanted to do. She was the one who kept the home fires burning.

She had to deal with fifteen kids—that must have been quite a battle.

She loved it. She was great. She was a fantastic cook, and we didn't have to worry about clean clothes or food.

These were the days of the March on Washington, which was memorably addressed by Dr. Martin Luther King, Jr. Did your speechmaking skills come from that experience?

I don't know if I could say they came from that experience. What I did realize at that time was the importance of the way words were put together, and not only the way they were put together, but the way they were delivered, with the energy that arose from inside of you, and not just from reading them off a piece of paper.

In fact, Mahatma Gandhi was a great inspiration, wasn't he?

From Gandhi I drew the knowledge, the acceptance, and the energy that the peaceful person with quiet determination and just a little bit of rebelliousness (all right—a lot of rebelliousness!) can move nations.

Two years later the Delano grape strike of Filipino American farm workers who were seeking better wages took place. Then your union, the NFWA, led a strike of California grape pickers. You marched 300 miles from Delano to the state capitol in Sacramento and started a nationwide boycott of table grapes. Tell me about that time.

That was the beginning of definition for Latinos—that in order to change things we had to be heard. We couldn't just sit in the fields, talk amongst ourselves, and have anything change. We needed to go to the government that had a voice on regulations. We needed to be recognized in the media so that the word disseminated about what was really happening in the fields. We needed to impact the common person, the one who was on the receiving end of the labor-intensive growing in which we were involved.

So you boycotted table grapes.

We boycotted table grapes, and made it very hard to get them out of the fields.

Did you have any support in Washington?

We had some support in Washington from some of the politicians who had fought injustice, particularly Bobby Kennedy. He and his family had always been involved in causes to balance the playing field, whether in economic circles or between the races, and he became a big supporter of getting our story out to the general public to put pressure upon the farmers and the government.

It took five years from the time of the grape strike to the time when new contracts were signed, and before that time was over you staged a hunger strike. Was it effective?

The hunger strike let people see and put a face to the workers (the idea, of course, arose from Gandhi's life). They saw that this was not something that could be taken lightly. This was a life-and-death issue for the Latino farm workers, and I let myself be center stage as the symbol of what needed to be done.

In fact, you led two more hunger strikes, one of 36 days. Did they take a toll on your health?

They took a toll on my physical health, but they strengthened my soul's energy.

One of your campaigns involving your "Fast for Life" was against pesticides used by farm workers. Now, from your position at Home, what do you think of the use of pesticides and herbicides on American farms in the current years?

This is an issue that still needs to be addressed. It is an uphill battle because the money is in the manufacturing of the insecticides and herbicides and in the additional profits that can be made by the growers who use them. The studies that show the effects of these chemicals are well hidden if they are done at all. But from a spiritual standpoint, it is still various lessons that are being played out on both sides of the coin by the souls directly involved in the situation.

Is organic farming an answer to this problem?

Organic farming, which is to say, going back to the way it had been for decades and centuries upon your planet, before money became involved in the mix, is the thing that is best for the human body. Is it the thing that is needed for the lessons that people have to learn? That's a case-by-case determination.

Your efforts resulted in the 1975 California Agricultural Labor Relations Act. This is still the only law permitting farm workers to unionize. Are you disappointed that other states have not followed suit?

I don't have disappointment up here for anything. I can evaluate that it is a real shame that our efforts were not mirrored in other locales, but there aren't as many locales that have the same situation with the migrant workers as in California. While there are not large laws, within some areas there are local laws that take care of how the migrant worker has to be treated. Some of those are prevalent in the Midwest.

In your day, the United Farm Workers wanted immigration restricted, concerned that illegal immigrants would undermine the hard-won gains in pay and conditions. What do you think about illegal immigration in America today?

Again, you would be asking the body of Cesar Chavez for an opinion. The soul has no opinion. The soul can only see that that is the next step in the issues that I dealt with when I was in body form.

And does the body of Cesar Chavez have anything to say?

The energy that was in the body still says that there must be protection for those who do the work. If all of our efforts can be circumvented by importing people from other countries more cheaply, that is going to be done for purposes of profit by the farmers. Why do you think it took five years for my efforts to come to fruition? Those grapes were still picked and still packaged, but not by us.

Your motto was "si se puede" *(yes, it can be done). If you were here on Earth today, what would you tackle that still needs to be done for Latinos and other farm workers in America?*

The thing that I would tackle first is a type of amnesty program for those illegals who have been in the country for so many, many years providing vital services that nobody else wants to do, and give them an option to become citizens if they choose instead of always having the sledgehammer over their head that they can be sent back at a moment's notice at the whim of the INS.

Thank you, Cesar Chavez, for talking with us.

Commentary

Toni: Cesar had such a calm and calming energy. In talking about something you would think would make his blood boil, his attitude was a very matter-of-fact "yes, that's the way the human body reacts, but the core, the soul, just has the purpose of carrying through with the lesson that is provided by this." It put a lot of things into perspective.

At the end, when Peter was pushing him about the way that he would react now to what's going on, I felt a sense of his unease—that's kind of strange to say because I usually don't feel unease from a spirit. It was almost a feeling of "Why do I have to go back and repeat what I've done? That's somebody else's turf, somebody else's lesson to learn. I want to move on to something else." But he was very aware of everything that's going on right now, almost as if he has monitored to see the drift of what he started: Has the course of the river changed, or is it edging back toward where it was when he was here?

Peter: This seemingly simple story was stamped with the hallmark of a deep spiritual humility: a great and lasting human achievement which was quite understated by an immensely successful leader. Cesar's life is a classic in its field. The open discrimination against poor Latinos, even those with rights of American citizenship, was brutal. His father, who cleared a huge acreage of land only to have his promised reward denied him by the white racist con man, suffered greatly. One felt the young Cesar, a tightly coiled spring, ready to express his outrage. Or was he more in control than that? In our discussion, direct action, not anger, was the order of his day, together with a deep empathy for the millions of hard-pressed and suffering fellow farm workers.

That Cesar took a fledgling migrant movement and crafted it from weakness into a force to be reckoned with in the California corridors of power reveals his dedication. As his lengthy fasts testify, he had a very rare kind of personal courage. With little formal education he developed his understanding and speaking skills by reading widely; he learned leadership by leading. Above all he learned the lessons his soul had assigned itself with modesty and gentleness of spirit.

The big disappointment for me was when his soul side-stepped the thorny immigration issue, though he did eventually advocate an amnesty program. But workers' rights remain a huge issue in a greedy society that continues to take the labor of the poor for granted. Perhaps it is just as well that most of our lives as incarnated souls are spent among the poor of the Earth. Otherwise some of us might learn nothing.

An interesting footnote: The day I made my final revision of this chapter, an unsolicited appeal from the United Farm Workers (the first ever sent me) arrived on my desk! It felt as if Cesar Chavez were still actively involved in his great campaign.

"I found something that the general public loved.
It was easy to produce, it was easy to market, it was easy to rake in the cash."

Andy Warhol

1928 - 1987

Andrew Warhola, you were known to the world by the name Andy Warhol for a lot longer than "just 15 minutes." You and your two older brothers grew up in a tiny Pittsburgh apartment, and your family had a tough time in the Great Depression. A sickly child, at the age of six you were confined to bed with St. Vitus' Dance, and you had a lonely time at school when you finally returned. Tell me about those days.

It's a period that I don't really like to spend too long thinking about, but I'll spend a little time on it now. At first, I thought that life was difficult but manageable. Then when I became ill, it was like any contact I had outside of that tiny abode was ripped away from me, and I was put into a very dull, drab place. The good part about it was that it caused me to go inward, where I saw my garden. I saw what could be painted there, what could be manufactured there, and I could make within my garden a world that would take me away from everything that seemed so heavy and ponderous around me. The sickness, I now know, occurred so that I could be in a position to go inward, to get out of the affection I had for things outside of me and to be able to start drawing, developing, painting, manufacturing inside of me. When I went back to the real world outside of my bed, I was in a totally different group of people from those I had started out with, and I was the outsider. I was the outsider who saw things and talked about things that they couldn't imagine, so I became known as the weird one.

What kind of things did you talk about?

I talked about the colors I saw, the magnificence of what could be had inside of yourself. The other kids, who were only concerned about trying to pitch pennies or snatch an apple from the corner stand or things like that, couldn't see any significance or any importance in my world.

Your family helped you to become an artist, didn't they?

As I talked about what I saw and began describing it for them, it seemed to enlarge their world as well as enlarging mine. So they said, "Do you think you can show us what it is you see?" and that was how it all began.

Another thing which began at the same time was a lifelong fear of doctors and hospitals, wasn't it?

Well, the hospitals were cages and the doctors were the zookeepers. They were also the ones who told me that what I saw inside of my head was brought on by the fever, the tremors, the itches, the situation that I was put into, and that it wasn't real. Not only did I rebel against their way of "helping" me, but I also rebelled against their "closed-ness."

When you were only 13, your father, a construction worker, died in an accident. What was your relationship with him?

During the time I was ill, my father and I became quite close. My older brothers were off trying to help the family out in any way they could find—shining shoes, delivering things—and I was always there at home. When my dad came home, he would spend a short period of time each day with me, and he allowed me to see the outside world through him, what he was doing, how he was changing the landscape with what he did.

His death must have been a big blow.

It was like ripping out my heart.

Did you then, at that point, make a decision to try to escape from poverty?

I don't know if it was an instant realization that poverty was making everybody work so hard and so relentlessly that they became tired and didn't watch as carefully as they should have, as happened with my father. Or perhaps the misery that I felt around me propelled me toward the desire to be out of that. Or maybe it was just having visions of those around me who didn't worry where the next loaf of bread was coming from. But yes—I decided, however I had to do it, that I was not going to spend my entire life in the gutter.

You bonded closely with your mother, Julia, who later shared your New York home for nearly two decades. She was quite a good artist, wasn't she?

Mom in a lot of ways was better than I, but she wasn't as daring as I. She was more conservative in her approach to art.

In fact, she described herself as your mother, didn't she, in some of her work?

Yes, she did. She was an inspiration for me, again showing that you could take yourself out of drudgery, out of the darkness, and go into a light, bright, beautiful, happy world.

Was she accepting of your homosexuality?

My mother accepted me exactly as I was. She did not make any distinctions one way or the other between my lifestyle and the lifestyle of my siblings.

Did you choose to be homosexual before coming to planet Earth?

I chose to experience ambivalence, which was the period of time before I accepted and told others that I was in fact homosexual. It was a constant battle of: Am I doing this to be different? Am I doing this because I'm actually being accepted by a male partner rather than a female partner? Or am I doing it because that is what my body and my mind need at this time? I did put all of those patterns together for something I wished to experience in this lifetime.

Did you ever have any past lives as an artist?

Not as entire lifetimes. There were lifetimes in which I was a hobbyist or I was on the fringes of art, such as being a decorator or things of that nature, but I was never a fine artist.

And were you in manufacturing?

Yes, that I was.

So did that past experience of being a manufacturer speak to you in terms of your art?

Well, it gave me the approach of having a pattern for getting from point A to point B. If you wanted your end product to have one type of an appearance, there were certain steps that you had to go through. There were also certain things that you aspired to do, such as reproduce things that were the same but different, and I played with all of these concepts from my past in my art.

At the School of Fine Arts at Pittsburgh's Carnegie Institute of Technology, you studied pictorial design. Then in 1949 you went to New York and quickly created a fine reputation as an artist working on magazine illustrations and advertisements. What did you enjoy most about New York, the work or the social scene?

I enjoyed the whole experience. I don't think one thing shone above the other. I was out of the dreary, drudging things that held me down from my youth, into a very vibrant, alive, fascinating area that not only allowed me to grow as a person but allowed me to socialize on a par with people, not being the odd little boy but being the accepted, proven artist and individual.

Then, as the orders multiplied, you took on the design of record labels for RCA, and exhibited your work at the Bodley Gallery. To increase your output, you began to manage a team of collaborators. One of these was Gerard Malanga. Tell me about him and how you now view the controversy about your team approach to art production.

[laughs] I don't really care, as I didn't then, what people think. What was important to me was taking the raw material that was available and accomplishing what I sought to accomplish. That raw material could be the paints and the canvas, or it could be the additional hands and minds of those with whom I collaborated. It was not unusual in many professions, such as songwriting and doing plays and movies, for there to be a collaboration. All of the energy that was spent criticizing and critiquing what I pioneered as an approach, I felt was very enjoyable. I now

see it as just another step of integration that I was going through in this lifetime.

Were you helped by Gerard?

I was very definitely helped by him because he had a broader base of where he came from and experiences he had had that helped contribute to the depth of what we could produce.

The crowd at "The Factory," your studio on 47th Street, Manhattan, was truly Bohemian. But you said, "I'm the type who'd like to sit home and watch every party that I'm invited to on a monitor in my bedroom." Were you truly an active participant in the sex-and-drugs scene you helped to create, or were you more often, as some have suggested, mostly a voyeur?

Truth be told, I was mostly a voyeur. That was precipitated by my early life, when I was a voyeur of the world—when I was taken out of it and put on the sidelines, and had to live it through the retelling of my brothers and the conversations with my parents. There was a certain degree of discomfort I felt when put into a social situation, that I was having to write the script as I went along. I was much happier when I could observe from a distance, see how it was done, and then maybe replicate it if it felt good to me.

Then came silk screens and a steady stream of mass-produced pictures including the famous cans of Campbell Soup, displayed at the Ferus Gallery in Los Angeles. You had bottles of Coca-Cola, portraits of Liz Taylor, Marilyn Monroe, and others, taken from photographs. Your American Supermarket had sculpted, oversized boxes of Brillo, pictures of mushroom clouds, and much more. It was termed "Pop Art." They were widely popular but was it really art, as you claimed, or just an easy way of minting money?

I guess you caught me. I decided I was going to have everything that money could buy, and the more money I had, the more things I could buy. I found something that the general public loved. It was easy to produce, easy to market, easy to rake in the cash.

You also called yourself "Andy Warhol, the underground filmmaker." Your numerous films stimulated and titillated the avant-garde, *and caused people to be shocked and bored in equal measure. You even opened porn cinemas. What were you trying to achieve?*

The majority of my life at that time was based upon stimulation—stimulation first of myself, doing what I wanted to do, experimenting with things, indulging myself, and then stimulation of those who utilized what I produced. I wasn't too choosy as to what I used to stimulate, whether it be the media or the subject matter. But nobody, once having seen something I produced, didn't have a definite opinion of it.

On a June day in 1968, Valerie Solanas came into your studio and shot you and the art critic Mario Amaya. He recovered quickly. You very nearly died. What was that experience like?

For me it was having reality catch up to me. My entire life was played out on flat surfaces—my pictures, my prints, my movies—anything that I produced. There was a sense of non-reality to the life I was leading until that day when a small inanimate object made out of metal put me in a situation where I could not deny that I was flesh and blood, that I wasn't just these reproductions that I put out as being who Andy Warhol was. It of course put me right back into all of those fears I had of doctors and hospitals, confronting the fact that others would have total control over me and could be critical of how I was doing and in their very action dictate whether I recovered or not.

It was being in the hands of others and being totally dependent upon them, something I had not done for a very long time. I had been in the driver's seat for many years at that point in deciding where I was going to go and what I was going to do, and now it was like a hand coming down from on top, putting a finger on my head, preventing me from moving, and saying, "Let's take an evaluation of where we're at, Boyo."

Did forgiveness come to you at that time, and how do feel about Valerie Solanas now?

I don't think I ever had a true hatred for her. I had a sense of outrage for having put myself in a situation where somebody was that incensed with what I did and how I was condemned or acclaimed, but to carry a grudge—no, I didn't, because it put me into a place where I really needed to be at that time.

Do you see this now as a contract?

No doubt about it—perfect example of how we make contracts so that when the time is right for us to be able to take an inventory, we're put into a situation where we face the stock.

Does that contract involve Valerie's soul?

Oh, absolutely.

Did it have to be that form of action? Did it have to be a shooting?

In my case it had to be a situation that would put me into some form of medical condition in which I needed to face my greatest fears, so whether it was a shooting, or pushing me in front of a streetcar or out of a window, or poisoning me—whatever it was, it had to be something that threatened the existence of my physical body.

You were very committed as a Byzantine Catholic all your life, but you appear to have been very frightened of death. After you were shot you said, "I always wished I had died, and I still wish that, because I could have gotten the whole thing over with." Was your faith no help to you?

Faith is a nebulous thing. Faith is what you make of it from time to time based on what you want to get out of it and what you want to give to it. My religion meant my family to me because it came through my family. It was a connection I had to a feeling of safety. But it was always a love-hate relationship. It was not something to which I could give myself completely, nor was it something that completely answered the questions I had. I did have a sense that there was something beyond life, and at that point in time, with my walls crumbling in around me, my perception was that I would be better off back in soul form.

What should religion say about physical death?

I don't think that any of us can stand up on our soapbox and declare what is best for everyone. Religion has to fill the need that each person has for it. It can't be one size fits all, so it would be very presumptuous of me to say that religion must provide us with this or that or must be our savior, must be our womb, must be our taskmaster. It is just to be used as part of the outer garment of each individual.

After being shot you were just as keenly involved in making money, but spent more time on portraits of rich people who were "somebody," from John Lennon to Mao Zedong. You and Gerard Malanga started Interview *magazine. You were criticized for being merely commercial and superficial. Or were you, as was said, "the most brilliant mirror of our times"?*

[smiling broadly] I think only my critics can answer that question. I was doing what I needed to do to make money. I was providing for people what they needed, and for some it was to be able to look at the perception that those outside of them had of them. I did not provide pictures that brought out the energy of the subjects. I provided pictures that were snapshots of the façades presented, and it was then for the subjects to decide if the portraits made them comfortable or uncomfortable.

You had two distinct sides to your persona: the very swish, camp, erotic artist, a Hollywood-tinsel-and-trashy-plastic-loving personality, who delighted in being "a deeply superficial person;" and the shy, meticulous, detached, religious man who went to church frequently, quietly helped out in homeless shelters, and lived with his mother. Who was the real you?

In body form I was both—I was schizophrenic, so to speak. I maintained within me the sensitive person who could feel and evaluate everything that the plastic person experienced. The plastic person could go out without fear, without worrying about repercussions, and sample of everything that was available, then bring it back to the sensitive person, who would decide what there was to learn from it.

What do you now think of the current avant-garde *art scene in Manhattan?*

I think they're having as much fun as I had.

Did you learn the lessons you came down to experience as Andy?

I fulfilled the majority of the commitments that I had made. I experienced and understood the majority of the lessons I set up.

Will you be returning soon?

Possibly sooner than most people think.

Thank you, Andy Warhol, for talking with us.

It has been my pleasure.

Commentary

Toni: Whoa!—that was really a kind of circus. I was seeing flashes of his life as it went along, from a very dreary apartment—very cramped and uncomfortable feeling—to flashes of the various paintings that he had done during the different phases of his life. I also felt a shifting of the energy from the two personas that he very definitely had: the private one that nobody ever saw and the professional one that was garish. Even at the height of the garishness, though, the parties and everything else, it was as if that were playing out on stage with him sitting in the audience in a little cocoon, eating popcorn, taking it all in. It was a sense that he was participating in both but never joined the two.

Peter: Untangling the complexities of Andy's personality does feel a bit like diagnosing schizophrenia, as he lightly suggested. But his soul was sane enough even if his human life seems quite crazy at times. Here was a soul who, beforehand, had loaded itself up with severe childhood illness that was bound to leave awful psychological scars, plus a loving father whose untimely death caused untold grief to the lonely teenager. Then as soon as he was moving out of chronic sickness, he became involved in the pain of the sexual ambivalence that his soul had chosen in advance of incarnating. That the sensitive Andy survived to maturity at all is something of a miracle.

How this famous artist learned to flourish socially and professionally brings more complexity. Admittedly he was a genuinely talented artist, but it was his drawing energy from an occult skill as a manufacturer in a past life that brought about his mass-produced, multi-million-dollar success as the icon of pop culture.

The little boy had learned to observe the world, its glitter and its façades. As an adult, it was as a skilled voyeur of the art and entertainment scene that Andy was able to patent his reputation. And he did not please everyone. "The Factory," his foil-lined bohemian art studio, was not only a notorious den of eroticism, but it had its fair share of drunks and nut cases. One of them, Valerie Solanas, founder of the "Society for Cutting Up Men" (SCUM), shot and nearly killed him. The complexity in that event was, I confirmed, that it had all been planned in a contract their two souls made before incarnating. Finally, Andy's lifelong fear of hospitals and doctors appeared to have been predictive, as he died in a hospital at age 58, apparently through post-operative negligence.

Ultimately, Andy's soul seems satisfied with the number of lessons learned during this incarnation. But, having been content for a while just to be a celestial voyeur of the Earth-scene, he now hints at gearing up for another course in our planetary school. It makes me wonder what kind of picture he'll paint this time around.

"I just hope that my message will continue to play in a loop, impacting each new generation, letting them see and feel that the struggles can be won."

Martin Luther King, Jr.

1929-1968

Martin Luther King, Jr., you were born into a leading ministerial family in Atlanta, Georgia. Your grandfather became the Ebenezer Baptist Church pastor in 1914. Your father succeeded him in 1931. At the age of 19, you were ordained there in 1948, and after serving the Dexter Church in Montgomery, Alabama, you returned there as co-pastor with your father for eight years until your death in 1968. It all sounds like a family business—was it?

It's hard to call it a business because that implies work for profit—for monetary gain—and our work, our business, was in enlightenment, encouragement, and bringing souls, while in physical form, into an awareness, into an enrichment of who they were. I chose to come into a family that had a history of service and preaching so that it was easier for me to slip into that mold, to get from an early age a sense of what it was like to be able to have my words express what I was feeling inside, what I wanted the energy around myself and others to be, and how with my words I could help to change the flow of rivers.

You didn't quite share the biblical literalism and religious emotion of your heritage. Did Benjamin Mays, the Morehouse College president, persuade you that the African-American churches' social outreach was an instrument for change, and it needed your service more than your scruples?

Well, I'm not sure exactly where "scruples" come in, but what I did get from my college experience was that I had two choices. I could stay within the pattern and only contribute to the lives of the black people. I could help them know and accept who they were and be happy within that frame. But that didn't do anything for how they were being treated outside of their own little communities. I saw as my goal, my passion, my pathway, to be able to pave a strip that would take them out of the bondage of their ancestry and their close-knit little community and give them the opportunity to go into the world, to be accepted in the world, and eventually to become no different from anyone else. Their heritage, their history, would be no more binding than that of an Irishman, an Italian, or a Pole.

The preaching style of black ministers and traditional spirituals appealed to you, but you were intellectually skeptical. At Boston University you studied the liberal theologians Tillich and Wieman, and seriously considered becoming an academic, didn't you?

At that point in my life I was searching for something that would have an impact, through religion, across racial lines. At first I believed the way to do that was to put the words on paper in a very rational, intelligent way, and to start with the academicians and have them disseminate the word to those who were broad-minded and educated.

Shaking the foundations?

Shaking the foundations—but my impression of what the foundations were, changed. There are the foundations of academia, which will always be there, can always be referred to, but impact a very small portion of the overall populace. It became very apparent to me that in order to bring about the change needed, it had to be in the "every-person"—the person out there on the street who didn't have the time nor the background to read the academic papers that I had thought would be my direction.

It was a little bit more than academic, though—you were more liberal than your colleagues in the black churches. How did this liberalism affect the style and content of your subsequent writing and sermons?

The liberalism you speak of that separated me was more a sense that blacks could be integrated—not lose their identity, but be integrated. The traditional feeling was that we were individual but separate, and I saw too much of that. I saw that that situation created a prison for my people, that there had to be a mind change within blacks that they *could* go outside of their neighborhoods—not lose their identity, but have more opportunities because of it. That was construed as liberalism because I was saying that we are all the same, that we don't have to stay within our little community—during the day go out and mingle with the rest of the world and then come back home to the safety of our little prisons.

In our day, the Rev. Jeremiah Wright has been talking about the cultural differences that the black community has with the white community, and how deep they go into music and art and everything. Is it fair to ask the black community to assimilate into the white community? Don't they have a rich culture of their own?

I didn't say, or mean, "assimilate." I said bring their culture with them, just as immigrants who go from their native country into another land take with them their vegetarianism or their particular type of meditation or music. They don't live that during the day while they interact with the general population, but they don't lose it, either, because it is a part of who they are. But in order to become a part of the world, there has to be a certain amount of integration, to take the black and the east Indian and the Eskimo and bring them together as a people to move forward and accomplish something. They bring the richness of their backgrounds and families to the table, and it is that richness that increases the productivity of the entire world.

1953 you married Coretta Scott. Tell me about her and about your family life with your four children.

Coretta was the most beautiful, loving, tolerant person in the entire world. She had a dream, just as I had a dream, of being able to make a difference in the world. She was a fantastic mother, but more than anything else, she was the organization that kept us together. They laugh now about the boards on the refrigerator with everybody's little job and how you have to take Johnny to soccer and Susie to music lessons and Jeremy to karate. She had it down, but all in her head, and she knew where everybody was supposed to be, what everybody needed, and what the next step was to enrich our lives.

Do you, Coretta, and your daughter Yolanda get together often at Home?

I wouldn't say often. After each of them had made the passage Home, we got together to discuss and celebrate things that were happening on planet Earth, but we each have our own projects to work on here at Home.

What is she doing now?

Coretta is actually organizing a lot of the children as they pass over—helping with their acclimation to being back home, the decision of what to do next, where to go, helping them understand some of the lessons that were stopped in mid-stream because they chose to return early.

We were told by Elvis Presley that he's doing a similar job. Do they see a lot of each other?

They're in different parts of the energy, but they do collaborate on occasion.

How is Yolanda getting on?

Yolanda is actually just about to come back. I am very happy for what she's doing. She is going to plan a life in which she holds her finger in the dike, but I'm not going to say more.

You said, "Injustice anywhere is a threat to justice everywhere." Tell me about the injustice you encountered during your ministry in Alabama.

The physical injustice was always that we had to follow somebody else's rules. We had no control over what we wanted to experiment with, what we wanted to try. We were told what we could and couldn't do. There were certain places we weren't allowed to go. There were certain opportunities of which we weren't allowed to avail ourselves. It was as if we were—I wouldn't say pets, but somebody's animals, allowed to feed ourselves, allowed to roam within the confines of established barriers, but not allowed to come out of that enclosure unless invited.

Was the issue of injustice one that you had dealt with in past lives?

I experienced a number of past lives in which I was the controlled person. I was a galley slave in Greek times during some wars when all I ever saw was the belly of the ship and the oar to which I was attached. There were times when it was all about physical activity—I helped to build the pyramids. There were many lives filled with the frustration of not being able to say what I wanted to say or practice what I wanted to practice if it was against what my owner, my controller, the "big man" decided to allow.

How did these lives relate to your life as Martin?

The life as Martin was a culmination of seeing all of the injustices that could be perpetrated upon a person—having categorized all of the things that I couldn't do, having enumerated all of the things that I'd always wanted to do, and now finding a way to put all of that into practice.

Life became tough for all of your family during the 382-day Montgomery bus strike. You were abused and arrested, and your home was bombed. But didn't you also gain recognition as a civil rights leader as a result?

Whenever a flare goes up, notice is taken. That was what the actions of those who fought against me did. They sent a flare up to the world, and right in the middle of that light was Martin Luther King, Jr., who then became the symbol. When you are a symbol, people recognize you, and if you have a voice and aren't just a symbol on paper, then you begin to be listened to. So it was the prelude necessary to authenticate, so to speak, my identity as one who knew what was going on and was trying to change it.

And had suffered.

The suffering, yes, was a part of it—that was all part of being that symbol.

Martin, I wonder if you can help me and many of the readers of this series of dialogues. You said, "I refuse to accept the idea that man is...unable to influence the unfolding of events which surround him. I refuse to accept the view that mankind is so tragically bound to the starless midnight of racism and war that the bright daybreak of peace and brotherhood can never become a reality." My first question is, do you still hold that view?

Absolutely.

The Ascended Masters and many souls I have interviewed have told us how at Home, together with our spiritual advisors, our soul freely plans the lessons we want to learn during our life on Earth. They indicate we sometimes choose to suffer negativity such as abandonment, oppression, or ill health; sometimes we decide to embrace negativity and become an addict, a thief, or a dictator. How does this fit with that "bright daybreak of peace and brotherhood"? Is being good and doing good something we just happen to have chosen in advance, or is goodness part of our soul's nature that will always emerge if we allow it?

To understand this whole thing, you have to appreciate that the sense of right or wrong is a judgment issue, and that judgment exists only in physical form. When we are at Home with our advisors, we decide what lessons we want to experience. The purpose of a lesson is to gain wisdom—what it feels like, how it enriches, how it enlightens, how it contributes to the growth of who we are as an essence.

When people decide to experience negativity, they can experience it in minor ways, such as not being in control of themselves, always being directed by others as to what to do, always being told in Earth terms that what they're doing is wrong, which crushes their self-worth. Or they can be instigators of negativity, such as the role chosen by Hitler, in which he took a form to cause people immense suffering and physical stress.

Once we decide what we want to do, we go down and experience it. Again, this is a lesson, so it may take us an entire lifetime, or more than one lifetime, to get to the point where we truly understand that lesson, where we can assume the wisdom of knowing what effect it has upon a human soul, how energetically it affects our essence. That point can come during our first lifetime experiencing it, or we can go through several lifetimes, learning pieces of it during each, and all of a sudden in one lifetime it clicks. The lights come on; we understand; we feel; we know; we become as part of the wisdom that we were seeking. Once that point is reached, we have the choice to continue to bask in the energy that we have come around to, or we may decide to change direction because we have the wisdom we sought.

The change in direction can be within the same energy source, concerning the same lesson, such as negativity, or since we know what negativity is, we can turn around and experience understanding positive influences upon people. We don't come down with a detailed plan: "I am going to understand what negativity is, and I'm going to do it exactly this way." We never have "exacts," and the reason we don't establish an exact formula is that if we do that beforehand, we are restricted by what we can experience, and if any of the other participants (with whom we come in contact as we learn our human lesson) change the parameters, we aren't flexible enough to be able to take that change as an enrichment of the lesson we're learning. We just ignore it and miss out on the opportunity to be enriched, and therefore we might have to come back and do the lesson again because we didn't explore all of the possibilities.

To sum it all up (because I know I've been a little long-winded on this), we decide what lessons we want to learn. We don't decide all of the facets of how we're going to learn those lessons. It is once we get here in physical form that we say, "Oh, that didn't quite give me the sense of what that emotion is; let me try this other way to sense it, to feel it, and see if it resonates more with me." So we have the freedom of choice of how we experience our lessons, and we don't decide that until we're here in physical form. The predetermination is the base outline of the lesson. The freedom of choice is how we choose to do it, which is constantly evolving while we are in physical form.

I must admit to being a little disappointed, because you have given us the usual answer from Home in terms of lessons and experiences, yet your life, Martin, was supremely dedicated to that "daybreak of peace and brotherhood." You lived a social gospel of action to better other human beings, and I don't see the answer that you have given me as tackling my question: Is it our inner nature that makes us want to do good, and does society progress at all, or is it purely by chance that any progression is made?

Well, you are talking about a number of different things here. You are talking about the individual soul's lesson, and then you wrap it all up in the framework of society in general. You can't compare the two. The thrust from society is that we would like everybody to be altruistic, to be giving, to be loving to everyone else, because to us when in body form, that is the ultimate—to have that pleasure, to have that relaxation, to have that "feel-good" sense. But each soul must experience what its lessons are.

Now you say that your impression of my life is contrary to what my soliloquy explained, but it's not. When I first came down, I was in a preacher's family. My life was the tiny community, defined by that church within that community. We discussed the outside world and how nice it would be if we were treated differently, but the primary purpose of that church was to give solace and comfort to the community.

I could have remained there, but I experimented with the possibility of changing those things we wished for in the church—that acceptance, that communion with the outside world. I first experimented with the possibility of doing it intellectually, of getting the intellectuals to recognize exactly what was happening, how things could be changed. But it came to me that this was theoretical and not something that would impact the world I was existing in right then. It would be a legacy that could be taken up and become a standard bearer in the future, but it would not have a force upon my family in my generation.

So I chose the next route, which was getting myself out there, getting myself on the end of that plank, sending up those skyrockets, saying, "I am going to see the world as it should be seen. I am going to show you what you are doing to me and my brethren. I am going to show you the discrimination that is so ingrained in you that you don't see it as anything that is potentially wrong." That was another choice that I made. So I did make choices throughout my lifetime to change the way my plan was going, and my plan was to help people of the race and color in which I came down.

In 1957 you became the president of the Southern Christian Leadership Conference and led the Coalition of Conscience in a huge protest in Birmingham, Alabama. You were jailed, and while there, wrote a famous letter asserting your right to disobey unjust laws non-violently. You wrote, "Human progress never rolls in on the wheels of inevitability. It comes through the tireless efforts of men willing to be co-workers with God, and without this hard work time itself becomes an ally of social stagnation." Tell us about that experience.

The experience of the discomfort of being treated as less than human, of being herded around and then being locked up in a pen, was to me the epitome of what I was trying to free the people from. This was a microcosm that was part of the macrocosm of the black-white problem. The sense that I had while I was there was to take the blinders off people, to let them see what was going on, to stimulate within the community a desire for balance, for freedom. I realized that this could be manifested by the actions of myself and others, joining with the God-Force we had inside of us and taking all of that energy and directing it toward change. I then chose to continue what I was doing because I saw that it was starting to have an impact. The reaction directed against us showed that the people who had always perpetrated the discrimination were afraid. Their very reaction to us showed their fear, and that was something we could turn against them.

Then a quarter of a million people came for the March on Washington, famous for your "Dream" oration. But the tenor of the speech was angry. The founding fathers had signed a promissory note for every American. "This note was a promise that all men, yes, black men as well as white men, would be guaranteed the unalienable rights of life, liberty, and the pursuit of happiness." From your perspective at Home, how much of this promise has now been fulfilled?

From Home we get a perspective of everything that is going on, and we are very aware of the cyclic actions that occur upon the planet. There are major changes that have been made since that time, bringing things more in tune with the intentions of the founding fathers, but there have been erosions again at the base of those great thoughts and intentions, which have been directed not solely against blacks, but against other groups, whether they be immigrants or people whose ideas and ideals differ from those of mainstream society. It is a battle that will constantly be waged upon the planet, because the planet is a duality. We can't get to a point where everybody has everything, because then you won't be able to experience anything.

Accepting the Nobel Peace Prize in 1964 you said, "I refuse to accept the cynical notion that nation after nation must spiral down a militaristic stairway into the hell of thermonuclear destruction. I believe that unarmed truth and unconditional love will have the final word in reality." Are war and terrorism still the biggest threat in the world today, or is the physical crisis of planet Earth worse?

They affect different things. Terrorism is the biggest threat against the ideologies of the people on the planet. The ecological demise of so much of the planet's resources will have—and is having—a drastic impact upon the population, which will then cause more of the former to flare up. Right now it is pretty much a balance as to which is more destructive to the physicality of your planet.

In your 1967 sermon "Beyond Vietnam: A Time to Break Silence," you spoke out against the Vietnam war and called the U.S. government "the greatest purveyor of violence in the world today." The media turned against you, and the civil rights campaign lost support. How badly was your work harmed by the rejection of your stand by those who had previously supported you?

[laughs] It was very interesting to see that, because I was now attacking the shaky pillars upon which they had based a lot of their economics, the politicians with whom I had begun to gain favor attacked me in response. In my entire existence, I always spoke as I felt, and there was a dual purpose in what I was saying. Not only was that war an injustice, it was a burden placed disproportionately upon the black people: those who couldn't buy their way out of the war, who couldn't put their children in college so that they didn't get shipped off to Vietnam.

I saw it as a further exasperation and frustration—as far as we had gone in getting equality, when cannon fodder was needed, they reached back into the bag that they had used before and put us on the front lines. It had an impact on the support of those to whose backyard I had taken the fight, those who kept their sons out of the front lines, but it brought the message more thoroughly back to my black brethren that there were many layers that we were addressing, that we weren't talking just about riding a bus with the whites.

In your last sermon before you were assassinated you said, "I just want to do God's will. And He's allowed me to go up to the mountain. And I've looked over. And I've seen the promised land." You were referring to Moses who, according to Numbers, chapter 20, had displeased God when he struck the rock and brought forth water and, in consequence, was only permitted to see the promised land from afar. Was your remark merely rhetorical, or did you feel that you, like Moses, did not deserve more because of something you had done?

It was totally rhetorical. It was also when I had a feeling that my time on the planet was coming to an end. I had accomplished the lesson of learning how to alter the direction of the water, and I sensed that the best way to ensure my legacy of continuing to help others see the same lesson was by my departure, so that primarily only what people on Earth would call the "good" part of what I had accomplished would be remembered.

I understand. Finally, who actually killed you, and was it a government conspiracy?

There are many things afoot concerning that fatal time, and I would rather not, in this book, go into that.

Thank you, Martin Luther King, Jr., for speaking with us.

I just hope that my message will continue to play in a loop, impacting each new generation, letting them see and feel that the struggles can be won.

Commentary

Toni: Wow! That was quite an energy—it was so dynamic. I know that during Dr. King's lifetime there were many times when he showed anger or frustration, but there was none of that during this interview. It was just a matter-of-fact representation of what he had accomplished and what he had done. I felt like a very eager little acolyte at the feet of a master, trying to get a grasp of how you do this thing called life, how you go through this learning of the life lessons, what you can accomplish—not only for yourself, but for those around you—while you're going through these lessons. It was, for me, a very fascinating but also a deeply emotional interview.

Peter: Martin's desire to influence future generations with his powerful message remains undimmed, judging from his concluding remark.

There was a wholeness in our dialogue that was very satisfying, and I felt as if the advance planning that had gone into his human life had been very thoroughly done before he incarnated. The choice of his strong family provided both the right training for his young mind and the springboard for his dynamic ministry. His first ministerial appointment in Montgomery, Alabama, helped him to put his cutting-edge theological views to the test (they were quite advanced for a black congregation), but possibly more importantly, to test his practical response to the daily, grinding, practical reality of racial discrimination and the scourge of segregation.

He clarified for me the underlying issue: previously blacks sought acceptance but a separate community. What Martin looked for was not that nor a faceless assimilation into white culture, but a true integration that celebrated the strengths and cultures of both communities and contributed to the maturity of the diverse American and also the world society.

We had two glimpses into his occult life. He mentioned how first his beloved Coretta, and then his daughter, Yolanda, on their transition Home, got together with him to celebrate. Then both of them went off on their individual assignments. Souls have quite different inter-relationships once human life has been completed. We were also reminded of that when Martin referred to past lives he lived as a galley slave and a slave-laborer building the Pyramids, that his preparation for life as a great civil rights leader truly ran deep—over several centuries!

There was a lot to chew on in our dialogue, but let me mention just one issue. Like many souls whom I have interviewed, Martin's soul seemed conscious of the dynamic cycles that the world goes through—not on this occasion about global warming on the planet, but the cycles between ethnic groups. His remark was revealing: *"It is a battle that will constantly be waged upon the planet, because the planet is a duality. We can't get to a point where everybody has everything, because then you won't be able to experience anything."* There have been positive changes certainly in our relationships, but we are in a training course on Earth. Polarization, wars, racism, discrimination, human angst, are all part and parcel of the tough course we are enrolled in. We must remain vigilant and try to do good whenever and wherever we can.

Much of the work of Dr. King and his followers represented a freely chosen path of action that many (but not all) people would consider "good," but which, for him, was accompanied by 30 imprisonments; the bombing of his house; attacks by police with sticks, dogs, and water hoses; a turning away by supporters in the media when he talked against the war; and, at the end, his assassination. It was a difficult journey, but his personal march to Zion was very well done and remains an inspiration to many.

Martin did not want to discuss his assassination, but I vividly remembered the day I heard the news. It was during the 1968 Prague Peace Conference, embracing religious leaders from East and West during the Cold War. I was privileged to be sitting between Canon John Collins, the founder of CND, the Campaign for Nuclear Disarmament, and Pastor Martin Niemöller, the German theologian who was one of the founders of the Confessing Church, which opposed the nazification of the German Protestant churches. The dramatic announcement was made from the platform that Dr. Martin Luther King, Jr. had been gunned down at his hotel. The dire news was received with a gasp by the assembled clerics, followed by profound prayerful silence in the hall. Then the 76-year-old determined opponent of Hitler leaned over me, jabbing his finger at Canon Collins, and said, "We must carry on his work." And so we will.

"When I played music, I let the music play my body."

Elvis Presley

1935-1977

Are you the real Elvis Aron Presley, or an impersonator?

I'm the real one. The one and only—the King!

It is believed by some of your followers that hours after your reported death a man using the name of Jon Burrows, which was your traveling alias, paying with cash bought a one-way ticket to Buenos Aires. Was that man you?

[laughs] Certainly not! That was somebody taking advantage of it. He actually was an old employee who had been called in to help clean some stuff up at the mansion.

Do you remember his name?

Jose.

Did he get to Buenos Aires?

Yes, he did.

Was he using your money?

Yes, he was.

Have you ever appeared on Earth since your death in 1977?

Yes. Primarily I appeared to my sweet wife and daughter, just to let them know that I apologized for not being very nice to them while I was around, and to keep (as you British would say), 'a stiff upper lip' [Peter, the interviewer, is British] with all of the problems that would be visited upon them because of the hoopla concerning my passing. I also told them to move on.

Was that the only appearance you made on Earth?

That was my only appearance in the flesh.

Are you planning a second coming as Elvis Presley? And could you do that anyway?

I could, but I don't choose to do it. I learned those experiences of the good and the bad, all the trials and tribulations of humankind. I don't need to go there again.

You say you could "come back' as Elvis. How would you do that?

All of Earth's linear time exists at the same time. There is no such thing as time for us, so I could go back and re-live that particular role as Elvis. I could do it within that time frame, choosing to alter slightly some of the experiences that were had.

So what are you doing back Home now—are you singing gospel, rock and roll, or country?

Mainly I'm just entertaining the kiddies; some of those who come over here are kinda confused. I help them transition [move from Earth to Home] into nice, smooth, comfortable existences—get them back to feeling who they are as a soul, so they get out of the mindset that they're anywhere from three to seven years old, and let them know their actual age. I do it through music, do it through play.

Do you appear physically to them when you are doing that?

Only if they're physical, which the majority of them are. I appear sorta as I did when I was in the army, a suave, debonair young man.

With a short haircut?

With a short haircut and no sideburns.

How do you take on physical form when you are back Home? Do you not normally have physical form?

Normally we do not maintain a physical form. In most cases we're just energy. We communicate by using our intention and create what you would call mind-communication. So the appearance of physicality is only used whenever some beings transition but don't realize they are energy. For their own self-identity and comfort they consider themselves to be in physical form. In order to communicate with them I have to be in physical form as well.

That's the point where you can sing?

That's the point where I can sing, but I can send music into someone's mind. Sometimes I have fun doing that. You know, when you're going down the street and you hear one of my songs, and it's not playing on the radio—that's me sometimes just having fun. I just put music in people's head when I think they need to have a good day.

Which song do you choose?

Well I like "Hound Dog." It kinda says what my life was like. I like the love songs and the ballads; some of the stuff I did in the movies is really good.

The music was better than the movies!

I made a lot of money on those movies but they were very restrictive to me. That time when I was doing most of the movies was after I got back out of military service. That's when I was, y'know, being all impressed with myself, picking up some of the self-medication rituals that I had. I lost whatever humility I'd had and it became very important that I be "The Man."

You became famous, but you were born into a very poor Mississippi family. Your father, Vernon, hardly spoke at all, and Gladys, your mother, was unusually and fiercely over-protective of you all your life. Did you have a choice of parents when you came down to planet Earth?

Oh, we all do. One of the lessons I wanted to learn was that of being able to build myself, within the framework of humankind, to be able to determine who I was, and to go from "rags to riches" (as you say on Earth).

As a mama's boy you were very shy and isolated at first. You seem to have been passionate about girls, not just in high school, and not only in your relationships with Dixie, Anita, June, Natalie, Connie, Ann-Margret, Linda, your wife Priscilla, and your fiancée Ginger, but also a number of young teenage girls. Can you explain the nature of your sexuality?

[chuckles] I was very confused by my sexuality. Being extremely protected, I never got social skills when I was young, concerning dealing with the sexes. When I started being adored by girls it was sorta as if my mama was there with me, and the affection that she always lavished on me was coming from outside sources. So it was multiplying and was very comfortable to me. I really got into that particular groove. In the beginning it didn't have anything to do with sex; it had to do with how I felt about myself. The image I had of myself was that I was shy and didn't have experience. Then to go out and be *adored* by people gave me a definition of who I was—who I was as this person everybody liked, everybody wanted to be with. It didn't go into sexual things until much, much later, because my whole sexual identity was kinda confused.

Eventually, did you have sex with minor girls?

Not all the way to intercourse, no. It mainly came to the point of liking to have them around because they adored me. I was "The King" and what was important to me was how I felt about myself.

In your last years there seemed to be a confusion in your sexuality because in concerts you began to look, dress, and act like Liberace. Were you ever actually bisexual or just confused?

Totally confused. I did have some cuddling time with males, but it never went much beyond that. I gravitated toward anybody who could make me feel good.

You were surrounded by so much feel-good stuff toward the end of your life—weren't you almost in a cocoon?

It was as if I was in this padded room and everything just came to me.

Going back to your early days, when you were 10 your mother bought you a guitar from Forrest Bobo at the local Tupelo hardware store. Soon after your family moved to Memphis and you attended the Pentecostal church. What did these early musical experiences mean to you?

Communication around my house was never very good, from my daddy, even with my momma. She would talk but she was over the top so I didn't know how to express myself. Once I started with music, I began to express myself through the music because that was accepted around the house. Rather than going around prattling like a little kid, I got my communication out through music. When I got involved in the church, I realized how you could move a person, how much you could say to a person in a single song or in a single piece of music, and it started to shape my life from the first time I picked up and sang.

Were you ever a musician in a former life?

Yes, mainly I was a traveling minstrel back in the fifteen hundreds. I had a lute and I went from town to town singing for my supper.

Did the girls gather round in those days?

Not as much as they did in my life as Elvis!

After your family moved to Memphis, you hung around Beale Street where African-American musicians such as B.B. King were playing. A producer called that area "the center of all evil in the known universe," but you found it musically inspirational. What did you learn there?

I learned soul there—by soul I mean, taking what was inside me and bringing it out in musical form. This was because B.B. and that whole string of people just knew how to speak, and what they spoke of were the emotions of their life. Now, that was feared by white folks at that time because they could *feel* the intensity of the music and they didn't want to. Those days everything had to be cut-and-dried, had to be categorized, programmed, but that music brought out the essence of a person. It didn't take what was written in "step 4" of your life ("this is what you'll be in step 1, in step 2, step 3, or 4"). It said "this is *who* I am." That "feared" a lot of people, but in me it awakened the energies within and I could feel more than I had felt anywhere else in my life—what was inside of me and what I had to offer to others.

It's obvious that Sam Phillips of Sun Records saw in you someone who could take black rhythm-and-blues music and make it popular with whites as well. You did that brilliantly, but immediately found you were in a racial storm about "race music." How did you feel about that?

I thought it was funny. You know, I was born at a time and in an area when whites didn't mix with blacks ("niggers," as everybody used to call them). To me they were beautiful people. I learned so much from them. They had a sense of who they were, and within their art of who we all could be, instead of those stuffed shirts, the white folks. We could, in baring our soul, give so much help to other people. Those [whites] who were around did not want to say that they could learn anything from people they considered their inferiors. For me, it was a key to expression, a key to the soul. I wouldn't listen to what anyone said about it being bad. I had to change it a little bit, morph it a little bit so it was more accepted, but it was the same core energy that I used. I reached people because they thought I was just this good old Southern boy and they accepted it from me because I was white.

In addition to the racial issues, you were fiercely attacked by lots of people, including your Pentecostal friends, for your being very provocatively sexual for the time. However did the shy schoolboy turn into the delinquent "Elvis the Pelvis," also called "that backslidden Pentecostal pup"?

[laughs] When I played music I let the music play my body. When you are talking, you talk with every energy that you've got and you talk with every muscle, every nerve, every bone in your body. When I wanted somebody to be happy, when I wanted to get that message over how good life was, how cheerful things could be, my body just played for me. I had advisors who said if you really wanna get known, you *really* wanna get that name out there, you wanna get the girls, you accentuate some things. [laughs]

You were a successful musician but no businessman. You even allowed your manager to write his own price, 50% of the take. Now the people running your estate fiercely control an enormously successful entertainment empire. In 1956 a business journalist wrote, "Elvis Presley is a business." From your position now, how do you view all this material success other people enjoy?

Good for them! I don't have any regrets, don't have any wishes. People are going to be who they are and are going to play the part that they've got. To me, getting the soul out of music was the important thing. So long as my needs were taken care of, I didn't care who else got the benefit. That wasn't important to me. When I was a child we had very little and I was happy. As I became this "empire" (as people say), so long as I had what I needed that was all that was important. I sometimes had a few extravagances. I loved my cars and things like that, but that was only because they were on my wish list as I was growing up. I didn't care what happened to them after I left. I don't need them up here!

You used the word "regret." What things do you regret doing, or would do differently if you could?

I really wouldn't do anything differently, because I learned exactly what I needed to learn. I needed to learn the value of life, to learn the value of taking the abilities and the tools we have and using them to the full in the physical format, and in so doing, if we have to help others, help others to feel good, too. I wouldn't have been in some of my self-destructive moods, possibly... but I learned from those as well. I learned that you have to be balanced as a person to have—I guess—a non-controversial human lifetime. But I learned everything to the full in all of my experiences.

Does everyone have lessons to learn?

Some 99.99% of the people have to. Every now and then there's one who comes down just to relax.

As the reputed "King of Rock 'n' Roll," what do you feel were your greatest accomplishments?

Opening people up to what music can do for them. Opening up that little boy, that little girl, from being a shy person to somebody who will go out in their back yard and sing a song, and with that to have a connection with the other little kids in the neighborhood. Music is a form of communication, one that bonds disparate people together, makes them forget their troubles, forget their races, religions, their sex—makes them forget everything, and combines them as one harmonic vibration. That's what the primary thread of my life was. Not all the problems I had, not all the human "mistakes" (as you would say) that I made. That legacy I was able to put down there was of giving people something to unite them.

Is there anything not widely known that you would like to tell us about?

Almost every aspect of me is known! I'm not sure how many people know how very, very shy I was as a child. I was so shy that if anybody came visiting I would hide behind my mother. Until I got that guitar I identified myself strictly as my mama's son. I never became Elvis until I got up there and let that part sing out.

Did you take that massive dose of pills deliberately to kill yourself?

Not to kill myself. It was just another way of deadening. I was into a very deep depression at that time. I had no direction. I felt I had played out everything I had to deal with then. I saw no excitement, I saw no future. I just saw this blob sitting there who was unable to make a comeback anywhere, and I was just trying to deaden everything that was in my consciousness.

What was death like for you?

Very peaceful, fell asleep.

Did you hang around a long time after that?

Not really, I was ready to move on. I was ready to rid myself of that ugly body at that time. It wasn't the nice svelte look that I once had.

Some people will probably want to know if you went to heaven or hell, and where you are now.

Well, there ain't no such thing as heaven and hell. After we transition, it's just a matter of what we choose to create with our intention. At first, I chose to punish myself for what I considered the mistakes I made toward the end of my life. Finally I realized I was being used by others, and things like that. Then, with the help of some transitional folks, I began to realize who I really was.

"Transitional folks"—you mean spirits?

Angels and other souls who provided the means of helping me to understand. It's like what the military call "de-programming."

Since there are angels, isn't it heaven?

No, it's just unconditional love, which a lot of people consider heaven, but there's no alternative unless you put yourself there.

Heaven implies a reward, but there's no reward?

There's no reward for us at Home because during our life's lessons there's nothing right and nothing wrong.

So does everyone goes Home?

Everyone goes Home. It's just up to them to decide what "Home" means—the storybook Heaven or Hell.

Even Elvis the Pelvis?

Even Elvis the Pelvis!

Thank you, Elvis Presley, for talking with us.

Commentary

Toni: This was a smooth interview. His spirit is very comfortable with its identity as an individual soul. It's a comfort level which he is trying to make available to others, especially children returning Home. I felt a little bit of underlying shyness, but also the bravado of the showman. As a showman he was saying you shouldn't pick apart his human difficulties and idiosyncrasies. Look rather at how his music turned people inside out to feel themselves, and how music helps souls speak to other souls, regardless of the color of the body that they are currently wearing.

Peter: The heart of Elvis was found in his childhood—the shy, over-protected little white boy who wandered into the cheerful presence of local black musicians and discovered himself as a person through listening to, and then playing, their evocative rhythms and sounds. This perennial boy—this Peter Pan—had no real sophistication, neither in the racial politics of the time, nor in the business issues that followed his meteoric climb to fame, and especially in the relationships of singing star and audience members. His talent was in making music—just the way his soul liked it.

Above all, Elvis, whose father was undemonstrative and whose mother was possessive, wanted—no, *needed* to be cuddled. And his self-centric desire for affection did not mean he was incapable of ever giving love to others. It was just that he did not fully understand the rules of the game. So he played his way through a life full of screaming teenagers (girls mostly), a big mansion, a collection of cars, and drugs to ease the aloneness and dissatisfaction with it all. But there was one passion which never left him, the passion for the beat and the melodies of his youth. And of that, one might say he was more than a star: he was the King.

So if you hear "Hound Dog" playing in your head, be happy and sing along, but don't look for the singer. There will be no more Elvis. He could come down to planet Earth but made it plain that it isn't his intention to do so. He would rather be playing songs upstairs for the kiddies returning Home. Rock 'n' roll, of course.

"There was this sense that I had
of the nearness of a transition back Home ...
somebody with a gun ready to send me off.
I did not care whether people hated me or not."

John Lennon

1940-1980

John Ono Lennon, you were born in Liverpool and named John Winston Lennon after Winston Churchill, Britain's wartime leader. Was your later name change not only a tribute to your wife, Yoko Ono, but also a symbol of your pacifist rejection of war?

It was solely a tribute to my wife. As much as I embraced pacifism, that was not what I was trying to say in dropping the Winston name, because Churchill was not only a wartime leader. He was also a terrific orator, a purveyor of words, somebody who could be looked up to for what he had accomplished, not just for the decisions he made during the time of our upheaval.

Where did your pacifism come from—seeing the effect of bombing in Liverpool?

It was more pervasive than that. It was seeing what those weapons could do to a people, but it was the energy that was contained behind the war, what happened to the small people, those who were pushed aside as the fighting men battled their way to the front, not only in my own country but in other conflicts throughout the world.

What was happening to those who did not partake was more egregious than what happened to the participants. They went to war in the knowledge that it was "you or me, do or die," and the mother, father, or child who stood in the way of the conflict was summarily brushed out of the way so that the conflict could continue. They had no interest in what was going on. They were not part of the politics. They did not benefit from the battle, but were the refuse that the victors, the conquerors, and the defeated pushed before them.

Your parents separated when you were very young, and your aunt Mimi became your caregiver. You had a harmonica and also learned to play the banjo; then your mother gave you a guitar when you were sixteen. Was making music important to you when you were little, or did you discover your talent rather late?

I always knew that in the music I could be carried away from what was around me. I could find a love within the music that I didn't feel I got from my parents. My aunt was great in taking care of me, but I was a bit too much for her. The music changed, though, as I became proficient with the instruments, particularly the guitar, because there was a sadness that could be conveyed with the music that told of the struggles, the possibilities, the dreams that I had as an individual.

Had you been a musician in a past life?

I had never concentrated on music. It had been something that was merely a hobby in past lives, and the music that became my life when I was John Lennon was just the means of conveying my energy and my art.

You and Paul McCartney met at a gig that your new group, The Quarrymen, had in a local church. What convinced you to invite him to join the group?

There was the same intensity and sadness within him, and also the same hope that I was beginning to feel. I felt the connection between the two of us and felt that together we could start to get our message across.

Your musical partnership with Paul developed quickly to be very fruitful. What drove your success as songwriters?

Again it was that inner urging, that inner need to be understood, to be able to say to people this is what life truly is, and here—this is what life can be: that you don't have to be under the yoke of something, that you can use music as leverage to lift those difficulties off of you to find the love and the beauty within.

Did you take it in turns to be the leader of the songwriting team?

I don't think that either one of us was dominant. The messages came to us at different times, and sometimes a message would come to one of us and we couldn't express it properly, and then the other would fill in the blanks. It was a total collaboration that most people didn't understand, and neither one of us really wanted to be out there as the leader.

Then Paul brought George Harrison into the Quarrymen. Tell us about your relationship with George.

Well, at first George was just sort of this silent person until the music began, and he came with a lot of fear and reservations. It was almost as if he had to make up his mind after he was with us that he truly wanted to open up and become a part of us. The energy in the group was in turmoil when he first joined us. There wasn't a distinct direction or purpose. We were floundering, running hither and yon trying to find something that would totally catch on with the people, and as George came and began to open up, it was as if a blossom that started to enfold us, to give us some support, had entered into our group.

Do the two of you get together often at Home now?

I don't know what your definition of "often" is. Do we exchange anecdotes about what we did together? Yes, because some of the things we did were completely outrageous, but yet some have become the mainstays for a generation. When we recall something that carried the hopes of a group of people, we like to relive it.

You renamed your group "The Beatles" and were booked to play in Hamburg pubs. Wasn't that something of a disaster?

It was, because we didn't know who we were at the time, and we were trying to be whatever we thought our audience wanted instead of just saying, "This is who we are." We found it was very difficult to try to take an idea that we had of an idea and carry it off.

In 1961 things began to improve. You started playing at the Cavern Club in Liverpool and signed Brian Epstein as manager. Tell me about him.

Brian was a true visionary. He also could read people very well. He could read the energy between people; he knew what worked; he gave direction to the group as to what would be accepted in various parts of the music world. We were at that time finally beginning to define who we were as a group. Even though we had our name, even though we thought we had a style, Brian showed us we in fact did not have a central style.

So he put you in Beatle uniforms with Beatle mop haircuts and gave you discipline, I suppose.

He did keep us toeing the line. He told us in no uncertain terms, "If I am going to represent you, and I am going to book you someplace to do something, I expect you to be there and do what has been promised. If you find you do not want to do that, or cannot do that, then we cannot remain together." The uniform was to set within us the idea that we were unified, not just musicians who had come together to jam, each one doing his own thing; that in order to be accepted and productive, we must have a sound; each one of us must have certain responsibilities that were reproducible. We had had the problem that when we went to a locale, one night we would be fantastic and the next night we would be awful because we had no discipline or unity or set pattern. Our outfits reminded us constantly that we had to be a group with a format in order to be recognized and to go outside of the neighborhood.

The next year you replaced drummer Pete Best with Ringo Starr, as he became known. Now the "Fab Four" were complete. Tell me about your relationship with Ringo.

Ringo was a character, by human standards. He brought to us a sense of discipline, as well, because although he could take off and do a reel like no one else could do, he was almost mechanical in the way he would create the sound. He showed us that we could put individuality into the pieces but still be a group, still be reproducible, and the energy that he brought was one of cohesiveness.

In August 1962 you married Cynthia Powell, a student with you at the Liverpool College of Art. You were idle and disruptive in class, and abusive of Cynthia. When your son Julian was born you remained distant from him. What was going on inside you?

I was frightened, scared, totally out of my element. I did not know what a loving family was like. I had only had my own experience, in which I felt deserted by my folks and sort of left to my own devices. I was afraid that Julian would be the same way, so in response to that, I fled. Cynthia was trying to get me to understand about family life, about home life, and I felt that she was trying to control me, whereas in fact she was just trying to instruct me. We were getting a little bit of notoriety at that time, and I thought that I was above and beyond what other people had to do, and I just would not listen.

The Beatles cut "Love Me Do" at the EMI studios, followed by the successful "Please Please Me," and then a series of hit singles which topped the charts in Britain. Money started pouring in; teenage girls were screaming; alcohol, drugs, and sex were plentiful. What was the impact on your mind of such fame and fortune?

It identified that I was somebody. I'd never thought of myself as anything other than just a bloke off the streets, and here I was recognized, I was idolized, I was given anything I wanted, and at that time I wanted everything. I wanted to prove that I was fabulous, that I could have the girls, that I could get myself silly with alcohol and drugs if I chose, and I was really a bore.

Later, you indicated that the song "Help!" referred to your own inner confusion. You said, "I'm not going to change the way I look or the way I feel to conform to anything. I've always been a freak." You also said, "Part of me suspects that I'm a loser, and the other part of me thinks I'm God Almighty." What was happening?

Pretty much as I just described. I was going through this transition phase where for the first time I did have the sense that I could be God Almighty. The acknowledgement that I thought I was a loser was very difficult for me to make. It was the beginning of a self-realization period that took many, many years to accomplish, in which the full sense of being human hit me—that we have these difficulties, these lessons, that we have to work our way through in order to be able to move on and really accomplish something in this life. That I was a pendulum going from extreme to extreme I would blame mostly on immaturity and lack of experience, but that was what I had set out for myself to do.

How much did LSD affect your mind?

For a period there I was pretty fried, as they say. I would have hallucinations. But under the influence I saw a beauty that I didn't see in the streets around me, even in those paved with gold that I thought I was entitled to and becoming a part of. It was at a time when I got my first true, deep feelings of myself. It was like stripping off the mask of being human and sensing a little bit of the unconditional love that comes from Home.

You got into serious trouble in America by saying, "Christianity will go. It will vanish and shrink. I needn't argue with that; I'm right and I will be proved right. We're more popular than Jesus now." You apologized profusely at the time for what you had said. Now back Home, how do you view what happened?

[laughs] I see a soul in human form influenced by the extreme egotism that can come from a little bit of fame and money—the need for that ego to be right, to be dominant. Now I see it simply as reaching the height of humanness so that I then could feel the richness and the depth of my soul.

Tell me how much you now agree with your statement: "I believe in God, but not as one thing, not as an old man in the sky. I believe that what people call God is something in all of us. I believe that what Jesus and Mohammed and Buddha and all the rest said was right. It's just that the translations have gone wrong."

I agree with that 100%. I wouldn't use those words to describe it, but it's the way things are.

What words would you use?

I would say that, in fact, we all are God—that each soul comes down to Earth to learn about the difference between being God and being something else, so that the magnificence of that sense can become known. There are a number of prophets, a number of very enlightened people who come to show us the way to this understanding of ourselves as being pieces of creation. Those people function within the dynamic of humankind at the time they are on the planet, so that the words of Jesus, the words of Mohammed, the words of any of the great prophets have to be viewed in the context of the time—what those people to whom they were talking and trying to show the pathway understood. You do not talk to a four-year-old with the same language you use to a 24-year-old or a 44-year-old or a 64-year-old. You take their experience and use that as a lexicon for the language.

Then in 1966, which was not very long after you'd all started touring, the Beatles stopped, complaining that the huge, screaming crowds drowned out the music. You said, "It was like being in the eye of a hurricane." Was this a point when you began to understand your art was more important than the crowds?

It was a point at which we were beginning to know that our message, contained within our art, was a vibrational pathway that some could use to learn more about themselves. We, of course, didn't understand it in those terms, but we just had this sense that if they came simply to scream at our physical form, they could not hear our message. But if they bought our recording and listened to it, maybe the first or second time, while they were still screaming, they wouldn't get the message, but with repeated use, the message would get through.

The group recorded "Sgt. Pepper's Lonely Hearts Club Band" in 1967, but you were personally ready to move on. Then you fell in love with Yoko Ono. Cynthia divorced you, and 18 months later the Beatles performed together for the last time. Tell me about Yoko and these changes.

Yoko was not impressed with The Beatles. Yoko did not see me as a Beatle, scurrying about, trying to excite the young girls. Yoko saw my soul. She helped me to feel who I was. She brought with her a peace and a tranquility that I had never before experienced, and a place in which I wished to reside.

How acrimonious was the breakup of The Beatles?

There were some accusations of "traitor" and "world-wrecker" and the idea that I would be taking money out of their pockets. I told them that the group could go on with a replacement if their whole mission was just to do shows, just to go out into the world of the screaming fans and bask in the adoration. But it was time for me to become more private, to become more my own person and not that figurehead that represented one of The Beatles.

Following your cannabis conviction, and the banned nude picture of you and Yoko on the cover of "Two Virgins," you married and shortly afterward held several "bed-ins" for peace. You recorded "The Ballad of John and Yoko" and "Give Peace a Chance." The focus of your life had changed. Was this infatuation with Yoko, or was it the real you?

That question was frequently asked of me, and my response is simply, "My entire life was the real me." But just as we change jobs, and identities with the jobs, in human life we go through phases. I had completed my egotistical, outwardly bombastic phase, was introduced to peace and tranquility, and saw that as something else I could introduce to the world. It was the real me at the time, just as the abusive drinker/druggie had been the real me of my youth.

In "The Ballad of John and Yoko" one refrain was: "The way things are going /They're going to crucify me." You also said, "You either get tired fighting for peace, or you die." Did you live with the thought that your opponents would eventually kill you?

There was this sense that I had of the nearness of a transition back Home. I took this feeling to be that there must be energies outside of me that sought my destruction, and I felt that it must be somebody with a gun ready to send me off. I did not care whether people hated me or not. I was in a position at that time where I had to be true to what I was feeling, and although I knew it ruffled a lot of feathers, I was as strong a proponent for what I believed in as I had been for the music that I almost deafened ears with.

Looking back, did your peace protests and songs achieve anything lasting?

There was an awareness created that someone such as I could go from being a bombastic, ne'er-do-well, egotistical person to someone who felt the pain of the common man's being oppressed, being put up for slaughter by his government. I knew—and I know—that the energy I put out there created an undercurrent, that nothing can be unaffected by putting the ideas out into space, into the universe, into the people. We can start a grass-roots effort.

You did in fact say that if everyone demanded peace instead of another television set, there would be peace. What can ordinary people do to bring peace to the troubled world?

Well, it's a little like prayer. If everybody prays for peace in the duality of the Earth plane, they are saying the energy of war is present. They are giving force and power to that energy of war. But if, instead, they start living their lives with the energy of peace, if within their common life they accept that everybody has an opinion that they don't have to refute, that is taking away war energy and creating peace energy.

In 1973 you and Yoko separated for 18 months, which you spent in Los Angeles. There you recorded your first #1 single, "Whatever Gets You Thru The Night," and your first #1 album, Walls And Bridges. *What triggered the split with Yoko?*

The split was triggered by the intensity of what we were going through. I wanted things to happen *now*. I wanted to have people follow my words and my ideals the same way they had followed The Beatles, with the same enthusiasm, the same outlay of their money in buying. I thought that if I was this great (having still a little of that god-complex), when I said we needed peace, there should be peace. Yoko was trying to get the intensity out of my emotions and show me that all we can do is, by example, put our beliefs out there. We can't change other people, but we can give them a way to rethink their beliefs and opinions. It can be very easily seen by the lyrics of the songs I produced during that period of time that they were pleas to her to get back together, to help me see what I wasn't seeing, to help me understand the whole human soul interface that she so well understood.

Your son Sean was born in 1975 and you retired to become a house-husband and to care for your boy. Five years later you published "Starting Over" and "Double Fantasy." Then, all of a sudden, it was over. You were killed outside your New York home by a mentally ill gunman. Tell me about those last five years.

From a human standpoint the last five years were the happiest of my human existence. I had a relationship not only with my darling Yoko but with a son—a small me whom I could help to see the problems I had overcome so that he did not have to face them. I understood for the first time responsibility for another individual, what the impact can be of the pathways that I had set out previously—on a smaller scale, of course—and it was a time for me to be able to go inside, not being distracted by all of the outside forces that had always entered into my life previously.

John, you said, "My role in society, or any artist's or poet's role, is to try and express what we all feel. Not to tell people how to feel. Not as a preacher, not as a leader, but as a reflection of us all." Did you achieve your objective?

For a number of people, I achieved exactly that. But there were millions who saw only that they could dance or sing to the same things that had an internal effect on the few.

Thank you, John Lennon, for talking with us.

Commentary

Toni: That was the first time that I have channeled one of these interviews where, when we were discussing his five years as a house-husband, the emotions were coming through so strongly about the love he had for his family, for his son, that there were tears welling up in my eyes from the change in his emotions. The whole conversation started out with the brashness of youth, the devil-may-care "it's my life, I don't care what others think," through the transition of coming into awareness, although first with the influence of drugs. There was a sense there when he talked about the LSD of how pleasurable it felt to his physical body, but also how it seemed to open up a door to the dimensions of Home, although he didn't understand exactly what it was. And then a transition again as he began, with the help of Yoko, to realize what was inside of him and what his connection was—not the egotistical "I am God," but the soul-felt "I am a part of creation." It was like a metamorphosis from a very ugly caterpillar just scraping along to a beautiful butterfly that not only was pleasing to the eye, but created a wave with its wings that began to have an impact on people in a quieting way. The symbolism and the energy behind the entire interview were just fantastic.

Peter: This soul's story confirmed the classic tale of a bright, restless, out-of-control young man who slowly loses his lack of self-worth, achieves artistic greatness, finds a soul mate, and finally achieves inner peace—all this in the bright lights of publicity, all this with acid, grass, alcohol, and total saturation in other people's sexual fantasies. Here is an artist who, at his most belligerent, defiantly dares to go eyeball-to-eyeball with Jesus Christ, but finds ultimate peace and salvation at home nurturing his baby son.

In his lifetime John Lennon attracted many young people to him who have remained deeply attracted by his life and art. He was a revolutionary who got young and old lustily singing the Beatles' songs all across the globe, a renegade whose constant passion for world peace made him respectable in the eyes of a whole generation and taught us that we should "give peace a chance." He showed in his life, and has now confirmed from Home, the depth of his conviction in the eternal truth that *"there's nothing you can do that can't be done—all you need is love, love, love is all you need."*

Living Souls

The human soul is eternal. There is little disagreement among the world's major religions about that idea.

When I was a boy it seemed to me that a soul was something you were given by God when you died. Maybe you got one if you were good, and if you were bad—well, then there was "outer darkness" complete with "wailing and gnashing of teeth" waiting for you. It never really occurred to me that you do not "have a soul," or "get a soul," but that you are a soul, that the Thing somewhere inside you, who (or which) is doing the driving, is your soul. Maybe when you are forgetful, it's having a nap and letting your brain do the driving instead!

Religious people don't talk that much about the soul; it is sort of uncertain territory for most folk—or it used to be, but perhaps not any longer. A good deal has changed in the certainty we have about the human soul. People have studied thousands of near-death experiences. Scientists have written detailed case notes about little children who vividly remember being someone else before they were born. There have already been many millions of past-life regression experiences in hypnosis, and a whole field of life-between-lives regression with hypnosis is becoming established worldwide.

All these tell the same basic story of the life of the eternal soul. It is a story that supports and amplifies the collection of dialogues in this book and in the rest of this series. Toni Ann Winninger's amazing channeling of our 21 leading men deals with the same issues as do thousands of researchers and therapists, to say nothing about other well-known psychics and channelers.

What is remarkable about these brief dialogues with leading men of the twentieth century is that they give us glimpses of what it is like actually to be a soul, alive and flourishing before, during, and after physical life. Our discussions have served to clear up many unsolved mysteries, and clarify issues that puzzled historians. More importantly, these encounters raise new questions about the life purpose each soul is working through on Earth, about soul groups and soul contracts, and the whole question of why, when we volunteer to come down here, we suffer so many problems of disease and death.

For the sake of those readers who may not have read the first book in this series, *Talking with Leaders of the Past* (and as a refresher for those who have), we now summarize the Masters' core teaching. For more details please read volume one—it's not really a good idea for us to write the same book more than once!

Summary of the Masters' Teaching

We should never think about God as the "supreme gentleman in a white beard and cloak who has ultimate power over everything upon the Earth," whose wrath and judgment are used to control people and punish evildoers. The Masters prefer to say "Creator," or "Source," or even "God-Force," which they clearly interpret as meaning the collective divinity of all the spirits in the whole universe, including our own individual soul.

All souls are separate energetic portions of the Source which have been "broken off" in order to extend the outreach and deepen the experience of the Source itself. Souls exist in the universal God-Force community, sharing all its knowledge totally, yet possessing individuality and personal wisdom gained from their past experiences.

All souls eventually return from planet Earth to Home, which is an energetic realm of unconditional love. Although there is self-evaluation of our lives, there is no judgment made of us there. All is unconditional love and service.

We have to give up the old ideas of Heaven and Hell: Heaven because our eternal Home, though filled with unconditional love, is not a place of celestial reward for our being and doing good; Hell (which exists only as a state of mind within the energetic dimension of planet Earth) principally because the divine force is non-judgmental. Every soul who incarnates on Earth will eventually return Home. There are no exceptions.

We all incarnate on planet Earth with a copy of the database of our soul's life in our DNA, though most of us are entirely forgetful of our origin and life purpose. Together with guides and counselors at Home, we have already identified those types of experience we need to have, during our time on Earth, for personal growth toward our soul's maturity. We select our parents, and our soul may make contracts with other souls who will provide us with challenges of various kinds during our lifetime.

Of whatever nature our physical experiences may be, they are always for a positive purpose within the life of our soul. The lessons will not necessarily be humanly judged to be pleasant or even experiences of goodness. They may involve our role-playing in a manner that human ethics consider profoundly negative or evil. We may have chosen to be subjected to physical or psychological pain and suffering which few human minds would ever regard as benign. Moreover, if we fail to deal successfully with the specific challenges that we have chosen in order to gain spiritual mastery, we will need to face something similar in a subsequent life. The experience of negativity is part of the plan to awaken our conscience, increase compassion, and gain an understanding of the opposite of negativity—the magnificence of unconditional love.

Our soul never dies because it remains always pure energy destined to realize its true identity in harmony with the Source. This fact affects many areas of human life and physical death. For example, abortion is seen by those at Home as a non-issue: The aborted fetus's soul (if, indeed, a soul has even been assigned to the fetus) is not involved in the destruction of fetal tissue and returns Home in advance of the procedure. You simply cannot kill the soul.

Likewise, tough life-support and euthanasia issues are challenges which everybody involved with the patient must face, yet the permanently vegetative patient's soul itself will have already substantially detached from the shell of the body and is only nominally connected until, finally, the body expires. With sudden death, as with lingering dying, the soul is unharmed but *transitions* back to the place from whence it came. So our role in the cosmos as incarnated human beings provides the means by which our spiritual selves may learn many lessons. Our egos and our body shells are designed simply as vehicles for this spiritual work, which we will continue to use until it is time for our souls to return Home.

The Authors

Toni Ann Winninger, JD, CH, is a Reiki master and metaphysical hypnotist. She has a flourishing international practice as a psychic channeler, and teaches shamanistic Light Language. A native of Chicago, Illinois, her working life included twenty-seven years as a prosecutor for the busy Cook County State's Attorney's Office in Chicago, before being called by the Masters to be a channeler.

Toni's task in this book was to channel accurately the thoughts and words from Home of 21 famous men of the twentieth century.

Peter Watson Jenkins, MA, CH, is a clinical master hypnotist, working in the metaphysical fields of past-life and inter-life regression, and energy release, and EFT. A Cambridge University (UK) graduate in theology, he was a parish minister, and is the author of: *Escape to Danger* (2001), *Training for the Marathon of Life* (2005), *Healing with thc Universe, Meditation, and Prayer* (2007), *Talking with Leaders of the Past (2008), Talking with Twentieth-Century Women (2008), Christy's Journey (*2008).

Interviewing the twentieth-century personalities was Peter's task. In making his choice of topics, he aimed to cover popular issues of interest and concern. He conducted the dialogues as an informed layman, with little background in the historical or academic disciplines involved in the study of each personality.

Celestial Voices, Inc.

We hope that you found this book a challenge and an inspiration. We are the human "voice" of the Masters of the Spirit World, working to promote their messages. We have two websites for your further enrichment. They promote the messages from the Masters and public discussion:

Messages from the Masters:
www.MastersOfTheSpiritWorld.com

This web log publishes the Masters' regular messages and provides a place for your comments on a variety of topics which are chosen from the many questions that people have asked them—from relationships to the behavior of domestic pets, and from discussion of various meditation techniques to UFO sightings. Informative and interesting!

Details of publications and activities:
www.CelestialVoicesInc.com

This website gives details of publications and the activities of the Celestial Voices team including media appearances and speaking tours, and ways in which supporters of the Masters can help them in their work.

Celestial Voices publications are detailed on the following pages.

Our booklist

Healing with the Universe, Meditation, and Prayer (2007)
This 96-page booklet is available from the publishers and Amazon.com. Retail: $6.95

The possibility of having a spiritual bird's-eye view from the Other Side on what we do down here on Earth is appealing, but not without difficulties. The Masters please many readers by their cool appraisal of society's current medical scene. Their dispassionate attitude views everything on Earth in terms of energy. Pills and potions do not cure us, let alone surgery. Healing only takes place when the soul of the patient intends its body to recover. At best, doctors or other therapists facilitate that internal, spiritual process. At worst, they hinder their patients' healing.

Dialogues with Masters of the Spirit World

I. *Talking with Leaders of the Past* (2008)
Now in Amazon's list and from the publishers. Paperback 272 pages. Retail: $17.95 or £9.99. The Masters' discussion of reincarnation is followed by dialogues with the souls of 15 prominent people born in the nineteenth century:

Andrew Carnegie, Winston S. Churchill,
Charles Darwin, Albert Einstein, Mahatma Gandhi,
Adolf Hitler, William James, Pope John XXIII,
Carl Jung, Dwight Moody, Florence Nightingale,
Eleanor Roosevelt, Bertrand Russell,
Margaret Sanger, and Oscar Wilde.

This groundbreaking book of amazing spiritual conversations has set a new high standard in channeled publishing. Intelligent questioning of the Leaders about their past life and their current opinions has revealed new material about their historic past, surprising changes in their current opinions, and challenges to the belief systems of today's philosophies and religions.

II. *Talking with Twentieth-Century Women* (2008)
Retail $19.95 or £12.99.
Dialogues with the souls of 21 prominent women:

Jane Addams, Marian Anderson, Maria Callas, Rachel Carson, Marie Curie, Amelia Earhart, Ella Fitzgerald, Anne Frank, Judy Garland, Barbara Jordan, Helen Keller, Margaret Mead, Golda Meir, Carmen Miranda, Marilyn Monroe, Georgia O'Keeffe, Selena Quintanilla-Perez, Sylvia Plath, Wilma Rudolph, Sharon Tate, and Mother Teresa.

III. *Talking with Twentieth-Century Men* (2008)
Retail $19.95 or £12.99 (this book).

The Masters' Publications

Wisdom from Beyond

A collection of messages from the Masters' blog, August 2007 – July 2008 (Fall 2008)

The Masters' Reincarnation Handbook: Journey of the Soul

The Masters' systematic analysis of the process of reincarnation (Winter 2008)

Please consult our website for details:
www.CelestialVoicesInc.com

Please visit the Masters' blog:
www.MastersOfTheSpiritWorld.com